HICKLING STAITHE

BROGRAVE
HICKLING Drainage Windmill
Staithe
HORSEY MERE
HORSEY
Drainage Windmill
Staithe

WAXHAM CUT

HICKLING
BROAD

MEADOW DYKE

HUNDRED DYKE
original course of
RIVER THURNE

SOMERTON
Staithe

HEIGHAM
SOUND

MARTHAM
Ferry
Brick Works

High's
Drainage Windmill
POTTER HEIGHAM

UDHAM

POTTER HEIGHAM Bridge
Staithe

Maltings
Staithe

RIVER THURNE

POTTER HEIGHAM BRIDGE

ORMESBY BROAD

Staithe
THURNE MOUTH

FILBY BROAD

MUCK FLEET
Not Navigable

WEY Bridge

STOKESBY
Staithe
Ferry

GREAT YARMOUTH

ACLE

RUNHAM SWIM

TUNSTALL DYKE

RIVER BURE

Fertilizer
Works

GREAT
YARMOUTH

BREYDON WATER

HORSEY MILL AND STAITHE

E.W. PAGET-TOMLINSON
FEBRUARY 2002

THE
NORFOLK & SUFFOLK
BROADS

Robert Malster

The Broadland village of Horning seen about 1880 in a photograph by George Christopher Davies. On the staithe at left is a malting that is said to have been built partly with stone from the nearby St Benet's Abbey, and on the hill is Jonathan Nicholson's windmill, reputedly the first mill to have been fitted with William Cubitt's self-regulating sails, patented in 1807.

THE
NORFOLK & SUFFOLK
BROADS

Robert Malster

Phillimore

2003

Published by
PHILLIMORE & CO. LTD,
Shopwyke Manor Barn, Chichester, West Sussex, England

© Robert Malster, 2003

ISBN 1 86077 243 9

Printed and bound in Great Britain by
THE CROMWELL PRESS
Trowbridge, Wiltshire

Contents

LIST OF ILLUSTRATIONS

Frontispiece: The Broadland village of Horning.

ILLUSTRATION ACKNOWLEDGEMENTS

The author is grateful to the following for the use of black and white photographs: Bolingbroke Collection, frontispiece, 1-5, 7-8, 14, 16-19, 21, 24-31, 34-7, 45, 49-53, 55, 57, 65-9, 71-7, 81-2, 86, 90-7, 100-1, 103-4, 107-9, 115; David Cleveland, 33, 47; R.N. Flowers, 116-22, 124-7, 129-30; Ted Gray, courtesy Mrs Jean Gray, 59; Anthony J. Ward, 42-4; The rest were either taken by the author or are from his collection. The colour photographs were taken by the author except for XVIII, which was taken by R.N. Flowers, and XVI and XIX, which were provided by the Broads Authority.

Acknowledgements

Writing a book of this kind is by no means a solitary occupation; rather it is a collaboration between the author and a host of friends and acquaintances with similar interests. The present author has certainly not lacked help from a great many people too numerous to mention individually.

Though the writing of this book has occupied no more than a few years, the work of researching and recording the subject has occupied a very much longer period. In fact I was nudged on my way by my experiences as a boy cycling around the Broads area in search of wherries and windmills, and in those days I received encouragement and help from people of an older generation such as Horace Bolingbroke and Philip Rumbelow, who both contributed a great deal to the writing of this book although both long since departed their old haunts. Many of the illustrations, including those photographs taken by George Christopher Davies in the 1880s, come from Horace Bolingbroke's collection.

During the writing of the book I have received invaluable assistance from my friend John Fairclough, who has contributed greatly to the early chapters from his knowledge of the archaeological background and has guided me throughout. We have shared a number of expeditions that would have had much less satisfactory results without his input. Special thanks go also to another friend, Edward Paget-Tomlinson, for the pictorial maps that have been reproduced on the endpapers, and to Richard Flowers for the use of some splendid photographs.

Members of the staff of the Broads Authority, particularly Jess Tunstall and Martin Joslin, have given me much help. I am indebted to Dr Martin George not only for pointing me to sources of information in his monumental volume *The Land Use, Ecology and Conservation of Broadland* but for writing a foreword to my book.

Others who have given me much help include Peter Allard, Brian Ayers, Jamie Campbell, David Cleveland, Eric Edwards, Mike Fuller, David Gurney, David Holmes, David Lindley, Linda and Vincent Pargeter, Vic Standley and Anthony Ward. To the many others who have helped in so many ways and whose names have been omitted from the list, my apologies and my thanks.

My thanks also go to Noel Osborne, of Phillimore, for asking me to write this book, to Andrew Illes for the care he has taken in producing it, and to other members of the Phillimore staff for the interest they have taken in the progress of the book.

When I was young my parents encouraged my interest in the Broads and did not complain when I arrived home late on a Sunday night after a weekend spent with my Sea Scout friends at Woodbastwick. Without their forbearance and encouragement in those days this book might never have been written. and it is to their memory that I dedicate it.

FOREWORD

Robert ('Bob') Malster, a publisher and a former journalist and now an acknowledged expert on local history, has long had a special affection for Norfolk, where he was born and brought up, and for Suffolk, where he lives today. Several of the twenty or so books he has written since the 1960s have been about the Broads, perhaps the best known of these being *Wherries and Waterways*, first published in 1971 and revised in 1986.

Over the years others have sought to describe the natural history of this wonderful region, the commercial and other pressures to which it is subject, the conflicts which have occurred in it between different user interests, and the arguments which have taken place about how it should be administered and managed. But with this latest offering from Bob Malster we have what has been largely missing up to now, namely a comprehensive account of the social history of a region which is widely accepted as lowland Britain's finest and most complex wetland system.

Here is a scholarly and yet eminently readable account of how human endeavour turned what was, in Romano-British times, an open estuary into the system of shallow lakes, fens and grazing marshes familiar to us today. And here too is a description of the people who have lived and worked in the region, and who have exploited it, at first as a source of peat, later for livestock farming and the production of reed, sedge and other fen crops, and today for water-based recreation and a multi-million-pound tourist industry.

I am quite sure that visitors to the region, as well as those who live and work in it, will find this splendid book just as informative and enjoyable to read as I have.

MARTIN GEORGE
23 SEPTEMBER 2002.

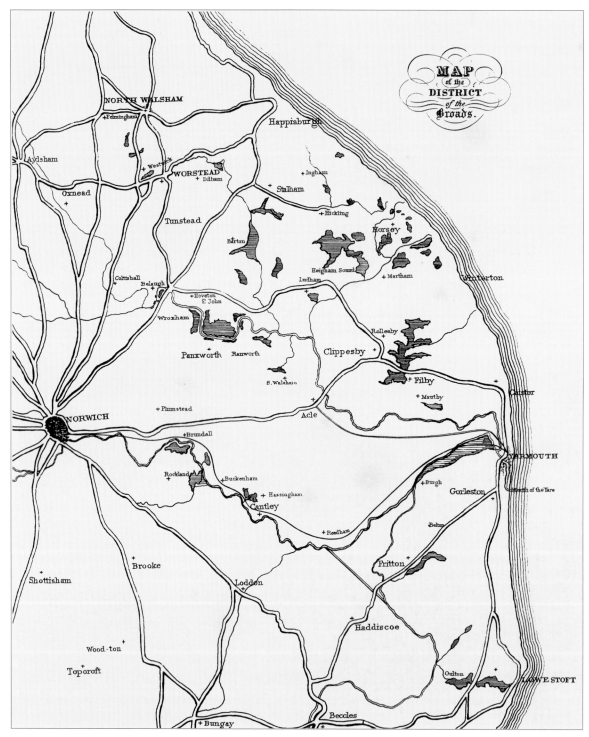

'Map of the District of the Broads' from the Revd Richard Lubbock's Observations on the Fauna of Norfolk, and more particularly on The District of the Broads, *published in 1845.*

One

WATERY LANDSCAPE

It is a happy coincidence that this book appears just 100 years after the first publication of William Dutt's classic book *The Norfolk Broads*, to which men such as Arthur Patterson, Claude Morley, H.E. Hurrell, A.J. Rudd and Nicholas Everitt contributed their special expertise to produce a work that has stood the test of time. It was not rivalled until Ted Ellis produced *The Broads* 60 years later, again with the assistance of other experts.

As was realised by William Dutt and Ted Ellis, the Broads, that area of waterways, marshes and shallow lakes to the east and north-east of the city of Norwich and along the Norfolk-Suffolk border, was shaped by man from prehistoric times onwards. The land was farmed even before the Roman takeover some 2,000 years ago; it is likely that had Britain been a primeval

1 *The Broadland rivers as William Dutt knew them: Postwick Grove on the Yare, with a timber-laden wherry bound for one of the Norwich timber yards.*

2 *The River Bure, on the left, and Salhouse Broad seen in a photograph taken by George Christopher Davies about 1880. In the distance can be seen Hoveton Great Broad. Today the view is very different, for trees that have been allowed to grow along the river banks and in the marshes have had a marked effect on the landscape and much of the marsh seen here is now alder carr.*

wasteland the Romans would not have expended so much effort to conquer and occupy it for some four centuries.

Within the past 1,000 years the Broadland marshes have been drained, river walls have been constructed to keep out the tides, and the rivers themselves have been manipulated in the interests of both land drainage and navigation, while the natural resources of the region were exploited for domestic needs and for industry throughout the Middle Ages and since. The monasteries, of which there were a number in the Broads area, played a significant part in the life of the region until Henry VIII appropriated their properties and their possessions for his own use.

It is interesting to discover the extent to which monastic establishments such as that of St Benet-at-Holme made use of water transport not only for carrying goods but for personal journeys around the region. Transport by river remained of prime importance until the coming of the railways in the latter half of the 19th century, and even then wherries continued to be used for the carriage of a variety of goods within the region and sea-going vessels traded to the inland ports of Norwich and Beccles until the mid-20th century.

Even today the Bishop of Norwich, who is by virtue of an historical anomaly also Abbot of St Benet's, travels by river once a year to conduct a service on the site of that once-important establishment, reminding us visibly of several aspects of the region's long and fascinating history.

3 *Postwick Grove was well known as a beauty spot, and in the late 19th century it was common for Norwich people to resort there to stroll among the trees. A party of ladies and gentlemen can be seen on the river bank in this photograph from the 1890s.*

Much has happened on the Broads in the century since the appearance of Dutt's book. On the debit side the remarkable growth of the holiday industry has combined with a variety of other factors, some natural but many created by man, to bring about a disastrous degradation of the local environment. On the credit side a great deal has been deduced about the origins and history of the Broads themselves by experts in various disciplines collaborating in the field to produce some startling and far-reaching discoveries. As a member of the Norfolk Research Committee, I heard these experts tell of their work, was present when they displayed their findings, and listened to them expound their theories as they pursued what was a pioneering piece of interdisciplinary research. The crowning achievement of this team was to prove that, contrary to long-held beliefs, the Broads were not a natural formation but were the result of man's activities over the centuries.

I was fortunate enough to spend my formative years around the Broads. Old enough to remember the last commercial wherries, admittedly not working under sail but with motors fitted in the cabins in which the crew of two had in times past been wont to live, I can recall sea-going ships bringing coal, timber and a variety of other cargoes upriver to my home city of Norwich. And I still tend to pronounce the names of towns and villages as they were rendered by the natives of years gone by – Hofton and Po'er Ham, Hazebro and Ranner and the rest.

As a young member of a Sea Scout troop I spent many weekends at Decoy Broad, Woodbastwick, clearing alder carr, working on the troop's somewhat aged boats, and sometimes sailing them. Occasionally we lads took part in expeditions further afield, as when a friend and I hired the Yare & Bure One-design *Scotch Argus* from Percival's boatyard at Horning and spent some days sailing on the Bure, Thurne and Ant, crossing Barton Broad in a near-gale and approaching Barton staithe cautiously and amateurishly under jib alone.

At the Research Committee meetings in the Castle Museum, usually in a somewhat claustrophobic meeting room at the end of the fish gallery, I heard botanist Dr Joyce Lambert giving progress reports on the programme of borings initiated by J.N. Jennings and then being carried on by her in the valley of the Yare and later in the other river valleys. Examination of the pollen grains found in the material brought up by the borers provided a great deal of information on the trees and plants that had grown in the region at different times in the past, but neither Dr Lambert nor those who listened to her descriptions of past flora realised then just how her work would change our perception of this fascinating region.

It had always been accepted that the Broads were areas of shallow water that were relics of the Great Estuary of Roman times, puddles left behind as the sea retreated in the post-Roman period. Dr Lambert's findings did not fit the old understanding, for they showed that the Broads had sheer sides and flat bottoms, which made them look very much like pits from which material had been dug. Having accepted the commonly held view, Dr Lambert puzzled over how it came about that the Broads did not have the expected shallow sides and concave bottoms, and realised that the explanation could only be that they had been made by man.

I was there one afternoon in 1953 when Dr Lambert revealed her hypothesis that the Broads had been dug out as peat pits. She pointed to the sheer sides dropping six feet and more, the level bottom, and the peninsulas and islands that were the remnants of the baulks between individual pits, most evident in Barton Broad. What she said fitted exactly with my experience of Decoy Broad, where there was at least one narrow island with an alder or two growing on it; I was convinced at once that her hypothesis, for at the time it was no more than that, was the true explanation for these areas of water.

Others were less easy to convince, and there are still some people who refuse to accept the evidence, overwhelming though it now is. Historical confirmation was soon provided by C.T. Smith, a Lecturer in Geography at the University of Cambridge, who found ample evidence in the account rolls of the Cathedral Priory at Norwich and in other historical records of the large-scale consumption of peat over the course of several hundred years, quite sufficient to explain the extraction of the estimated nine hundred million cubic feet that had been produced. Archaeologist Charles Green supplied the evidence of land and sea level changes that explained how the peat pits or turbaries became flooded in the later medieval period, creating that landscape of fen and water that we know as Broadland.[1]

4 *Before the deluge:* The Pleasure Boat *at Hickling advertises Bullard & Sons Norwich Ales on its sign and boats to let in hand-painted letters on the wooden door, but it was a very quiet spot when this photograph was taken about 1890. Some 70 years later, when the Duke of Edinburgh and young Prince Charles stayed at the inn during a visit to Hickling, the Broads were more crowded, especially in summer.*

Man had made the Broads, and now man was destroying them. I was blissfully unaware of the fact in the 1940s that I was seeing the area at a time of change, and that man's interference was combining with natural processes to bring about a disastrous deterioration in water quality, in the diversity of flora and fauna, and in the landscape itself. There were those who blamed all the problems of the Broads on the growth of the holiday industry and in particular on the increasing use of motor craft, whose screws were said to churn up the mud of shallow rivers and so turn the water into a muddy soup, whose wash tore away the reed fringe from the shores of the rivers, and whose toilets discharged straight to the water and created unpleasant pollution. Get rid of the motor cruisers and all would be well, they said.

If only it had been that simple. The increasing numbers of boats on the waterways were creating problems, but there were many other causes of the decline in water quality, the silting up of the Broads, the loss of aquatic vegetation, and the changes in character of reedbeds and grazing marshes. Pollution did result from the discharge of sewage from boats, sailing as well as power, but there were also discharges from sewage treatment works that were being built to take effluent from town and village homes that had not previously had the advantage of mains drainage. The stirring of mud by propellers undeniably resulted in sediments being washed down with the river flow, but far more turbidity resulted from enrichment of the water by the leaching out of fertilisers spread on the land and by other accidental additives. Enrichment encouraged the growth of algae which gave the water the appearance of pea soup, shutting out the sunlight from plants growing up from the bottom and so preventing their growth.

Another threat to the environment came from the escape into the wild in 1937 of coypu, large South American rodents that had been farmed for their fur, known in the trade as 'nutria'. These animals found in the Broads something of a counterpart to their native swamps, and the damage they did to riverside and dyke vegetation and to farm crops resulted in a campaign that eventually saw them exterminated from the region. It has to be said that the effect of the coypu was not entirely harmful, for while the outer fringes of reed beds were destroyed by their feeding, water was allowed into the further parts of the reed beds, improving the quality of considerable areas.

While their numbers were restricted the coypu did as much good as harm, helping to offset the natural processes which led to broads and waterways growing up. It is said that Ranworth Broad was enlarged by some 12 acres between 1946 and 1952 as a result of their activity.[2] They had few natural predators, however, and as sometimes happens with introduced species their numbers exploded to the point at which they presented a real threat to the local environment. When they began burrowing into river walls and marsh banks it became necessary to introduce measures to control them. Ted Ellis warned in the 1960s that many characteristic plants of the Broads were likely to be lost unless the coypu were controlled, for by the 1960s the cowbane (*Cicuta virosa*) and the great water dock (*Rumex hydrolapathum*) had almost disappeared from the Broads and marshes in which they had been so abundant.[3]

Ted Ellis, Dr Martin George and others pointed out from time to time at Research Committee meetings and elsewhere that there was a multitude of factors affecting the local environment. For one thing reed beds that had been regularly cut in the past were going out of use and marshes were no longer being mown for hay as the demand for thatching materials and animal fodder and bedding decreased, the result being that scrub invaded and, if left alone, the land developed naturally into carr, the wet woodland that is typical of the area. Broads that had been silting for centuries had reached that depth at which reed began to invade the open water, turning it into fen. And there was a complicated pattern of cause and effect that, if left alone, would inevitably lead to great changes in the landscape. This was to some extent a matter of the hand of man being removed and nature being allowed to take over; a man-made environment was being abandoned to nature.

[6]

5 *A black-snouted wherry and a yacht on the Bure near Horning Ferry, a photograph by George Christopher Davies probably taken around 1880.*

Research sometimes led to strange and puzzling findings. In one experiment carried out by the Nature Conservancy Council, the Norfolk Naturalists' Trust and the University of East Anglia's School of Environmental Studies in 1977 two butile rubber tubes, each 20 metres in diameter, were moored in Hickling Broad, with a rubber skirt dropped to the bed of the broad and weighted with about a quarter of a ton of chain to sink the lower edge into the mud, effectively isolating the water within the ring from the rest of the broad. It might have been expected that over time the water within the ring would prove less polluted than that in the rest of the broad, which received its daily dose of nitrogenous fertiliser run-off and sewage phosphates; instead the scientists found that the water inside gave much higher phosphate readings, the readings increasing throughout the course of the experiment.

It was only when the warden of Hickling reserve, Stewart Linsell, paid a visit one moonlit December night that the riddle was solved. As he approached in his punt he saw by the light of the full moon that black-headed gulls were standing shoulder to shoulder all round both tubes, all facing outwards. They were depositing almost pure phosphate into the water within the tubes as they roosted on this convenient perch that had been thoughtfully provided for them by the scientists.[4] I first heard the bare bones of the story from Dr Martin George at a Research Committee meeting; only later did I meet Stewart Linsell and learn from him just how that strange anomaly had been explained during one of his nocturnal ramblings.

Such experiments demonstrated that the situation was complex indeed, and that no simple answers would be found to the many problems facing the Broads. They also helped environmental scientists to develop ways of overcoming the very complex issues that were threatening to overwhelm a stretch of countryside that is not only very special but also valuable in terms of the holiday industry, nature conservation, landscape quality and a host of other considerations.

Complex situations require to be handled both expertly and sensitively. There are conflicting interests to be reconciled, and it is not always possible to achieve reconciliation when interests as diverse as yachting, angling, speed-boating and water-skiing, and birdwatching and nature conservation are involved in what is after all a severely limited area. The formation of the Broads Authority in 1978 was intended as a first step towards providing proper management of this fragile and already sorely damaged area.

The Authority's first important restoration project involved suction-dredging of Cockshoot Broad, a small non-navigable broad between Woodbastwick and Ranworth, to remove nutrient-rich sediment that was acting as a source of pollution. As a result of this work and of other restoration measures, Cockshoot Broad gradually recovered. As a related experiment, Alderfen Broad, a land-locked stretch of water between Neatishead and Irstead, was isolated from its main catchment to prevent the ingress of nutrients; it was not dredged, however, until in 1993 it became necessary to pump out the mud to prevent the broad from silting up entirely. Belaugh Broad, upstream from Wroxham, was the site of another suction-dredging experiment, and other broads have been dealt with since. Biggest project of all involves Barton Broad, whose rejuvenation is recorded elsewhere in this book.

After ten years of feeling its way the original Broads Authority handed over to a new statutory authority created by the Norfolk and Suffolk Broads Act, 1988. The new authority inherited the title of its predecessor, but it was given considerably greater responsibility. At last the government had realised that the Broads needed the same measure of protection as national parks such as the Peak District, Dartmoor and Snowdonia and, while stopping short of declaring the Broads a national park, it gave the new authority, which began operating on 1 April 1989, wide powers to deal with issues such as navigation which were specific to the area.

In 1997 the Broads Authority published an overall strategy for managing the Broads;[5] the draft version published five years earlier had been given the significant title *No Easy Answers*. Reporting on its vision for the Broads, the Authority faced up to the daunting task ahead and declared that its objective was 'A future which safeguards the well-being and special character of the Broads, and sees life and vitality restored to a vulnerable and damaged area'.

Amen to that.

Two

THE GREAT ESTUARY

There were people living in the region centuries before the Broads themselves were formed. The earliest inhabitants were hunter-gatherers who lived a fairly precarious life, but farming began in the area some 6,500 years ago. Whether the earliest farmers were the descendants of the indigenous Mesolithic population who had adopted a new and more settled way of life or were immigrants is unknown; perhaps farming was introduced by people from the continent, as used to be supposed, and was quickly adopted by those among whom they settled.[1]

These early farmers might also have been the first industrialists, for it was they who learnt to mine the floorstone, the lowest of three levels of flint found in the East Anglian chalk, at the great Neolithic industrial site of Grimes Graves, near Brandon, and at Whitlingham, beside the River Yare just to the east of where Norwich was later to develop.[2] Perhaps they used their flint axes to build dugout canoes which they launched on to the rivers – the first Broadland watermen?

Some of them had, after all, already made their way across the North Sea in craft that were either of this kind or possibly of animal skins on a light wooden framework.[3] If the craft they used were skin boats it is quite likely that they were not dissimilar from the curraghs still in use on the west coast of Ireland at the beginning of the 21st century. While it is true to say that these settlers were at the beginning of that development which led to the Agricultural Revolution of the 18th century A.D., the degree of industrial organisation manifested at Grimes Graves demonstrates that they were by no means the primitive, unknowing beings generally assumed from the description 'stone-age man'. While their tools were crafted from flint, they were certainly not simply-made implements but demonstrated a very high degree of skill in the fashioning. Sometimes they were given a keener edge by being polished on a block of stone such as the block of quartzite found with a group of such axes at Lound, in one of the side valleys of the River Waveney.[4]

So far as the area of east Norfolk and north-east Suffolk is concerned, there are few visible monuments from this period apart from a Neolithic long barrow or burial mound on Broome Heath, Ditchingham, in the Waveney Valley. Broome Heath also has a C-shaped enclosure defined by bank and ditch enclosing more than a hectare and containing pottery fragments and worked flints that are clearly indicative of a settlement of some size.[5]

Flint implements of various kinds continued to be utilised after the use of bronze, an alloy of copper and tin, had been introduced about 1700 B.C., there being no sources of either metal in East Anglia. Early bronze tools used in the region were imported from elsewhere, bronze-founding only coming into East Anglia when there were sufficient obsolete bronze tools to be recycled. It is noticeable that until the late Bronze Age the area of the later Broads seems to belong to a cultural group with links along the east coast as far north as Yorkshire and at times to the opposite shore of the North Sea, emphasising the importance of communication by sea even at so early a date. Whatever the position with regards to the rest of Britain, this part of East Anglia has enjoyed close ties with Europe for well over 4,000 years.

Archaeological evidence of the lifestyle of early residents of the area is sparse and hard to find, but there are sufficient indications to show that the area was fairly extensively settled by the end of the Bronze Age, around 800 B.C. There are, for instance, the Bronze-Age round barrows on Belton Heath, some four miles south-west of Yarmouth, survivors of a much larger number of burial mounds that have been ploughed out and remain as buried ring ditches visible merely as crop marks on aerial photographs.

More impressive is the woodhenge monument at Arminghall, just south of Norwich, that was discovered by aerial photography and excavated in the 1930s. We can have no idea of the rituals that might have been performed at this religious site when it came into use about 2500 B.C., but there can be no doubt as to its significance. The main feature is a ring ditch, 28 feet across and enclosing an area 90 feet in diameter, interrupted by a causeway giving access to the circular central area. When first cut the ditch had been at least eight feet deep, and the surrounding bank was 50 feet across at the base. Outside this bank was a shallow outer ditch cut into sand and gravel.

All that remained to be seen of the eight massive oak posts that had been erected in the central area were the holes, excavated some 7½ feet into the gravel, into which they had been set. The holes indicated that these great posts were some 2½ feet in diameter; we can only guess at their length, but Rainbird Clarke surmised that they must have stood at least eight feet above ground level. It appears from the ramps dug to insert them that these heavy tree-trunks were dragged downhill to the site from a southerly direction, and that they were erected before the digging of the inner ditch, which provided material for the surrounding bank.[6]

When this henge monument and its associated barrows stood in isolation on the slopes of the River Tas they must have formed a most impressive part of the landscape. It is difficult to be sure what the landscape was like at the time of the henge's construction, but we are fairly certain that by the time of the Roman occupation of Britain the site overlooked the head of a wide, shallow estuary occupying much of the area now occupied by the marshes inland from Yarmouth.

Archaeological excavations in 1999 on the line of a new gas pipe from Bacton to serve a gas-fired power station at Great Yarmouth produced unexpected evidence of extensive activity in the coastal area before the Roman period. A circular timber house dating from the Bronze Age, about 3,000 years ago, was found at Witton, inland from Walcott, together with such indications of farming as the remains of barley. Cereal remains were also found at Rollesby and Ormesby St Michael, where a series of ditches suggested arable field systems, while quantities of burnt material at Hemsby were the result of some industrial activity employing high temperatures. Unusual ditched enclosures at Caister-on-Sea, on the other hand, appear to have been nothing to do with farming but to have been designed for some ceremonial purpose.

It is likely that the whole of the land in this area was intensively farmed during the Iron Age, a period which began a little before 600 B.C. when a wave of immigrants from the Netherlands brought with them a knowledge of iron.[7] Those people already inhabiting the area doubtless soon absorbed this knowledge and made use of iron-bearing stone found in parts of Norfolk to produce iron that could be turned into effective tools and weapons.

The pipeline investigations showed that farming and settlement continued during the Iron Age. A large timber roundhouse at Ingham, between Stalham and the coast, produced barley, rye and wheat grains indicating extensive arable farming some 2,000 years ago, as well as clay loom weights that provide evidence of the weaving of woollen cloth, an indication that sheep were presumably part of the local economy. Further evidence of farming during the Iron Age was found elsewhere in Ingham, at Repps-with-Bastwick and Ormesby St Margaret-with-Scratby, while signs of some ceremonial or ritual activity were found at East Ruston, just to the east of the River Ant.

Farming spread widely in what appears to have been a continuous process starting in the New Stone Age more than 6,000 years ago and continuing through the Bronze and Iron Ages. By the time the Romans arrived in Britain large areas of land were engaged in food production. Although at Ingham the Iron-Age field system was replaced by new fields on a different alignment late in Roman times or early in the Saxon period, evidence has been put forward suggesting that in places the field system that still existed at the beginning of the 20th century had its origin in the Iron Age. East Norfolk and north-east Suffolk were at that time occupied by the Iceni tribe, almost certainly the people named by Julius Caesar in 54 B.C. as the Great Ceni.

Evidence found during the construction of the gas pipeline shows that at Repps farming continued after the Roman conquest. There was probably a timber roundhouse there, while activity in the Roman period was also observed at Hemsby, Caister-on-Sea, East Ruston and Ormesby St Margaret. However, compared with the unexpected extent of activity in the Bronze and Iron Ages, which suggests farming was well developed at that time, there was less visible evidence found of occupation in the Roman period. It has to be borne in mind that this particular investigation was based on the study of 14 sites,

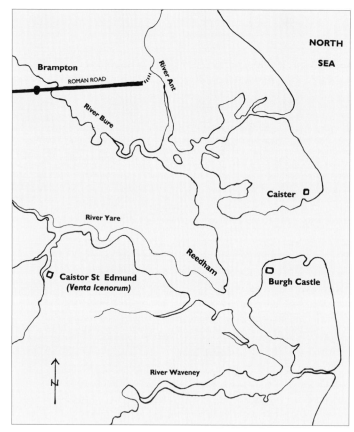

6 *The Great Estuary as it was in the Roman period, with the forts at Burgh Castle and Caister (either or both of which might have been known as Gariannonum) on either side of the entrance. Venta Icenorum lies towards the head of the estuary and the settlement at what is now Brampton lies not only on the River Bure but also on a Roman road connecting with the Fen Causeway. This road apparently crossed the Ant at what is now Wayford Bridge, but its route onwards from here, presumably to Caister, is at present unknown.*

and the negative elements might be the result of a random sample of locations rather than of any real reduction in activity during this period.

The conquest of Britain by the Romans in A.D. 43 probably brought no great and immediate changes at least until the death in A.D. 60 of Prasutagus, client king of the Iceni. It was the action of the Emperor Nero in enforcing direct Roman rule over the tribe that led to the revolt of Boudicca, Prasutagus's widow, in A.D. 61, a rebellion that at first dealt the Roman occupiers a severe blow but in the end resulted in the defeat and subjugation of the native population.

Thereafter East Anglia became part of the Roman province, and for more than three centuries Roman rule and culture governed the pattern of life in the area. Roman culture permeated down into the indigenous population, the more prestigious and more affluent of whom became virtually indistinguishable from their Roman rulers. It is not unlikely that some of the larger and more spacious properties in the region were occupied not by Roman officials but by well-to-do Romano-British landowners and farmers who owed their wealth to the sale of grain and other farm produce to the occupying army. Unfortunately for the archaeologists, East Anglian farmhouses were most likely either timber-framed structures or clay-walled buildings with thatched roofs; such materials melt back into the ground as they decay and leave few if any traces after almost 2,000 years.

Where people have looked for the evidence they have found intensive occupation during the Roman period, suggesting that this region was a good source of agricultural produce; Alan Davison's fieldwalking in Loddon, Hales and Heckingham, on the southern shore of the Great Estuary, has produced ample evidence of occupation,[8] and similar evidence has been found by Mike Hardy in the Waveney Valley parishes, demonstrating intensive farming on the southern edge of our region. It is known from Strabo[9] that even before the Roman conquest Britain was producing an agricultural surplus, some of which was sold to the Roman empire, and we can assume that one source of this surplus was East Anglia. The income derived from efficient farming could well have been a source of the Icenian wealth seen in the gold torcs or neck-rings found at Snettisham in west Norfolk.

This surplus, which would have been seen by the Roman government as a valuable asset available to feed the army, could easily have been transported to units in the field by way of the Great Estuary and thence by coastal ship-ping routes. Much later the Romans were shipping British grain to feed the army based on the Rhine, and there is also evidence of communication between East Anglia and Hadrian's Wall. Local products might also have been sold through merchants at Domburg and Colijnsplaat in the Netherlands who recorded trade with Britain on altars dedicated to the goddess Nehalennia. Pottery was produced in some quantity in our region, 141 kilns having been found at Brampton alone. Some of the mixing bowls or 'mortaria' made by potters in the Waveney Valley found their way to garrison troops on Hadrian's Wall, and examples from Brampton, on the Bure below Aylsham, reached the Antonine Wall near Edinburgh.

It has often been said that a fleet of barges, perhaps similar to those ex-cavated in the Thames by Peter Marsden some forty years ago, must have been used on the Great Estuary to carry cargo between the various Roman settlements and forts. So far, however, no archaeologist has discovered the remains of a Roman vessel in this area.

The exact extent of the Great Estuary is a matter for speculation, but it is worth noting that Venta Icenorum, the presumed post-conquest regional capital of the Iceni at Caistor St Edmund, is at the head of one branch of the estuary, while the only other defended town in Norfolk, at Brampton, might well have been on another branch. The shipping of grain and other supplies by way of the Great Estuary could well have been one function of both these towns. What appear to be Roman tiles and other building materials are to be found both in Brampton church and in neighbouring Oxnead church.

Brampton is not only on the River Bure but is also on a Roman road that is an eastward continuation of the Fen Causeway. This road can be traced as far as Smallburgh and apparently crossed the River Ant in the vicinity of Wayford Bridge, a point which was above that reached by the waters of the Great Estuary; a series of bores taken across the valley showed conclusively

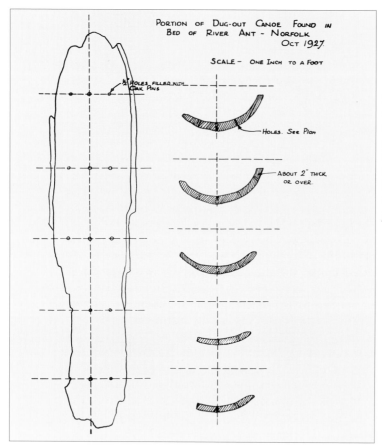

PORTION OF DUG-OUT CANOE FOUND IN
BED OF RIVER ANT - NORFOLK
OCT 1927.

SCALE - ONE INCH TO A FOOT

5 HOLES FILLED WITH
OAK PINS

HOLES. See Plan

ABOUT 2" THICK
OR OVER.

7 *Plan and sections of a dugout canoe found in the bed of the Ant in October 1927. The oak pins in the bottom would have been fastenings for ribs, suggesting that the craft might have had additional planks above the dugout section; it is probably medieval.*

that the estuarine water did not penetrate that far. Finds made in the vicinity of the bridge in the early 19th century were interpreted as a 'Roman encampment', but the eventual termination of the Roman road is unclear; the late second- or early third-century fort at Caister-by-Yarmouth is the most likely destination.

This fort is one of two sited north and south of the Great Estuary and well placed to control and protect traffic leaving the estuary, the other being Burgh Castle, which lies on a promontory that today overlooks the confluence of the Waveney and the Yare. At the time of its building the latter fort would have looked out over the Great Estuary towards Reedham, where there might have been a lighthouse providing a very necessary navigation aid for those negotiating the shallow waters of the estuary. To seaward of the forts was the wide mouth of the estuary, soon to be obstructed by the formation of a sandspit on which the town of Great Yarmouth would spring up hundreds of years later.

The Caister fort, whose square, round-cornered walls were still standing above ground in the 17th century, appears to have been established in the late second century or in the early part of the following century; unusually high numbers of coins dating from A.D. 192 to 222 have been found in excavations on the site. The discovery of central Gaulish samian pottery and coarser wares from northern Gaul suggests that Caister might have been supplied by the Classis Britannica, the Roman fleet which from the period of the invasion in A.D. 43 until some time after A.D. 245 played an important part in affairs on both sides of what the Romans could have called the Mare Saxonicum – the Saxon Sea. During later Roman times the soldiers responsible for the security of this coast came under the command of the Count of the Saxon Shore.

The construction and design of the Caister fort suggests similarities with others at Reculver in Kent and Brancaster in north Norfolk (the stone fort which was possibly preceded by an even earlier fort). These could all have been supply bases linked to the campaign of the Emperor Septimius Severus, who struck into northern Scotland in A.D. 208-11 and restored Hadrian's Wall; he also built a new granary at Corbridge and probably extended the granaries at the South Shields supply base, which was certainly in use at this time as shown by imperial lead seals,[10] besides building coastal supply bases in Scotland.

The finding of coal in Roman deposits at Caister could be taken as evidence that the ships taking grain to the north found a return cargo in the products of early mines on the banks of the Tyne. Caister also has what might be a cattle-processing area, possibly preparing meat for shipment. Occupation at Caister, at least by the late third century, apparently included women and children, perhaps the families of the garrison, and rubbish found just inside the rampart during excavation of the site suggests that spit-and-polish in the Roman garrisons might not have extended to the surroundings of the buildings.

Burgh Castle, a near-rectangular fort with ten external bastions, was probably built in the late third or early fourth century,[11] fairly late in the Roman period. The bastions are bonded only into the upper parts of the wall and not into the lower courses, suggesting that they may have resulted from a change of plan during the building of the fort. If this is so it makes the fort transitional in design between the early playing-card-shape forts with internal towers and rounded corners, as seen at Caister, Brancaster and Reculver, and the less rigid shape with projecting bastions apparently introduced at the end of the third century.

Enigmatic layers of foundations, including stonework and decayed oak piles extending over a width of 11 feet and apparently a length of some 200 feet, excavated by Harrod in the mid-19th century might represent a harbour.[12] Harrod interpreted what he found as the missing west wall of the fort, which had slipped down the slope at some time in the past, but in fact the site of the collapsed wall was located in 1961 at the top of the cliff.[13]

It had always been supposed before the military nature of Caister was recognised that Burgh Castle was the Roman Gariannonum, and that this was the site of St Fursa's early religious settlement, known as Cnobheresburgh.

8   *The massive flint-and-tile walls of Burgh Castle, photographed by Thomas Ayers of Yarmouth about 1890.*

However, it is equally likely that the fort at Caister bore the name of Gariannonum, and the assemblage of Middle Saxon material at Caister, including two cemeteries, one inside the fort and the other outside the walls, supports the idea of a monastic site comparable with Butley and Brancaster, so it could have been here that Fursa founded his monastery. Both at Burgh Castle and at Caister there is evidence from aerial photographs of Roman settlement outside the forts, but unfortunately no investigation was carried out at Caister before the evidence was wantonly destroyed by building operations some years ago.

Reedham is said to be the site of a Roman 'pharos', a lighthouse with a circular base, and there is a 19th-century report of foundations 'in a field near the church'. The church, which stands on a bluff overlooking the confluence of the rivers Yare and Chet, does indeed contain a good deal of re-used Roman material, both tiles and stone, some of it of the same type as used at Brancaster fort. Where the stone originally came from is uncertain, but it is definitely not local. It would have been an excellent position for a navigational beacon enabling mariners to obtain bearings when sailing on the estuary. It might be significant that the adjacent parish to Reedham is

9 *The south and east walls of Burgh Castle in a print dated 1831 after a picture by James Stark. The bastions like that seen at the junction of the two walls might be a late addition to the design during building, as they are bonded only into the upper section of the wall; the lower part of the bastion is merely butted up against the wall. Burgh Castle church can be seen in the distance at right.*

Wickhampton, which could be one of the Wickham names that Margaret Gelling has established suggest significant Roman settlement.[14] Possibly there was more than just a lighthouse at Reedham; the amount of Roman material in the church walls seems to confirm that there could have been other substantial buildings in the vicinity.

One looks in vain for signs either of the lighthouse or of other Roman sites, but the explanation is to be found in the pages of *Norfolk Archaeology*:

> There can be no doubt that Reedham was a place of Roman occupation. Coins are found there still, but not so frequently as formerly, for the earthworks which formerly existed there have been levelled: indeed, a considerable part of the hill on which they were erected has been altogether carried away, for the sake of the sand or clay which composed it. Chance has thrown my way a piece of information which is too important to be passed over without notice. The late Mr Leighton, in the course of some excavations, discovered on the low cliff of Reedham the ground-plan or foundations of a circular tower, which he believed to have been a

10 *The north wall of the nave of Reedham Church with a blocked arch made almost entirely of re-used Roman material, apparently derived from a nearby site, possibly a military one, that has now disappeared.*

Roman Pharos. It is impossible at this distance of time to gain any further particulars of so curious a discovery: I will only observe that a lighthouse on the hill of Reedham would have been visible from the Roman station of Garianonum [Burgh Castle], and from a large extent of the estuaries of the Yare and Waveney.[15]

Slight as the evidence for the pharos might be, it is much more convincing than the folklore concerning a 'Roman dock' cut out of the hillside at Brundall. This excavation, some 100 feet long and five feet deep, is mentioned by G.E. Fox in his article 'Roman Norfolk'[16] published in 1889, but in giving a some-what enigmatic description of this feature he does not suggest its having been a dock, and from what he tells us this seems not at all likely. It sounds more like a tank for some kind of industrial process, or a swimming pool – and Roman swimming pools have been found elsewhere in Britain. Fox is careful not even to ascribe a Roman date to the basin, though he does record the finding of Roman pottery in the vicinity.

George Levine in his village history sheds some light on the matter when he records that, during the 1880s, when Dr Michael Beverley was laying out

11 *A close-up of Roman tiles and other material incorporated in the wall of St John the Baptist Church at Reedham.*

the grounds of Brundall Gardens he came across various Roman and Saxon remains, but the excavations were 'casual and inconclusive and left a number of questions unanswered'. It was Dr Beverley's theory, 'advanced on the scantiest evidence', that what he had found was a Roman dock. Part of the evidence was that the area was known as Dock Close in 1839, but Levine comments that 'the possibility that the word Dock may have applied to the weed of that name should not be overlooked'.

Illustrated on the village sign erected by the Women's Institute to celebrate its jubilee, this Roman shipbuilding yard on the shore of the Great Estuary seems to be unsupported by any real evidence. Of slightly better repute are the Romano-British cremation burials found about 1820 in the area just to the north of where Brundall railway station was built some two decades later. The urns in which the ashes were interred were taken to line a garden path, and being unglazed they crumbled away through rain and frost within a few years; nothing survives of what could have been a most revealing discovery.[17]

Three

SETTLERS AND INVADERS

Roman rule in Britain ended about A.D. 410, though the influence of 400 years of Roman government must have survived for a good deal longer. It is possible that there was rather more continuity of life and religion than has often been supposed.

Under the Romans eastern England had been an integral part of the Roman empire, but with the end of their rule East Anglia took on a separate identity. In the south the Angles of East Anglia were separated from the Saxons of Essex by the River Stour, and in the west the boundary with the Mercians was marked by the Fleam Dyke, now found to have been dug first in the late Roman or early Saxon period, and the Devil's Dyke, running from Newmarket to the edge of the Fens at Burwell. To the east the region was bounded by the North Sea, which was less a rigid boundary cutting East Anglia off from its neighbours than a highway of communication with the continent and Scandinavia.

It was people from Angeln – roughly that part of northern Germany now known as Schleswig-Holstein – and the west of Norway, identified by the pots used for their cremation burials and by the use of wrist clasps,[1] who settled in this region. Contrary to long-held beliefs, they seem not to have slaughtered all the existing inhabitants nor to have driven them out but to have settled down alongside them, becoming the dominant people and producing a dynasty of East Anglian kings that had its royal cemetery at Sutton Hoo in Suffolk. Agriculture, so well established during the Iron Age and the Roman occupation, seems to have continued without interruption.

These immigrants were pagans, though by the seventh century they were being converted to Christianity. There is a chance that the Christian religion survived among some of the people among whom they settled, for towards the end of the Roman period Christianity had become the official religion of the Roman empire and the forts of the east coast might have contained Christian churches, though no archaeological evidence has been found of this. If there were churches inside or adjoining the east coast forts, it is not impossible that some might have survived in recognisable form until the seventh century.

If we can take the place-name Walton as indicating a population of Romano-British ancestry surviving to be called 'wealas' by the Anglo-Saxons, and accept that the Bran in Brancaster is directly derived from the Roman name Branodunum and that the river name Yare derives from the same root as Gariannonum, there appears to be an element of continuity that encourages the notion of Christian communities surviving to meet the incoming St Felix, brought to Dommoc (Walton Castle, Suffolk) by King Sigeberht in 631. Could there have been a remnant Christian community when St Fursa arrived on the Great Estuary about the same time, to settle at Cnobheresburgh as recorded by Bede? Both these missionary saints might have been more sympathetic to the British 'Celtic' tradition than the 'Roman' Augustine at Canterbury, who we are certainly told did take over an existing church.

A quiet Christian community surviving among the subject people would not attract attention in the Anglo-Saxon record, but there is a possibility that King Redwald saw the value among one group of his subjects of adding the Christian god to his Anglo-Saxon pantheon. Could that have been the motivation behind that well-known story of his setting up a dual-use temple with two altars, one pagan, one Christian?

The parish church of Caistor St Edmund stands in a corner of the Roman walled site, and there might have been a continuous Christian presence there. Unfortunately we do not know what lies beneath the present medieval church, though there is a suggestion that a predecessor of the existing church might have been an early minster, with its territory bounded by the rivers Tas, Yare and Chet.[2] Another early church, perhaps a Roman one even, might have been at Eccles, between Palling and Happisburgh, where the round-towered church has fallen on to the beach; the name of Eccles is thought to derive from the Latin *ecclesia*, a church.

Medieval sources record the tradition that St Felix founded a church at Reedham, which would have been close to Fursa's Cnobheresburgh, whether that were at Burgh Castle or at Caister-on-Sea. Felix is also linked to an early church at Loddon, on the south side of the Great Estuary, where the present church is a 15th-century replacement of a Norman building. Both the Flixtons in the Waveney valley are related to St Felix by Norman Scarfe, who ascribes Homersfield to Bishop Humberht.[3] With Hoxne being held by the Bishop and named in Domesday Book as the seat of the diocese in Suffolk, and a minster at Mendham, we have an interesting focus of episcopal activity in that area.

Danes and Vikings
Reedham also comes into the legend of St Edmund, the last independent Anglo-Saxon king of East Anglia who was killed by the Danes in A.D. 869/870. According to a version of the story told in the early 13th century by Roger of Wendover,[4] a member of the Danish royal family, Lothbroc, went hawking in a small boat and was driven out to sea in a storm. He landed at Reedham, and was received with honour by King Edmund. One of the king's huntsmen, a man named Bern, envied the Dane's hunting skill and the fact that Edmund so favoured him, so he killed him and hid the body in a wood, where it was later found by the dead man's greyhound. The murderer was

cast out to sea in Lothbroc's boat and in due course was washed up on the Danish coast. Taken to the Danish court, Bern told Hinguar and Hubba, the two sons of Lothbroc, that Edmund had killed their father, and persuaded them to embark on a search for revenge that ended in Edmund's death. Though this story is recorded only in a late text, one wonders why anyone should have invented a reference to Reedham. Possibly the story originated in a real misunderstanding over an embassy or trade delegation, or even some secret communication between the rulers of Denmark and East Anglia.

By the time of Edmund's death the Great Estuary had shrunk, due to the rising of the land in relation to sea level and to silting that followed the growing up of a sandbank across the mouth of the estuary, that bank on which Yarmouth was to develop. Where in Roman times there had been a shallow inland sea there was in Anglo-Saxon days an area of marshland that could be used for grazing animals, with the rivers meandering through it towards the sea.[5] We do not have sufficient knowledge to paint a detailed picture of the landscape at that time, and there is disagreement as to quite how much of the land was dry and how much was bog, but we do know that eastern England was approaching its highest level since the Romans were here. From the 11th century the land began dropping again.

Whatever the truth behind the story of Lothbroc landing at Reedham, Edmund's death at the hands of the Danes – also known as Vikings – was the result of a prolonged campaign by those hostile people who are recorded as first raiding East Anglia in 865. The earliest visits by the Danes seem to have been piratical raids seeking gold and silver, and as they were not at that time Christians they attached no special respect to churches and monasteries, which they discovered to contain much of value. When monks and priests resisted the sacking of their establishments they were killed and the buildings set on fire, so Christian writers saw these raids as an attack on their religion. Edmund was seen as a martyr who had died for his faith, and soon became a saint to whom numerous East Anglian churches, including those at Acle and Thurne, were dedicated.

It is ironic that after settling in England the Danes quite soon adopted Christianity, and within 25 years of Edmund's death the Danish rulers under whom the region became part of the Danelaw issued a memorial coinage in his honour as both saint and king. The Danes seem to have adopted him as their own saint, but it has to be said that as long as they controlled the Danelaw they continued to deprive the monasteries of their lands, which were restored only under English rule in the middle of the 10th century.

According to the Anglo-Saxon Chronicle, the Danes shared out land in East Anglia in 880, and it would appear that their visits were not confined to raids in which they raped and pillaged. A tradition that the Blood Hills in Somerton was the site of a battle in which the invaders slaughtered the local inhabitants has been disproved by Barbara Cornford, who discovered a much more recent origin of the name, rendered as Bladwells Way in 1740.[6] Viking settlement is indicated by the presence in the regional dialect of many words and usages derived from the Norse language and by a concentration of –by place-names in the Flegg, but the newcomers do not seem to have confined themselves to this area. A wider spread of Viking field-names suggests that peasant farmers from Scandinavia occupied a much more extensive area of Norfolk; finds of jewellery and dress fittings of Scandinavian origin likely to belong to farmers and their wives also points to a wide distribution of settlement.[7] The archaeological evidence of peasant farmers occupying land across Norfolk provides a balance to the biased and very limited documentary record which refers only to violent raids and massacres.

It would seem that the newcomers settled down among the existing inhabitants, and it is probably reasonable to regard the resulting population, both in the countryside and in the growing town of Norwich, as Anglo-Scandinavian. This Danish influence is thought to be the origin of the large number of free men recorded in this area in Domesday Book, as the Danish system of government recognised the rights of individuals speaking in the governing assembly, known as the Thing.

A new series of violent raids on the region under joint Danish and Norwegian leadership began in the late 10th century and culminated in the Danish king Cnut (Canute) ruling as a Christian king over England as well as Denmark and Norway from 1016 to 1035. Then in 1066 the Normans, descended from another group of Vikings that had settled in France, introduced a new group of rulers who took control of all the land but brought comparatively few new settlers.

The survey carried out for the Conqueror in 1086 provides a most interesting picture of who owned what land in the area and, to some extent at least, of what was being done with the land. The illumination it sheds on life in the Norman period is, however, somewhat patchy, and the information given in Domesday Book is open to varying interpretations. It has been averred on the strength of the payment to Bury Abbey of 60,000 herrings that Beccles was at the time a significant fishing port lying at the head of an arm of the sea, but this seems most unlikely. Blomefield makes a similar claim that 'in ancient days, before the retreat of the sea', Norwich 'was a great fishing town as Yarmouth now is'.[8] What is far more likely is that both were important markets for herring brought from the coastal settlements, the Beccles payment being on account of the market there being three parts owned by Bury Abbey, the other part belonging to the king; no market at Yarmouth is recorded in Domesday Book.

The preservation of herrings, and the preservation of food generally, required salt, and the Broads area was one of the main centres in East Anglia for salt production. While we have no clues as to the amount being produced, we do know from the Domesday survey that there were 23 villages in the Flegg and elsewhere in the Broads that had saltpans in which salt was produced by boiling seawater over fires which were almost certainly fuelled by peat. As the salt crystals precipitated out they were removed from the pan and shovelled into wicker baskets to dry.

Though some villages were credited in Domesday Book only with a fraction, presumably because they shared a single saltpan with other nearby settlements, the place that seems to have been at the centre of the industry, Caister-on-Sea, had forty-five. Other Flegg villages with salterns included Hemsby, Winterton and Somerton on or close to the coast and places such as Filby, Mautby, Thrigby and Runham just a few miles inland. There were three 'salinae' at Burgh Castle and three more at Gorleston, but none recorded for Yarmouth itself. More surprising entries in the list are the inland villages of South Walsham and Sutton, with half a saltpan each, and Halvergate, with a single saltpan. It is generally assumed that the salterns belonging to these villages were in the coastal area or in the marshes adjoining the lower reaches of the rivers; the parish of South Walsham has a detached portion in the marshes to the east of Halvergate between the River Bure and Halvergate Fleet.

It was possibly one of these salterns that was excavated by members of the Norfolk Research Committee in 1948 on marshes at Ashtree Farm north of the Acle New Road, a mile west of Yarmouth but actually in a detached portion of Acle parish. Beneath a long mound was found a layer of slag containing pottery dating from the 11th to 13th centuries, which seemed to indicate the period the saltpan was active, if that is what it was.

St Benet's Abbey

There is little doubt that in the 10th to 11th centuries the area later known as Broadland, including Flegg and that part of Suffolk known as Lothingland in which the Danes had settled, was among the most populous areas of England. That could account for the number of monastic houses, some fairly large and others distinctly small, that existed in the area during the Middle Ages.

Earliest of these must surely be the Abbey of St Benet (St Benedict) at Holme in the parish of Horning, which might have been founded as early as 800. A medieval tradition recorded by John of Brompton in the 15th century attributes the establishment of this house to a hermit, Suneman, and others who joined him at a place beside the River Bure then called Calvescroft or Couholm. Suneman lived there for more than 50 years until his death, but the hermits were killed and their dwellings destroyed by the Danish followers of Inguar and Hubba, those same Danes who later killed King Edmund at Bradfield St Clare.

St Benet's is said to have been re-established somewhere about 960 by one Wulfric, who with seven followers held it for 60 years. Then in 1019 or 1020 it was refounded as a Benedictine monastery by King Cnut, who endowed it with his manors of Horning – 'the vill with its meadows and woodlands' – Ludham and Neatishead, as recorded in a charter whose authenticity is doubted by some scholars. Antonia Gransden makes the point that both the St Benet's charter and one relating to Bury Abbey could be medieval forgeries and suggests that both abbeys were re-formed from Ramsey Abbey, in the Fenland.[9] C.R. Hart expressed uncertainty whether the charter was genuine

Ecclefiæ Cænobialis S. Benedicti
de Hulmo in Agro Norfolcienfi, cænobio
nondum everfo delineatæ, et in quodam
codice MS. in Bibliotheca Cottoniana
repertæ, Figura.

12   *This engraving of St Benet's Abbey that appeared in the first edition of Dugdale's* Monasticon *(1655) is based on an earlier drawing bound up with the chronicle of John of Oxnead in the BL Cottonian Collection. It appears to show the north side of the abbey church from the direction of the fishponds; the cloisters and other buildings stood to the south of the church. The central tower appears to be a timber lantern, rather than a masonry tower, and there is no sign of the west tower that is known to have been completed by the fifth abbot, the Norman Richard, in the early 12th century; had it fallen down by the time the sketch was made?*

but suggested it might be,[10] saying that it was apparently issued at the same time as the one establishing the Benedictine abbey at Beodrichesworth, today's Bury St Edmunds, as it has the same witness list. It was probably drawn up soon after the death of Aelfgar, Bishop of Elmham, on 25 December 1021, it being noted that the abbey was to be independent of the bishop; it was witnessed early in the time of Bishop Aelfwine of Elmham.

13 *An etching by John Sell Cotman of the inside of St Benet's Abbey gateway, made in 1813. The 14th-century gateway must have been a most impressive building when it was complete, the standard of finish being very high. The 18th-century windmill builders who used the gateway to provide a secure foundation for their tower unintentionally provided protection for the fine carvings on the outside of the gate, though the weather has still rendered the design something of a puzzle to historians.*

Whether or not the charters are genuine, W.R. West describes a confirmation by Edward the Confessor of the abbey's possessions in various places as 'spurious' in his calendar of the abbey's 11th- to 12th-century documents, published by the Norfolk Records Society in 1932.

A delightful tale of how Cnut came to endow St Benet's is told by a 17th-century historian. It seems that one of the king's officers had taken a violent dislike to Wulfric and accused him and his companions of many crimes so as to turn the king against them. Determined to investigate these accusations for himself, Cnut went in disguise to the abbey accompanied only by a servant or two, thinking to take the occupants unaware. As he walked along the causeway that led from Horning to the abbey the king was met by Wulfric, who greeted him loyally with 'God save your majesty, King Canutus'. 'How do you know me to be the king?' asked the disguised Cnut in some surprise. 'Three days since an angel of God told me that the king would at this time come hither and richly endow the place', replied Wulfric. Retelling the tale in his *Index Monasticus* of 1832, Richard Taylor admitted that it was 'somewhat too marvellous to be offered as historical evidence'.

14 *The ruins of the St Benet's Abbey church, a photograph taken by George Christopher Davies about 1880. This view shows clearly how the earth has been removed from the interior of the nave, undermining the walls and leading to the collapse of a section of the south wall.*

That might be no more than legend, but it could be that the story reflects the fact that St Benet's was sited on a royal estate. The parish church of Horning, dedicated like the abbey to St Benedict, stands at the west end of an earthwork that once ran from the River Bure to the Ant, though it has now been levelled, and Tim Pestell has suggested that this earthwork, too massive for a monastic vallum, might have been the boundary of a royal estate which the king had granted to the monastery. He compares the parish of Horning containing the St Benet's site with Horningsea in Cambridgeshire, which is a similar peninsula cut off by the Fleam Dyke, an earthwork with Anglo-Saxon burials in it. The church of Fen Ditton, which was within Horningsea, stands at the western end of the Fleam Dyke, just as Horning church stands at the western end of the Bure-Ant earthwork.

The coincidence of name might be significant, though Eilert Ekwall gives divergent origins for the two names, suggesting that Horning is from Old English for 'the people at the bend of the river'. There is, however, another derivation that might fit both places, bearing in mind that both are in effect peninsulas: it could be that in both instances the name is derived from the word '*horna*', a tongue of land, as between two rivers.[11]

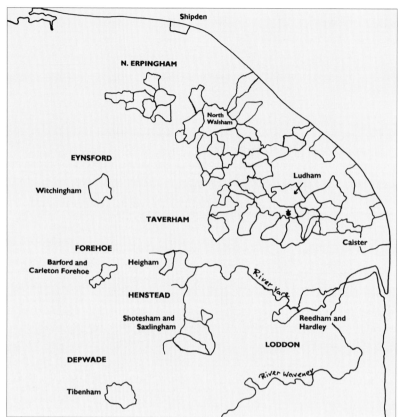

15 *St Benet's Abbey held land in no fewer than 13 hundreds, including the manor of Heigham on the outskirts of Norwich. The parishes in which the abbey had holdings are shown in outline on this map, the main holdings being in the hundreds of East and West Flegg, Happing, Tunstead, North Erpingham and Walsham.*

Whatever the possible links between Horning and Horningsea, there is certainly a link between St Benet's and the Abbey of St Edmund in Suffolk. In 1021 Cnut took half the monks from St Benet's – 13 out of 26 – together with half their books, vestments and vessels to set up the new abbey at Beodrichesworth, which replaced a college of secular priests who had looked after the shrine of St Edmund up to then. He also made the prior of St Benet's, Uvius, first abbot of Bury. It sounds as though St Benet's was already a flourishing institution before Cnut's charter, if the king was able to take half its monks and its furnishings without endangering its survival, so it would seem there is some truth in the story that it was re-established as early as 960. The renewal of St Benet's would fit in the context of the religious recovery in East Anglia initiated by Bishop Theodred of London and continued by Bishop Aethelwold of Winchester.

The two abbeys, St Benet's and Bury, certainly had a very close 'confederacy' of supporting each other by the 1260s, the abbots attending each other's elections, installations and funerals; they would help each other in times of poverty or trouble, if necessary harbouring half the inmates of the stricken house. When the people of Bury attacked St Edmund's Abbey in

16 *Although the sails were destroyed by a gale in 1863, the cap of the windmill remained for some years more, as seen in this photograph from the 1870s taken by Dr W.T. Bensly.*

1326-7 William Stowe, the sacrist, and others fled to St Benet's, whose abbot was appointed by the Pope to enforce restitution of the abbey's property afterwards, and to excommunicate the rioters.

Elsinus, the first abbot of St Benet's, replaced the existing church with one of stone, and the work of building was continued by his successor Thurstan and by the third abbot, Alfweald. Richard Taylor tells us how the Anglo-Saxon monks such as those who chose the low island of Cowholme for the site of St Benet's sought solitude amidst the marshes in which to construct 'their almost inaccessible habitations', and this remains a popular view. In a period when water transport was much used in preference to overland carriage, however, St Benet's on its 15-hectare island at Horning was anything but

17 *Looking west across the site of St Benet's Abbey, with the windmill rising above the gateway on the right. In this picture by George Christopher Davies a wherry can be seen sailing down the Bure and on the left a lateener, with lateen sails on both masts, is proceeding upriver.*

inaccessible, and there is little doubt that the stone for the new church of St Benedict was brought to the site by river. Much later, in the 15th century, the abbot of St Benet's sought by court action to preserve his right of passage downriver from his manor of Heigham, on the Wensum west of Norwich.

The strategic position of the abbey presumably had something to do with King Harold's appointment of Abbot Alfweald to take charge of coastal defence (*marina custodia*) at the time of the Norman invasion. After the Conquest he fled to Denmark to escape William's wrath, but he seems to have remained in exile for only a relatively short time before returning to resume his work as abbot; he died at St Benet's in 1089. St Benet's had a cell at Rumburgh in Suffolk, established in the 11th century by Bishop Ailmer, who was brother of Archbishop Stigand of Canterbury.

St Benet's is the only Norfolk monastery in Domesday Book, which records its holdings of property in Norfolk, much of it in the Broads area. It retained the key holdings of Horning, Neatishead and most of Ludham, and held in total 86 carucates (ploughlands) in demesne, 316 sokemen with 15 carucates and 87 acres, and 81 freemen with five carucates and 101 acres. On the lower-lying land scattered through surrounding parishes the abbey grazed sheep, but there were also holdings of rich arable fields in North Erpingham, Tunstead and Henstead hundreds. Some properties, including a number in Norwich and Yarmouth, were given by monks on joining the monastery.

About 1147 Abbot Hugh leased the Marsh of Fulholm in a detached part of Postwick with 300 sheep, and also some salinae or saltpans, from Philip of Postwick for five marks a year. He paid 15 marks down and was acquitted of rent for seven years 'from the setting out of the King of France and other barons and the said Philip to Jerusalem' – that is, Philip was raising funds to pay for his participation in the Second Crusade. In 1175 Abbot Thomas was leasing out the Postwick marsh at five marks and four shillings a year.[12]

Terms of holding tenancies and the field systems in use seem to vary in different villages, probably as a result of the individuality of Scandinavian settlers in the region. J.R. West compiled a list of nearly 140 personal names appearing in the abbey register in the 12th century and found 81 Old English names and 58 Scandinavian. The abbey held its own court at Hare Hill in South Walsham and also held the Hundred Court of Tunstead, which in 1128 was leased out at 20 shillings a year; there is a Hare Fen near South Walsham and also a hill locally known as St Benet's Hill.[13]

The second abbot set a pattern for the future, for he was a local man, to judge from his surname of de Ludham. In spite of its undoubted importance nationally as well as within Norfolk, the abbey seems to have adopted a policy of bringing on its own men to positions of authority. Ethelwold was succeeded by Ralph, the first Norman abbot, when he died in 1089; one cannot be certain about the origins of succeeding abbots who do not have surnames, but surnames from the 12th century onwards indicate that most of those who were elected to the abbacy were Norfolk or Suffolk men. Robert de Thorkeseye, elected in 1237, is likely to have come from the Lincolnshire village of Torksey, at the junction of the Fossdyke navigation and the Trent, but his successor as abbot, William de Ringfeld, was presumably from the Suffolk parish of Ringsfield, near Beccles. Adam de Neatishead, Richard de Bukenham and Nicholas de Walsham are likely to have come from nearer at hand, as did John and Robert de Aylsham, William de Hadesco (Haddiscoe), Robert de Sancta Fide (Horsham St Faith) and Richard de South Walsham, whose tomb-stone landed up in Norwich after the abbey was dismantled. Then there was Thomas Pakefield (Pakefield, south of Lowestoft), and the last abbot was William Repps, who was also known as William Rugge.

Its position in the midst of the marshes did not save the abbey from serious damage in the rebellion headed by Robert, Earl of Leicester, and Hugh Bigod, Earl of Norfolk, in the reign of Henry II. Austin Poole, who trawled very successfully through the Pipe Rolls to tell the story of the 12th century in *The Oxford History of England*, found that in 1176 the abbey was still in a state of partial devastation 'owing to the war of Earl Hugh'.[14] From 1168 until 1175 the abbey was in the king's hand, Prior Adam being in charge of ecclesiastical matters and Wimar the Chaplain accounting to the king for the revenue. Abbot Thomas, who had been Prior of Tofts (Toft Monks) until his appointment to St Benet's, had to do a good deal of building work as, according to William of Worcester, the property had suffered while in the king's hand. Small wonder that many years later, in 1327, the abbot was granted a licence to enclose the abbey with a battlemented wall, part of which still remains along the northern perimeter of the site, with a short section at full height alongside the oft-photographed gatehouse.

St Benet's withstood an attack during the Peasants' Revolt of 1381, when some 400 local rebels laid siege to the abbey in the mistaken belief that their great enemy Bishop Despencer was inside. Unfortunately for today's historians, the rebels did manage to secure the abbot's court rolls, which they burnt.

18 *The* Chequers Inn, *last inhabited building on the St Benet's site, was a popular waterside hostelry until its destruction by fire not long after this photograph was taken by George Christopher Davies about 1880. The photograph is entitled 'Mrs. Jones, Bure'; presumably she was the licensee, but her name cannot be traced in contemporary directories. On the right can be seen the chimney of the South Walsham steam pumping station.*

The flushwork facing of the exterior of the 14th-century gatehouse and the carving over the arch – happily protected for the past 200 years or so by the brick windmill tower – is of a very high quality, and the size of the gatehouse would have made it a most impressive entrance to the abbey. Having entered the gate visitors would have looked up the hill at the magnificent church, which would have seemed to tower above them. Although the elevation of the church site is probably no more than ten feet it is enough even now to raise the eyes; with a large church crowned by a central lantern rising from the little hill the view would have been awe-inspiring.

The gatehouse and a small adjacent section of the perimeter wall form the most spectacular survival from the medieval abbey. The walls of the church crowning the summit of the low hill on which the abbey stood are now so low as to give little idea of the imposing size and nature of that building, which measured some 340 feet from the west tower to the chapel of the Holy Trinity at the east end. Not only were the materials of the church recycled but the area of the nave had at some time been excavated by the tenant farmer, the earth and the many bones it contained being used as top dressing for some of the neighbouring fields. This excavation had so undermined the south wall of the nave that it fell over, and the surviving remnant of the north wall was underpinned with rough masonry by a 19th-century tenant.[15]

The site of the high altar is now marked by a large wooden cross, made of oak from the Sandringham estate, given by Her Majesty the Queen. Nothing at all is to be seen of the cloister, the guest hall, refectory, dormitory and infirmary and other buildings lying to the south of the church and chapter house. Few people visit the site apart from holidaymakers who come upon it while cruising on the Broads, but in future it may be given a higher historical profile by the Norfolk Archaeological Trust, which was in 2001 given a grant of £20,000 by the Town Close Estate Charity, the Norwich freeman's charity, and the Scarfe Charitable Trust to help buy the land on which the abbey remains stand; it took possession the following year.

Far from being an isolated place ignored by the local inhabitants in the Middle Ages, St Benet's was much frequented not only by those well-to-do local gentry who gave generously in hopes of later advantage but by the ordinary people of the area. There were two fairs held each year on the Fairstead outside the abbey gates, one on 25 July, St James the Greater's day, and the other on 21 March, St Benedict's day. In 1247 King Henry III granted the abbey the right to hold these two fairs at Grabbard's Ferry – later known as Horning Ferry – so as to avoid the noise disturbing the tranquillity thought appropriate to the daily round of the monks.

Many of those who attended the fairs at the abbey would have come by the causeway from Horning, but many more almost certainly came by boat along the river. The Ant had flowed along the northern boundary of the abbey to enter the Thurne, but after the course of the river was changed, cutting the causeway, a wooden bridge was erected to restore communication; the timbers of this bridge were still to be seen in the 18th century.

Although the abbey was not a very large one, there seldom being more than 25 monks in addition to the abbot and prior, it enjoyed an importance out of all proportion to its complement. The abbots were not infrequently called away to the king's court to give their counsel to the king, leaving the prior in charge of affairs at the abbey, where administrative matters must have taken up a good deal of time; the abbey was, after all, the centre of a considerable estate which extended over a very wide area of Norfolk. A fairly typical piece of business was transacted in the 1130s when Walter Halteyn granted to the abbey an acre of meadow at Hellesdon for making a millpool for the monks' mill. In exchange Walter received six marks and a meadow for which he used to render 16 pence a year, and he was accepted into the fraternity of the monks. Then there was the grant to the abbey by Walter de Bessingham of four weys of salt annually, to be taken from the saltpan of Symon Grehte, a reminder that salt for preserving as well as savouring food was an essential commodity in the Middle Ages.

The cellarer, who was in charge of food supplies and saw to the housing of the many servants employed at the abbey, could have gathered up much of the necessary food from the abbey's own holdings. Fish were brought in from the fresh-water fisheries owned by the abbey and were kept in the fishponds or stews which can still be traced from their earthworks north of the gatehouse, which faces on to the causeway from Horning. During the 12th century Abbot Daniel, a married man and a glassworker before entering the church, built a guest house, the Hostel of St James, for travellers on this approach about half a mile from the abbey. Both this hostel and another at Great Hautbois (Hobbis), near Coltishall, were controlled by the almoner of

St Benet's, who dispensed charity and hospitality on the abbey's behalf. The barn near Horning Hall which is today referred to as St James's Hostel is a 15th-century replacement for the original building.

Monastic Mission
The part played by the monastic houses in looking after travellers, sick and aged people and more generally in the economic life of the countryside was little appreciated until these social services were removed as a result of the Dissolution in the 16th century. Those who were wealthy enough to do so often contributed to the abbey's funds to ensure that they might live in the abbey in their old age, and be buried in the abbey church when they died. Sir John Fastolf, who built Caister Castle in 1432-5, was a great benefactor of St Benet's, building a chapel south of the chancel in which he and his wife were later buried. He apparently used the abbey as a safe deposit, because the inventory taken at his death included three thousand ounces of silver plate stored there.

Even a relatively minor monastic establishment such as Carrow Priory, a Benedictine nunnery founded in 1146 beside the River Wensum on the south-eastern outskirts of Norwich, played a significant part in the life of people in the surrounding area. Not only did the nunnery have an educational role in the local community but it also owned the manors of Crostwick and Wroxham as well as that of Carrow, the right to present incumbents to or to take the tithes from 15 churches in the area, and lands, rents, tithes and interests in some 80 parishes in Norwich and the county. This involved much more than a source of income for the priory, for with the manor of Wroxham went rights of fishery in the river and of taking rabbits on the land, providing a ready source of food for the nuns. The Wroxham fishery led to a dispute with the abbot of St Benet's, who claimed similar rights.

More than that, in 1335 the prioress received royal licence to accept in mortmain – meaning a permanent transfer of ownership to the priory – 34 properties, 80 acres of land, six acres of meadow and 12 acres of turbary in Wroxham, Rackheath, Crostwick, Beeston, Bastwick, Blofield and Ranworth which she bought from John de Hecham.[16] The turbary, ground containing deposits of peat that could be cut for fuel, is particularly significant, for this land would provide a ready supply of fuel for heating and cooking in the priory. Is it too great a leap of imagination to suppose that this 12 acres of turbary might be the infant Wroxham Broad?

Carrow, with its prioress and nine to a dozen nuns, was a very small place compared with the Norwich Cathedral Priory with about sixty monks. The Revd Francis Blomefield devotes more than six pages to listing the revenues and liberties of the prior and convent; let it be enough to say that among their possessions were the 'towns' of Martham and Hemsby, St Nicholas's church at Yarmouth and all belonging to it, and – among many others – the churches of Ormesby St Margaret-cum-Scratby and Ormesby St Michael, St Andrew and St Peter. The widespread properties of the priory also included grazing marshes on the Yare and Waveney.

The administration of estates of this size required a large staff, and it has been said that half the members of any monastic community were fully engaged in administration at one level or another. At a visitation in 1308 Bishop John Salmon was extremely critical of those monks who excused themselves from attendance at services because of pressure of administrative work.[17] In fact the monks formed only a small proportion of the priory population, Dr H.W. Saunders arguing that the total community of the Norwich priory in the 13th and 14th centuries must have been some 270 people, including the clerks of the church as well as cooks, grooms and other servants.[18]

The cathedral priory also had five cells or out-stations, one of which was at Aldeby, not far from the Wheatacre marshes that were part of the priory possessions. The existing parish church at Aldeby, with its central tower and fine Norman west door, appears to have been used as the priory church. Although the Ordnance Survey map shows the remains of the priory as being close to Aldeby Hall, some distance from the church, it would appear that the priory was immediately to the south of the church; possibly the site marked on the map was a grange, or monastic farm. There is no doubt that this priory was engaged in farming, for by an agreement of 1310 the prior of Aldeby was allowed to take marl from the great common of Aldeby 'to marle his lands'.

Not far away from the Aldeby priory was another Benedictine house at Toft Monks – the second element of the name remains as a reminder of this alien priory, which belonged to a Benedictine abbey in Normandy and was suppressed, with other priories whose parent houses were French, in 1415. This priory held the marshes on the Haddiscoe side of the Waveney across which travellers had to pass to reach the early ferry at Herringfleet, which was in existence at least by the end of the 13th century.

Religious houses were thick on the ground, for just up the road at Haddiscoe was a preceptory of the Knights Templar, of which Henry III is said to have been a considerable benefactor; however, the order of Templars was abolished in 1312 and the possessions of the Haddiscoe preceptory were taken into the hands of the sheriff of Norfolk and Suffolk. On a 'holm' or area of rising ground about ten feet above sea level on the Suffolk side of the Haddiscoe-Herringfleet ferry was a house of Augustinian canons founded by Roger fitzOsbert about 1216. Situated in a northern part of Herringfleet parish, this priory was dedicated to St Olave or Olaf, the Norwegian king and martyr who died about 1030, and it thus gave a new name to the locality in which it was built. In 1225 the priory was granted the right to hold an annual fair at Herringfleet on St Olave's day.[19]

The Augustinian or 'black canons', so called from the black cloaks they wore, were ordained clergy who lived a common life in the priory and owned no private property. They were therefore able to officiate at services in local churches and to devote their time to the spiritual welfare of the people among whom they circulated. In some cases the canons were indeed put in charge of churches that had been appropriated to their priory.

Suppressed with the smaller monasteries in 1537, St Olave's was first leased and later sold to Sir Henry Jernegan or Jerningham, who converted the buildings into his private house. Much of the priory was destroyed in 1784, a good deal of the material going towards the restoration of Herringfleet church in 1823. Little now remains apart from the undercroft of the refectory, constructed in the 14th century of brick; it is particularly interesting as being a very early use of this material. One of the undercroft columns rests on an old millstone, said to be of Roman date.

Another Augustinian priory was established at Hickling by Theobald de Valoins, lord of the two Hickling manors of Overhall and Netherhall, in 1185. It has been suggested that this was actually a reorganisation of an earlier foundation. Although Richard Taylor tells us that it held eight lordships and the advowson of nine churches and was granted a Friday market in Hickling in 1204,[20] this small priory seems to have found difficulty in making ends meet, for in 1397 'in consideration of impoverishment through frequent hospitality and great exactions' the Pope confirmed the permission given by the Bishop of Norwich for one of the canons to be appointed to the parish church of All Saints at Hickling on the death of the existing vicar.[21] Mention of 'frequent hospitality' does not necessarily imply a degree of high living but simply reflects the role of the religious houses in the Middle Ages, when they provided many of the social services that proved so significantly lacking after the Dissolution.

Remains of this establishment were still to be seen about 1860 'in the outbuildings of a farm-house, about half a mile north of the church'. The last window of the priory, we are told, was taken down in 1825 'and forms a porch to the farm-house'.[22]

At Langley, just south of the Yare between Loddon and Norwich, was a house of white canons, so called from their white habit. When this Premonstratensian house was founded in 1198 the first canons came from Alnwick Priory, in Northumberland, of which it was a daughter house. Is it a coincidence that there is in St Mary's Church, Surlingham, a brass to Master John of Alnwick, dated 1460? Although its complement was small, only an abbot and 15 or so canons at most, Langley Abbey was generously endowed by its founder, Sir Robert fitzRoger Helke, and by 1291 it had possessions in 62 parishes in Norfolk and 13 in Suffolk.

All the same, Langley Abbey does not seem to have been an altogether successful venture, for in 1343 it told the Pope that income from the market had been reduced by floods both from the river and the sea, as well as by the number of people seeking hospitality. The canons requested appropriation of the church of Thurton, to be served by one of the canons. At a visitation in 1488 the place was reported to be better run than at a previous visitation, when there had been references to the canons' visits to common taverns near the monastery, but 14 years later it was in financial difficulties and the abbot was removed from office. Nonetheless, on the credit side it has to be said that one of the Langley monks was responsible for the Sarum antiphoner on display in Ranworth church. With its illuminated capitals peopled by kings,

19 *The ruins of Bromholm Priory, seen from the south-east in a 19th-century photograph. This small monastic house gained fame and fortune when it came into possession of an alleged piece of the True Cross.*

monks and musicians, this lovely manuscript was restored to the Broadland church in 1912 after it found its way into a London bookshop, from which it was bought for the then very considerable sum of £500.

Bromholm Priory, overlooking the sea in the parish of Bacton, which began life in 1113 as a cell of the Cluniac priory of Castle Acre, would probably have been no more notable than Langley had it not been for its acquisition of a cross said to have been made of wood from the very cross on which Jesus had been crucified. The cross was among relics brought from the emperor's chapel in Constantinople by an English priest who had escaped with his two sons when that city fell to the Turks. The story goes that on reaching England he offered his relics to the monks of St Albans, but they, doubting their and his authenticity, turned him away. The poor canons of Bromholm were more welcoming, accepting his relics and admitting the priest and his sons as members of their community.

Matthew Paris, who tells the story, says that from the time the relics arrived at Bromholm,

> divine miracles began to be wrought in that monastery, to the praise and glory of the life-giving Cross; for there the dead were restored to life, the blind recovered their sight, and the lame their power of walking; the skin of lepers was made clean, and those possessed of devils were released from them; and any sick person who approached the aforesaid Cross with faith went away safe and sound. This said Cross is frequently worshipped, not only by the English people, but also by those from distant countries, and those who have heard of the divine miracles connected with it.[23]

[37]

The cross became a famous destination of pilgrimage. King Henry III visited the priory in 1256, at which time the monks began new building work. The Holy Rood of Bromholm is mentioned by Chaucer in 'The Reeve's Tale', when the miller's wife calls on it to save her. In the 15th century it was claimed that it restored the sight of 19 people and raised 39 from the dead, but it was sent to London for destruction in 1537.

Henry Harrod, in his *Gleanings Among the Castles and Convents of Norfolk*, published in 1857, tells how in the 19th century the remains of the priory had been taken into farming use and 'made a sort of hospital for maimed agricultural implements'. Today the site is being investigated by Tim Pestell, whose fieldwalking and metal detecting has recovered 5-6,000 objects, including a 13th-century gold ring, 47 silver coins and a good deal of lead. A close study of the locations of coins and lead weights clustered in certain areas of the precinct at different periods suggests movement over time of the area where trade took place and into which visitors were channelled.

The suppression by Henry VIII of the various monastic houses in the 1530s must have been traumatic not only for the monks and canons but for the many lay officers and servants employed within these establishments, and for many more people less intimately connected with the monasteries and priories. Besides bringing to an end centuries of social work provided by the religious houses, the Dissolution brought a revolution in land ownership, transferring sometimes large estates from the Church to the king, who disposed of them very largely to those who could afford to pay him handsomely for their new possessions.

Only one major religious house survived, and then only in a somewhat tenuous form. The last abbot of St Benet's, William Reppes or Rugge, was appointed Bishop of Norwich by King Henry in 1536, thus combining the bishopric and the abbacy. The Act of Parliament by which the two were united stipulated that 'the saide bishoppe shall have, finde and keepe within the saide monastery of Seynt Benet at the leste twelve monkes over and besydes the said priour ... for the mayntenaunce and kepying of dyvyne servyce there ...'.

Thus, alone of all the monastic houses, St Benet's escaped dissolution. For many years the Bishop of Norwich sat in the House of Lords not as a diocesan bishop but as Abbot of St Benet's, until in modern times it was decided that this historical anomaly could not be allowed to continue, thus arousing the ire of no less a man than M.R. James, the Provost of Eton. Red tape, he said, had 'wiped out a nice little harmless piece of history'.[24] The incumbent of Horning is now titular prior of St Benet's.

The king granted to the Bishop the estates of St Benet's, but in exchange took from him the much more valuable properties of the diocese. Perhaps the mitred abbot simply could not afford to keep up the abbey in the marshes, and the last monk is said to have left the site in 1545.[25] For all practical purposes the abbey had been as effectively suppressed as all the rest, and the abandoned buildings became a quarry from which stone was acquired for a variety of building work all over the area.

The Parish Churches

There is a curious link between St Benet's and the parish church of St Edmund at Thurne, a mile and a half from the abbey across the River Thurne. In the west wall of the square flint tower is a tubular squint so aligned that, in theory at least, a priest standing at the altar would be able to look down the length of the church and through the squint and see the abbey church. In practice one feels that it would be necessary for an assistant to be stationed at the squint, able to pass on any signal to the officiating priest, if indeed it was intended for such a purpose. Expla-

20 *An exterior view of the squint in the tower of Thurne church which is aligned on St Benet's Abbey.*

nations that it was a leper squint, enabling those excluded from the church by reason of their illness to see the elevation of the Host at Mass, or that it could be used to call for assistance from the abbey by lighting a candle in the tower are just not satisfactory – from personal observation it is plain that the draught through the squint would have put out any candle. Having regard to the careful alignment of this squint, it would appear that its purpose must have been to enable the priest at Thurne to co-ordinate Mass with the celebration in the abbey church; but just how it might have been done remains a matter for speculation.

The extraordinary number of churches in this area of east Norfolk and north-east Suffolk is partly at least a reflection of the relatively high population in the early Middle Ages. The Revd Alfred Suckling claimed that with the aid of a telescope he could see 70 churches from the tower of Burgh Castle church, and the proximity of one church to another is sometimes surprising. The apparent superfluity of church buildings might be the result of the number of freeholders, identified as freemen or sokemen in Domesday Book, and the fact that many places did not have one single lord of the manor, a situation that created a large number of individuals in a position to assert their status by establishing their own church.

Some quite small communities even had two churches, sometimes standing together in the same churchyard. The case of South Walsham is well known: St Mary's is still in use for worship, and the adjacent church of St Lawrence is now an arts centre after many years of dereliction following a fire in 1827 which destroyed not only much of the church but also a house and five barns, three wheat stacks and a haystack. The fire was caused by a careless cottager's wife throwing out a shovelful of hot ashes that set dry grass ablaze. The church was repaired and put back into use in 1832, but when the two livings were united in 1890 St Lawrence's was used as a Sunday school. In

21 *The ruined tower, all that remains of Repps church, in a photograph from the 1880s.*

1946, however, a decision was made to close the building and allow it to decay naturally, and it was in a very sad state when restoration began in 1992 with the idea of using it as a centre for training and the arts. Surlingham in the Yare valley and its neighbour Rockland also at one time each had two churches with separate parishes, but in both cases one of the churches fell into decay centuries ago. The same applies to Antingham, where lies the source of the River Ant.

Already by the time of Domesday Book there were many churches in the region, and it is likely that the majority of these were built of timber, some-times possibly on sites that had been of religious significance for centuries. In a few places it has been possible to prove by excavation that the original church was a timber building, but in most cases any possible evidence is concealed by the existing building. In surviving stone buildings it is difficult, and frequently impossible, to distinguish pre-Conquest work from that done

soon after the arrival of the
Normans, and it seems very likely
that some typically Saxon work is to
be found in churches that were
erected after the Norman takeover.
The magnificent west door of Aldeby
church is unmistakably Norman, but
it contains a capital whose decoration is so typical of Saxon work that
one feels it could only have been
done by a native carver, perhaps
even one who was cocking a snook
at his Norman overseer.

Not a few of the churches in the
Broads area stand in commanding
positions on the edge of the upland

22 *Intricate carving on the capitals of the Norman north
doorway of Hales church, including what appears to be an
owl's face.*

overlooking the marshes. None is more impressive than Haddiscoe, whose
round tower has two encircling bands of freestone and a slightly projecting
battlemented upper stage, with chequerwork below the battlements that was
added in the 15th century; the building stands on a bluff, giving it a most
dramatic appearance, particularly from the south-west.

A good many of the churches in the area have round western towers, some
of which were surely built before the Conquest, though many more are certainly post-Conquest. In the Lothingland peninsula nine out of the 14 churches
are round-towered. Stephen Heywood considers that the function of the round
tower was no different from that of other western towers, the principal use
being to house bells, and he suggests that the round tower was not only
characteristic of East Anglian churches but was almost obligatory during the
Romanesque period.[26] There is, he points out, only one other region in Europe
where single round western towers are used, and this is in Schleswig-Holstein
and the area around Bremen and Luneburg Heath, a district with which our
own region has strong cultural links. A few examples are to be found in
southern Sweden, whence came the Wuffinga kings of East Anglia.

A feature of certain of the early round towers is an entrance high in the
east side of the tower that could only be reached by ladder; this has led many
people to believe that the towers were used as a refuge at a time when Danish
raiders were pillaging the area. 'That many towers now attached to churches
were built for defensive purposes admits of no doubt whatever,' says the church
architect H. Munro Cautley, stoutly.[27]

> Even so late as the 13th century towers were provided for this purpose on the
> turbulent borders of Scotland and Wales, and if this were so, how much more
> necessary would such towers have been on the east coast in pre-Norman days? I
> have little doubt that many of the round towers of Suffolk and Norfolk are of the
> period of the Danish invasions and were built for defence.

23   *The Norman apse of Hales church.*

Others might disagree with Munro Cautley's expression of certainty, but in this respect we might also note the round towers built in fine ashlar masonry in Ireland in the early Middle Ages and allegedly intended to protect the church's books, plate and vestments from risk of fire and theft. Could this be evidence of the religious links of all these areas with the Church in Ireland, including St Fursey directly and St Felix indirectly?

These towers took some time to build, since it was necessary to leave the mortar to set thoroughly before laying further courses of stone; if the mason tried to hurry the work the whole thing might collapse. In some towers such as Mutford it is still possible to see the annual stages of work and to count the number of years it took to complete the structure.

There were probably many more round towers to be seen before the spate of new building in the 14th and 15th centuries that resulted in fine Gothic churches such as St Catherine's at Ludham, St Mary's at Martham – sometimes dubbed the cathedral of the Fleggs – and St Helen's at Ranworth, now considered one of the showplaces of the Broads. Almost all trace of the earlier church was sometimes swept away as the new structure took its place, but occasionally remnants turn up, as happened at St Edmund's at Acle, where parts of a Norman doorway were recovered in 1927 and rather roughly re-erected in the former rood loft stair turret. At Ranworth, also, there is a fragment of a Norman arch re-set in a buttress, presumably a relic of an earlier church whose foundations were found beneath the chancel during repair work in 1910.

24 *The sumptuous screen of Ranworth church was little regarded when this photograph was taken on 3 July 1881 and the church itself was slipping into dereliction. Within a few years the congregation was sitting under umbrellas to protect them from water dripping from the leaking roof.*

It is the magnificent screen that brings many visitors to Ranworth church, for it is considered to be one of the best – if not the best – in Britain. A statement from a report by the Society of Antiquaries, quoted in the many-times-reprinted guide by Canon H.J. Enraght, may be taken in evidence of its superlative quality:

> The magnificent painted Rood Screen and Reredoses to the Nave Altars form a composition which is unequalled by any now existing in a district famous for its Screens. As a whole, it may be said that there is nothing of the sort remaining to equal it in England. East Anglia still contains a considerable number of Painted Screens, some of much merit, in its churches, but for delicacy and richness of detail, that of Ranworth is unsurpassed.[28]

The screen not only cuts off the chancel from the nave but is extended to form partitions separating off the side chapels, whose altars have their own reredoses bearing the figures of saints. Another very fine screen can be seen at Barton Turf, where the saints depicted include St Olaf, who can be iden-tified by the punning emblem of a 'whole loaf' of bread.

The neighbouring parishes of Hales and Loddon offer an opportunity to examine some aspects of the church story. The church at Hales, whose round tower is probably the earliest part of the building, is some distance from the village, which has presumably moved at some time since a site was chosen for the church. Inside the lowest stage of the tower it is possible to see the imprint of the wickerwork formers that were used to create the splayed openings of the round windows. Although the main windows were probably inserted in the 13th century, the curving exterior of the apsidal east end retains much of its Romanesque arcading and its flat buttresses.

The north doorway into the nave is a very fine piece of Romanesque work: while most of the decoration is abstract patterning there is an owl's head at the lowest eastern end of an arch. Inside traces survive of painted decoration applied to the walls between the 13th and 15th centuries, reminding us that even small churches like this were richly ornamented and brightly coloured before the 16th-century Reformation. There on the walls are St James the Great with his staff and wallet, St Christopher carrying Christ across the river, and patterns of foliage that survive from a former riot of decoration. Similar wall paintings have been found in a number of other churches in the region.

No trace survives of the church that was founded at Loddon by East Anglia's first bishop, St Felix, but it almost certainly stood in the same prominent position in the centre of the village as the present one, overlooking the little River Chet. The church was totally rebuilt about 1490 by Sir James Hobart, who lived at Hales Hall and was Attorney General to Henry VII; he died in 1507 and was buried in Norwich Cathedral. Having been built all at one time, Holy Trinity church provides a fine example of a complete church in the Perpendicular style. While Hales church is no longer in regular use, Loddon's remains very active, being part of a local ecumenical project involving Anglicans, Methodists and Roman Catholics.

A painting to be seen in the church shows Sir James Hobart and his wife. It is apparently a reproduction of the design of the east window of the church as it was before its destruction by Puritans in 1642; the churchwardens' accounts for that year record, 'Laide out to Rochester the glaser efasinge of the images in the church £0 6s. 0d.' The reference to the glazier implies that the images were in glass. A Latin inscription at the foot of the picture asks us to 'pray for the soul of James Hobart, Knight, who built this parish church of Loddon from the foundations at his own cost, and for Dame Hobart his wife who built the bridge of St Olave's, together with the road leading to it at her own expense, for the public good'.

Four

THE RIVER CROSSINGS

The painting in Loddon church links the Hobarts to the important river crossing at St Olave's and to the bridge that was built about 1490, perhaps to replace the earlier ferry or just possibly to replace an earlier bridge. The history of that river crossing is not entirely clear.

There was probably already a ferry in operation when the Augustinian priory of St Olave's was founded about 1216, but the earliest record appears in 1295 when King Edward I sent a writ to William de Kerdeston, sheriff of Norfolk and Suffolk, to inquire what harm it would cause to any person for him to grant leave to Jeffery Pollerin, of Yarmouth, to build a bridge over the river at St Olave's Priory. A jury was empanelled, and it returned that one Sireck a fisherman had begun several years before to carry over passengers in his boat there, and received for his pains bread, herrings and such like things to the value of 20 shillings a year; after his death his son William made it worth 30 shillings a year; and after him Ralph, his son, performed the same service and received in payment from his neighbours bread and corn, and from strangers money; and because the prior of Toft (the Benedictine house of Toft Monks) hindered passengers from going through his marsh, Ralph purchased from the prior a causeway through the prior's marsh with a fleet or ditch on each side, paying 12 pence per year; and from the commoners of Herringfleet he purchased a way through their common, and was to carry them over at all times free, and then it became worth £10 per year. After Ralph's death his son John had the ferry, and it was valued at £12 a year. John sold it to Roger de Ludham, who then held it, and he gave it to his grandson Roger de Ludham, who valued it at £15 a year. The jury said that if the king allowed Pollerin to build a bridge across the water there it would cause no loss to the king, but it would cause a loss of £15 a year to Roger de Ludham and a loss of 12 pence to the prior of Tofts. It would, however, be to the great benefit of the whole people.

The jury's return gives both a concise history of the early ferry and an insight into the medieval economy, with the ferryman being paid in items of food by his local passengers and in cash by travellers from further afield. What it does not reveal is whether a bridge was built, though we do know that leave was given. If it were built it did not survive for very long, as we know

25   *Surlingham Ferry in a photograph of about 1880, with the pontoon in its dock on the extreme right.*

that a ferry was operating in the 15th century. In 1400 Henry IV granted his esquire Ralph Ramsey licence to operate and take the profits from the ferry called 'Seint Tollow Ferye' between Norfolk and Suffolk on the death of Sir George de Felbrigg, who had held it previously.[1] Then in 1421 Henry V granted a patent for building a bridge over the water between Norfolk and Suffolk at 'Seent Tholowes Ferry' alias 'St Olcoff fery' to Sir Thomas Erpingham, who had previously obtained the property of Toft Monks when the king dissolved it as an alien priory in 1415. The bridge, it was said, would be to the benefit of the adjoining country and would provide for the safety of the king and himself and Joan his wife and for their souls after death – a reminder that the Church designated the building and repair of bridges 'pious and meritorious works before God'. Sir Thomas was to repair the bridge whenever necessary, and the king withdrew all his claim over the passage and ferry, with the provision that whenever the bridge was broken, so that the king's lieges could not cross, the king and his heirs would control the passage and ferry, taking the income until the bridge was repaired.[2]

Sir Thomas had to buy out the interest of the ferry operator, because we find in the patent rolls confirmation that William Ramsey was to receive an annual payment of 20 marks from Sir Thomas in return for surrendering the letters patent of Henry IV granting him and his brother the ferry.[3] William and his brother Ralph had quoted these letters patent in the previous year[4] as entitling them to the ferry on the death of their father Ralph Ramsey, when Henry V had granted the ferry in 1419 to Giles Thorndon and his wife Alice.[5] The Ramseys won their case, and the king granted his esquire Giles Thorndon and Alice his wife £23 per year in lieu of the ferry.[6] From all this we still have no evidence that the bridge was actually built at that time.

The first certain record of the building – or rebuilding – of St Olave's bridge comes from the record in Loddon church that Margaret Hobart built a bridge about 1490. The stone bridge of three arches illustrated in the painting was either rebuilt in similar form or repaired in 1768, by which time the timber piles on which the stone piers stood were in a fairly parlous state, to judge from a report quoted by Dr W.A.S. Wynne.[7]

The stone bridge was replaced in 1847 by a single-span tied-arch bowstring bridge of cast iron built by George Edwards, of Carlton Colville, who had earlier been involved in the construction of Lowestoft harbour. A classic example of its type, the bridge has a clear span of 80 feet and is of considerable interest as a surviving example of 19th-century technology. The deck was originally supported on cast-iron cross girders suspended from the main girders by wrought-iron hangers, but the deck girders were replaced by steel joists in 1959 when it became necessary to strengthen the bridge to cope with increasing weights of traffic.[8] The bridge was again strengthened in 1998 to enable it to carry the 40-tonne lorries then being introduced to British roads.

With the making of the Haddiscoe New Cut as part of the Norwich and Lowestoft Navigation in the 1830s, a small lifting bridge was built near the St Olave's crossing to carry the Beccles-Yarmouth road. A toll was charged to river traffic using the New Cut, this being collected by the bridgekeeper, who would extend a linen bag – it had probably begun life as a flour bag – on a long cane so that the boatman could drop the appropriate coin into it. By the time this bridge was replaced by a high-level viaduct that strode over both railway and New Cut the little lift bridge was becoming rather ramshackle, rattling and shaking as road traffic passed over it.

Not only is the early history of St Olave's bridge somewhat obscure but we have no idea of the nature of the ferryboat that preceded it. Since the ferry

26 *A load of stone is unloaded from a wherry close to Acle bridge. The early history of this river crossing is obscure, but there is evidence that the earliest bridge had been preceded by a ford.*

was almost certainly used only by foot passengers it is reasonable to suppose that nothing more than a marshman's boat, or perhaps a reed lighter, was required. Elsewhere larger craft were used to carry horse-drawn vehicles and, in later days, mechanically propelled vehicles over the rivers. There were in the 19th and early 20th centuries 'horse ferries' – so called because they could carry a horse and waggon – at Reedham, Surlingham and Buckenham on the Yare and at Stokesby and Horning on the North River as well as a number of other ferries for foot passengers.

These 'horse ferries' were large wooden pontoons that were hauled from one side of the river to the other by a chain laid from bank to bank. In earlier days a rope would have been used, hauled hand over hand by the ferryman, but later a simple hand-cranked winch was used to wind in the chain; since 1986 the last chain ferry in operation, that at Reedham, has been operated by a diesel-hydraulic winch. The existing ferry pontoon at

Reedham was built by Richards Ironworks, but the origin of earlier pontoons seems not to be recorded beyond the fact that they were the product of local boatbuilders.

Grabbarde's Ferry at Horning is recorded as far back as the 13th century; the antiquity of the other ferries is uncertain, though some of them at least must have been working in the Middle Ages. Until the building of the Norwich southern bypass and Postwick bridge there were no bridges on the Yare between Norwich and Yarmouth, so the ferries played a major role in local transport until in the mid-20th century all but one went out of use. Reedham ferry has, in spite of discussions as to the viability of a bridge in the vicinity, continued to provide a very necessary link, being kept busy in the sugar beet season with lorries laden with beet from farms south of the river bound for the Cantley sugar factory – the alternative is a 20-mile detour.

On the North River the horse ferry at Horning had already ceased work when the *Ferry Inn* was destroyed by bombing in 1941, although a passenger ferry continued to operate until 1967, two years after the rebuilt inn had been gutted by fire as a result of smuts from a chimney igniting the thatched roof. This passenger ferry was a large marshman's punt with a light chain that was hauled hand over hand, a wet, cold operation in the depths of winter; the charge was an old penny, though that often went unpaid when those using it had to haul themselves across the river.

These later ferries were all on minor local routes, for major crossings like that at St Olave's were all bridged either in the Middle Ages or later. St Olave's lay on the road that seems at one time to have been the main land route between Norwich and Yarmouth, though it has to be remembered that for both goods and passengers the dominant route between these two was the river. A secondary road seems to have been that which ran from Norwich to Halvergate and then followed the winding Halvergate Fleet across the marshes to a ferry that carried travellers over the Bure into Yarmouth; it was almost certainly a route mainly for walkers and perhaps for pack animals, but little used by wheeled vehicles. The road layout in the area generally was determined by the available river crossings.

A particularly valuable river crossing was that just to the north of Acle where the Wey bridge carried the old road from Norwich into the Flegg and to Caister-by-Yarmouth over the Bure. Linking a promontory on the south-western corner of the Flegg to solid ground at Acle, the road had to be carried on a causeway two feet above the marsh. In Roman times the estuary was probably a mile and three-quarters wide at this point, so the Roman road into Flegg crossed the river a dozen miles or more to the north-west at or near Brampton, just below Aylsham, but by 1101 when there was a reference to the Weybrigg at Acle the sea level had receded and this crossing was in use.[9] Whether the crossing was a bridge or a ford at that period is uncertain, since there is evidence from another part of East Anglia that use of the word 'brigg' or 'bridge' sometimes implied a fording point rather than a structure above water level. Certainly in 1958-9 Charles Green and members of the Norfolk Research

27 *The Wey bridge at Acle, in a lithograph from Francis Stone's book on Norfolk bridges. If it is true that the bridge was built in 1830, it must have been almost new when Stone made the drawing from which this print derives, unless this shows an earlier bridge surprisingly similar to its replacement.*

Committee found evidence of a gravel ford under the bridge, and it was suggested that this ford might have been constructed in late Saxon times.

Until its replacement in 1931 Acle bridge was a three-arched stone bridge with the two piers supported on oak piles driven closely together into the river bed. The heads of the piles were sawn off and a platform comprised of a double layer of oak boards carefully dowelled together at right angles to each other was constructed on top to form a base for the stonework. The building of this bridge has been dated to 1830, but nothing seems to be recorded of its predecessors, though a bridge is certainly shown on Faden's map of 1797. The old bridge with its three quite narrow arches would have proved a barrier to any vessel other than keels and wherries.

Some of the upriver bridges certainly proved an impediment to navigation even by wherries, which were able to lower their masts to pass through the low, narrow arches. Ludham bridge, which is said to have been provided and maintained by the Abbot of St Benet's and to have become the responsibility of the Bishop of Norwich after the Dissolution, had a particularly bad reputation. A statement which was repeated in successive directories during the 19th century is surely a great exaggeration, yet it does give a good idea of the difficulties faced by watermen in getting their craft through the bridge in extreme conditions: 'Ludham bridge ... has but a very narrow waterway, and after much rain at certain states of the tide, the wherrymen have as great a difficulty in forcing their vessels through it as formerly the lightermen had at Old London bridge.'[10]

28 *A pleasure wherry is framed in the arch of the old Ludham bridge, which was well known as a hazard to navigation on the Ant. It is said to have been built in 1811, and was replaced by a girder bridge in the 20th century.*

That unsatisfactory bridge, which is said to have been built in 1811, proved in the 20th century to be as inadequate for road traffic as it was unsuitable for wherries and was replaced by a steel girder bridge of almost unparalleled ugliness; the new bridge was itself replaced in 1959-60. If the bridge were preceded by a ford, as seems likely, the 20th-century building operations have removed all trace of the former crossing, but at Wayford bridge higher up the Ant, where the Roman road from the west to Caister-by-Yarmouth had its river crossing, Charles Green and members of the Norfolk Research Committee found a compact stony layer that might well be the paving of an early ford. Another stony ridge across the river some sixty yards above the bridge seems likely to represent a medieval cattle crossing used at a time when the fen was relatively dry; a medieval stirrup dredged from the river to the west of the bridge and now in the Norwich Castle Museum was probably lost by someone crossing this ford.

The same road that crosses the Ant by Wayford bridge crosses the Thurne at Potter Heigham, a village that takes the adjectival part of its name from the medieval pottery whose kilns have been discovered not far from the parish church. Until the mid-20th century the name was pronounced Po'er Ham, the first element of the name being shortened by the glottal stop that is so noticeable a feature of the local dialect, but with the settlement of many newcomers in the village and the surrounding area this distinctive pronunciation has been all but lost. The A149 now flies over the river on a modern concrete bridge, by-passing the narrow 14th-century stone bridge that survives thanks to its status as an Ancient Monument.

The history of this three-arched bridge, whose central arch of 21 feet span has a clearance to the crown of the arch of a mere seven feet, is obscure. Jervoise, whose pioneering *The Ancient Bridges of mid and eastern England* was

29 *Wroxham bridge before being widened in 1897, in a lithograph from Francis Stone's book on Norfolk bridges published in 1830.*

published in 1932, considered that the round-topped central arch was later than the two pointed side arches, and it might well be part of a post-14th-century rebuilding.

As the holiday trade built up it was increasingly considered that this bridge was a serious impediment to development of the hire fleets, and suggestions were put forward more than once that it should be taken down and replaced by a modern bridge. A wartime army officer who was in charge of arrangements for demolishing bridges in the area in the event of a German invasion in 1940 claimed that he was offered a considerable sum by one of the local boatbuilders to stage an 'accident' on Potter Heigham bridge; he solved his personal billeting problem by borrowing a motor cruiser from Herbert Woods, but declined the offer to 'blow' the bridge.

This is not the only Broadland bridge to have been declared an Ancient Monument, the other being Mayton bridge over the old course of the Bure at Little Hautbois, named after the nearby Mayton Hall. A red-brick structure, apparently of 17th- or 18th-century date, with two four-centred arches of unequal span, this bridge has a brick-and-tile shelter at each end of the upstream parapet.

While nothing at all seems to be known about the building and subsequent rebuilding of Potter Heigham bridge, we do have an extremely interesting record of the rebuilding of Wroxham bridge in 1576-7, thanks to the survival of the account book in which the two overseers responsible for the work recorded every small item of income and expenditure, right down to seven shillings and eightpence for two wheelbarrows.[11]

30 *Wroxham was an undeveloped village when this photograph of Wroxham bridge was taken by H.C. Bolingbroke in 1882. The building on the Hoveton side of the bridge with a large chimney is the steam roller mills operated by Horace Howlett, who described himself in his advertisements not as a miller but as a wheat meal manufacturer.*

Several people had in earlier years left bequests for the repair of the bridge at Wroxham, including John Spendlove, who died in 1432 leaving one mark to the 'Brygg in Wroxham' and was almost certainly of the same family as Hugh Spendlove of Wroxham, one of the two overseers responsible for the 1576-7 rebuilding. The wording of the will of Richard Brymley of Hickling, proved in 1506, in which he left 6s. 8d. to 'Wroxham Bridge, if it be repaired', suggests that the bridge was already in a decayed state in the early 16th century, while Katherine Crow of Catfield in her will dated 1568 left money 'to the repair of the bridges of Flegg Bastwick and Wroxham', the first-named presumably being that at Potter Heigham.

By the 1570s the bridge at Wroxham seems to have been beyond repair, since a mason was twice paid to inspect it in the two years leading up to the rebuilding. A Norwich freemason, John Waterman, was put in charge of the reconstruction, and much of the preliminary work seems to have been carried out at his yard in Norwich, for he was paid 'before the first daie of June 1577 for worke done by him & others at Norwich in hewing & working of freston [freestone] before the same daie' and 6s. 8d. was 'payde to diverse men for the carryeng of freston unto the keele' which delivered it to the site. It would appear that the piles of the old bridge, which might have been built of timber, had to be withdrawn from the ground before work could proceed on the new bridge: one of the items was 8d. 'for a roape to drawe up piles' and a more expensive item was 3s. 'for ii greate hawseropes broken with pullyng up of pyles'.

In addition to the time spent working on the stone at his yard, John Waterman spent 276 days working on the bridge site, together with his two apprentices, Robert Padd and Robert Potter. Another freemason, John Clason, worked 94 days at a shilling a day and 28 days at 10d. a day, earning £5 17s. 4d. Besides the freemasons the workforce included a number of roughmasons, among whom were John Pratt and John Horne who were retained on 26 January 1576 for 10d. a day. The former worked for 137 days and John Horne and Robert Horne – perhaps his brother – spent 98 days on the bridge work, other roughmasons spending shorter periods on the job. There were also at least 40 named casual labourers employed in the work for varying periods, in addition to unnamed workers from Salhouse, Wroxham, Hoveton and Belaugh, who seem to have been paid around 8d. a day. Some of the workers received rather more when they were doing a particularly skilled or particularly uncomfortable job, as when Robert Edon was paid 3s. 6d. 'for laboring iii daies in the ryver'.

Presumably lodgings had to be provided for some of the men while working on the bridge, since a house named Grosses was rented for two years at a cost of five shillings a year. Also appearing in the list of expenses is an item for building a house at the bridge foot 20 feet long and 11 feet wide, though whether this was to accommodate some of the men, to provide a secure store for materials or to serve as a watchman's office is unclear. It is surely no more than coincidence that this item appears immediately beneath one relating to the boarding of John Waterman and Robert Paddes (referred to earlier as Robert Padd) for five days, perhaps before the house called Grosses was available.

The building operations entailed the construction of cofferdams apparently made of poplar and alder planks caulked with clay; a considerable amount of labour was expended on 'casting water' – baling out the cofferdams – and Hugh Spendlove charged 2s. 6d. 'for the slytt and wearing of my pompe', no doubt worn out in keeping the cofferdams clear of water. The piles of poplar and alder purchased were perhaps used to form the cofferdams rather than for the foundations of the bridge. Sums of 16s., 9s. 4d. and 10s. were spent on these piles, making a total of 39s. 4d. according to the overseers' reckoning; where did the other four shillings go, one wonders?

31 *The iron bridge over the Waveney at Beccles was new when this photograph was taken; it had replaced the old stone bridge in 1881. Just below the bridge on the Beccles side a steam launch lies alongside a wherry, the occupants of the launch all keenly interested in the antics of the photographer.*

Some 130 'greate pyles' were no doubt those used in the foundations of the bridge, and one would expect them to be of oak. The cost of these came to £1 5s. 4d. Another £11 12s. 6d. was spent on lime, £17 16s. od. on 'bryck' and £7 16s. 5d. on 'Carryage'. Some of the materials came by river, for the entry reads: 'Itm. to dyverse persons for carryeng Lyme sande Bryck Pyles gravell stone & dyverse other thinges as well by water as by lande'. The £10 2s. od. laid out for freestone included a payment of £1 6s. 8d. to the executors of the late John Parkhurst, Bishop of Norwich, who had died in 1575, for eight tons of stone. Ten shillings was also paid to the bishop's executor for four tons of squared flint. It cannot be proved, but it seems very likely that both the freestone and the flint came from St Benet's Abbey, which was owned by the bishop and had been standing empty for some years. It would, of course, have been brought upriver by keel from the abbey site at Horning.

The total cost of the rebuilding amounted to £202 2s., just £8 18s. more than had been received from a special county rate, from a donation sent by the town of Yarmouth, from the tolls collected at the ferry that operated during the building operations, and from other minor income including a small legacy under the will of William Howse of Salhouse. Possibly the balance was rectified by 'Sartayn thynges Sowld Syns the yeildyng of thacownt', but one cannot be sure since that page is torn and the sum raised is uncertain. In any case, there were 'Charges layd owt Abowt the brigg sins thacount' including an unspecified payment 'to Jhon Watarman & hys prentys for makeyng A gayn that whiche was broken down w^t a cart'.

After all that work, lasting some two years, the bridge had to be rebuilt again in 1614, judging from a datestone that survived on the upstream side until fairly recent years. On the downstream side there was another datestone recording the widening of the bridge in 1897. Both datestones disappeared when the superstructure of the bridge was cut down so that a steel arch could be laid on top to carry the weight of road traffic. A steel footbridge has been erected on the downstream side of the old bridge, and altogether the present state of Wroxham bridge can only be described as a mess, neither historically intact nor entirely suitable for modern needs.

On the south side of the river the bridge was approached along a causeway lined with trees. In later days roadside trees in such situations were normally pollarded; that is, the head or poll was cut off so that new growth sprouted from the trunk or tod. Not only did the new growth provide a useful crop of 'loppins and stowins' every few years, but keeping the tree low reduced the chance of its being blown down in a gale and encouraged it to produce a good root system that would bind the causeway together.

Five

THE MAKING OF THE BROADS

Brushwood peat laid down at a period when the Norfolk rivers flowed through a wooded landscape provided medieval inhabitants of the region with a fuel that was not only burnt on their domestic hearths and in the kitchens of various monastic establishments but also served industrial processes such as saltmaking. Over the course of perhaps 400 years an estimated nine hundred million cubic feet of peat was extracted,[1] a considerable portion of this being carried by river to the city of Norwich.

This peat was formed at a time long ago when the eastern part of Norfolk was covered with dense woodland and scrub. As the plants and trees died they fell into water retained by the underlying clay and there slowly changed into peat; because of the anaerobic conditions (conditions in which there is a lack of oxygen) this vegetation did not rot but instead was partially broken down by bacteria, fungi and other agents into a compacted form that could be used by man as a fuel. The trunks of fallen trees survived in these conditions, to be dug out and dumped by the peat diggers and in more recent times by mechanical excavators working on deepening marsh drainage channels.

Exploitation of this important natural resource may have begun as early as Saxon times, though the production of turves finds no mention in Domesday Book, possibly because it was not thought to be something productive of a tax income for the king. Domesday does, however, reveal that in the 11th century Norfolk and Suffolk were the most densely populated counties in the whole of England, and that the area of the Broads was one of the most densely settled parts of Norfolk.[2] In the two Flegg hundreds and in neighbouring Happing hundred there was an average density of more than 20 recorded persons to the square mile, compared with a figure of around five to the square mile on the lighter lands in the west of the county. Perhaps significantly, the Domesday survey also showed that the Broads area was almost devoid of woodland, suggesting that the population would need to look for an alternative source of fuel to the normal brushwood.[3]

The poll tax returns of 1377 not only show that this region remained densely populated but indicate that it was a particularly prosperous area in a county that was the most highly assessed in the kingdom. In this regard, C.T. Smith points out that the parishes around the Ormesby-Rollesby-Filby

Broads, which together cover 464 acres, were especially prosperous, with an average parish assessment of £6 15s. compared with an average of £4 15s. for all the Broadland parishes, and it was there that the turf-pits were dug more deeply and the turf more thoroughly extracted than elsewhere.[4]

It is surprising that the large-scale excavation of peat was neither recorded in historical writings nor remembered in local tradition and folklore, in spite of the fact that peat-digging continued on a much smaller scale until at least the 19th century. It was not until Dr Joyce Lambert postulated the artificial origin of the Broads as a result of her investigations in the Yare valley and elsewhere that documentary research by Mr Smith brought to light a wealth of evidence of an industry that over some four centuries had a significant impact on the landscape of east Norfolk and north-east Suffolk and on the economic well-being of the region.

It is in the records of the monastic houses that the earliest references to the industry are to be found, for it was to a large extent on the estates belonging to the monasteries that the peat was dug and it was on the hearths of those institutions that much of it was burnt. Although it is likely that men had been digging turves since Saxon times, the earliest references date only from the 12th century and are to be found in the register of St Benet's Abbey, which had acquired turbary rights over a wide sweep of territory between Beeston St Lawrence and Waxham. The right to cut turf was just one of the rights that went with a grant of land, although in some instances turbary did achieve a special mention, as at Ludham where there is a specific mention of '10 acres of land and Wynnock turbary and the turbary which Wilfrid held in Ludham'.[5]

With the sea having retreated from the Great Estuary as a result of the land rising since Roman times, leaving only Breydon Water sealed behind the Yarmouth spit as a relic of that impressive inlet, there should have been little difficulty for workers in digging down through the overlying clay to reach the thick bed of brushwood peat, which had a much higher calorific value than the more recently deposited *Phragmites* peat on the surface. For all that many of the turf pits were dug close beside the rivers, drainage would have presented no great problem, particularly as the digging of the turves was a summer job. In some places such as the Ormesby-Rollesby-Filby Broads the excavations were eventually as much as 15 feet deep, though some of the pits close beside the rivers were no more than six or eight feet in depth.

There would have been no shortage of labour to dig the turves, since the bond tenants of the manor had an obligation to spend a certain length of time working for the manorial lord. Tenants of Stalham Hall in Burgh owed their lord a total of 23 days' labour in the digging of turves, while those of the manor of Burgh were liable to a total of 14 days' digging in the turbaries or to the payment of 14d. in lieu of that service. Manorial tenants were allocated strips of turbary from which they could cut the requirements of their own households.[6]

The St Benet's account roll makes it clear that it was not always the tenants who had to dig the turves as part of their obligations to the lord of the manor.

It is recorded that in 1240 ten men were paid for the digging of turves at Witemore in Neatishead. The situation of Witemore is unknown, but there can be no doubt that the Alderfen Pyttes in Irstead, mentioned in 1209, are the turf-pits which later formed Alderfen Broad, a landlocked broad in a side valley west of the River Ant.

The link between turbaries and the Broads themselves becomes obvious when it is seen that of the 20 places where turbaries or turf production are mentioned in the 13th century, 15 now have broads, or parts of broads. Of the 29 parishes mentioned in this respect in the 14th century, all but four now contain broads or parts of broads.

Production was not limited to Norfolk, for in Suffolk Fritton Lake, Flixton Decoy and Oulton Broad owe their existence to the extraction of peat. These broads are all to be seen on an Elizabethan plan of Lothingland, made as part of a survey for the defence of the coast in 1584. Of other broads early cartographical evidence is at best sparse; Christopher Saxton's map of 1574 shows only Fritton Lake and a complex of lagoons in the Flegg area that is not named but is almost certainly meant to represent the Ormesby-Rollesby-Filby group. Despite this lack of firm evidence there can be no reasonable doubt that the other broads were in existence by this time, for the land had been dropping since at least the 13th century and there are indications in plenty that the peat-pits had been progressively flooded either as a result of catastrophic floods such as those described in the next chapter or through gradual seepage as the water table rose.

In the early period of turf production, when loads of turves were being sent to the Norwich Cathedral Priory and elsewhere, the peat blocks were being cut out, probably, by special tools known in more modern times as beckets, thereby forming the vertical-sided, flat-bottomed pits that became the Broads. Baulks of peat were carefully left between individual holdings, no doubt to arrest seepage of water as well as to mark out the holdings; some of these survived into modern times, notably in Barton Broad and also in other broads. The turves would have been thrown from the pits on to adjacent ground and piled to dry before being loaded into carts or into keels for transport to wherever they were needed.

As the pits filled with water there was naturally a change in the production method which is reflected in the records, the description 'turbary' becoming increasingly uncommon in the 15th century and being replaced by 'fen' (the Latin *mora*) and later by such words as 'water and fen' and 'water and marsh'. The lands of the Great Hospital at Norwich in Wroxham and Salhouse were said in the 14th century to contain turbary, but by the 15th this had become 'water and marsh'. This change in nomenclature is accompanied in the records by references to the use of an implement known as a 'dyday', in other words what has been termed in more recent times a dydle, a long-handled tool with an iron ring at one end to which is fastened a piece of net. Used in the 19th and 20th centuries to clear mud from a marsh dyke, it was obviously employed in the 15th to dredge pieces of peat from the bottom of the flooded turf-pits.

The records show that, while at some places the large-scale digging of turves was declining in the late 13th and early 14th centuries, at Barton Turf (which acquired the suffix to its name in the Middle Ages) the extraction of 'fen' continued well into the 15th century. Account rolls for Bartonbury Hall, a Barton property of the Norwich Great Hospital, in 1432 mention '15 lasts, 2000 of fen taken with a dyday' and in the following year '4d. for ½ last of fen taken with a dyday'.[7] A last, or as it was more often written, a 'lest', was generally 10,000 turves. Manorial records at Hemsby that in 1294-5 contain the entry 'In cutting 2 lests turf 7s. 4d. 3s. 8d. per lest' change the formula in 1312-13 to 'In making 1½ lest of turves with ferrying 12s. 9d.'. In 1324-5 the wording is even more explicit: 'In ferrying fen 10s. In making turves of the same 5s.'[8] It seems from the way it is put that rough pieces of peat were being dredged from a flooded pit and were being brought ashore to be moulded into blocks which could be dried for the fire. The fact that 'fen' and 'turves' were by no means the same thing is underlined by one of the Bartonbury Hall references in which the word 'turves' was written, then crossed out and replaced by the word 'fen'.

It is from the entries in such documents that we can see the Broads in the process of being formed. As references to turbary and turves became fewer, so the number of mentions of fisheries proliferated. The abbot of St Benet's held turbaries at Hoveton that were still active in the 14th century, when large amounts of turves were being produced there, but after the Bishop of Norwich acquired these lands in 1535 we find no mention of turbary, no reference to turves. A detailed survey of the bishop's properties made in 1649 contains no evidence whatever of turbary; instead there were various waters and the fisheries on them which brought in a useful income. It is a fair guess that the valuable 17th-century fisheries were in waters that had flooded into the turbaries of earlier centuries.

With the flooding of the pits the cost of producing turves rose, and as the price went up so consumers looked for other fuels to burn on their hearths. The Norwich Cathedral Priory rolls appear to record a transition from turf to wood as fuel for the priory kitchens starting in the final quarter of the 14th century. Sea-coal brought from the mines of north-east England was known in Norwich by the beginning of the 14th century, though it was only in the 16th that Yarmouth and other East Anglian ports played so prominent a part in developing the seaborne coal trade. Once that was well under way sea-coal quickly replaced other fuels, the coal unloaded by coastal colliers at Yarmouth being distributed throughout the area by keels and wherries. In 1585-6 more than 25,800 tons of coal were landed at East Anglian ports, 5,000 tons at Yarmouth alone.[9]

While most of the Broads can reliably be considered to have originated as peat-pits, there are some in the Thurne valley that seem to have produced clay as well as fuel. While most of Hickling Broad appears to have provided fairly pure peat, Whiteslea and Heigham Sound to the south-east seem likely to have produced clay, presumably used for building. The basins of Horsey Mere and Martham Broad are likely to have provided both peat and clay.

When these excavations were first in progress the clay might well have been used in its raw form for the building of cob walls and perhaps for making clay lump, but it is quite possible that some of the clay was burned to produce bricks, since tiles and bricks were being made in East Anglia at least by the 14th century. Is it just possible that local peat was used in the firing of early bricks? In a much later period the brickworks at Martham turned out large quantities of bricks which went downriver in wherries to supply the Victorian development of the rising seaside resort of Yarmouth, though then the clay came not from Martham Broad but from pits close to Martham Ferry.

Salt Working

The various salt production sites on the lower reaches of the rivers which in their early days depended so much on peat as a fuel had ceased production by the beginning of the 17th century, but a major salt works on Cobholm Island continued to produce salt into the 19th century. The works with its saltponds, in which the brine stood prior to boiling in lead pans, can be seen both in James Corbridge's prospect of Yarmouth and in the later prospect by Samuel and Nathaniel Buck.

Just when this salt works was established is unknown, but it was in the hands of Nicholas Murford and Christopher Hanworth in the reign of Charles I. At the beginning of the 18th century the works was operated by the redoubtable Mrs Bridget Bendish, granddaughter of Oliver Cromwell and widow of Thomas Bendish, who had himself run the business until his death in 1707. According to the Yarmouth historian C.J. Palmer, Mrs Bendish, who is said to have greatly resembled her grandfather, was 'accustomed to give her personal attention to business' and 'might be seen from early morning till the decline of day superintending her workmen and labourers at her salt-pans, not disdaining herself to take part in the drudgery'.

She seems to have been an impressively strong character, and she did not hold herself in any way aloof from the social scene in Yarmouth. 'When the labours of the day were over, she would eat and drink heartily,' Palmer tells us,

> then throw herself on a couch, and fall into a profound sleep, from which she would rise with renewed vigour, dress herself in silk which had probably appeared at the court of her grandfather, the Lord Protector, and then drive in her chaise or ride on her pad to Yarmouth, and there join the assemblies at the Town Hall, where all gave her place and precedence; or she would visit the houses of some of her numerous friends, at which she was always a welcome guest.[10]

After her death at the age of 76 in 1728 the salt works with its reservoirs, pans and cisterns, and the cinder ovens and brick kiln on Cobholm Island, were in the hands of a Robinson Farrow. He was declared bankrupt in 1771, however, and some time thereafter they came into the hands of Jonathan Symonds, at whose death in 1803 they passed to his son-in-law, Edmund Preston, who continued to work the saltpans well into the 19th century.

As rock salt from Cheshire became readily available, the Yarmouth salt works used what was known as the 'salt on salt' process, dissolving rock salt in the brine to produce a much more concentrated solution which was boiled in the pans. Eventually, however, the availability of imported salt made it no longer profitable to manufacture salt at Yarmouth, and the works closed.

Post-Medieval Turf-Cutting

Long after the large-scale excavation of brushwood peat had come to an end, turves were still being burnt in the cottages of the poorer people, who dug them on the commons or on the 'poor's allotments' that were set aside when the old commons were enclosed. Although this digging of fuel from shallow cuttings went on well into the 19th century, relatively little remains either in the folk memory or in the literature of the Broads area to tell us of either the technical details about how the peat was extracted or the manner in which the digging was controlled by those who were in charge of the land from which it came.

White's Directory of 1845 has many references to the poor's allotments awarded in the various Enclosure Acts of the early 1800s. That at Horning was no more than 30 acres, 'upon which the poor cut yearly 3000 turves for each cottage', whereas at Burgh St Margaret and St Mary, more usually known as Fleggburgh, there was no less than 460 acres set aside for the poor. Forty acres was let, bringing in about £60 a year, the rest of the land being used for digging fuel and cutting reeds and sedge, the poor cottagers also being allowed to turn their cows on to it. At Catfield, Ludham, Neatishead, Smallburgh and Stalham the poor's allotments were all used for cutting fuel, but that at Sutton was said to be largely covered with water and to afford 'but little turf or rushes'. It is interesting to see from this directory that even at so late a date there was a turf dealer, John Hudson, at Hoveton and another, William Skipper, at Horning, suggesting that by no means all the turves were burnt by poor people cutting them from the poor's allotments.

William Dutt, writing at the beginning of the 20th century, remarks that in the vicinity of Horning 'a few marshmen may occasionally be seen cutting peat by the riverside. The peat, locally called turf or hovers, is cut into square blocks, which were formerly sold at a shilling a hundred'.[11] In writing about his adopted village of Horning, yachting journalist Charles Carrodus recorded that at one time there had been a turf staithe where the turves were sold to people who came with their carts and wheelbarrows. On this staithe the turves were first left, tilted at an angle, for the water to drain out of them and then stacked five or six feet high in what were known as hales to dry out more thoroughly, the stacking being done carefully to allow the circulation of air between the blocks.

Recalling that turf was in fairly general use in the district late in the 19th century, Carrodus says that even the local vicar piled turf on to the vicarage fires, both in the dining rooms and in his study. One of his informants told of a hard winter during which there was a pile of turves on the Woodbastwick side of the river and stocks in the village were getting low; when the river froze over and the ice became thick enough, the turves were brought over to the village by wheelbarrow.[12]

He also tells the tale of a wager between two turfcutters, 'Jack' Skipper and 'Bob' Allen, over which of them could cut a thousand turves in the shortest time. Old-timers in the village gleefully recounted how the contest took place on the Woodbastwick side of the river, which was 'Jack' Skipper's normal place of work. When 'Jack' proved the victor he not only pocketed the ten shillings wager but also the money he received for the turves cut by his opponent, who customarily worked on the Horning side.

Just how many turves did each of the contestants dig? In the Fens a thousand could be anything from 1,260 to 1,320 'cesses', or blocks of peat, but there seems to be no record of how many the Broadland men cut to the thousand. As for prices, the accounts of the Trustees for the Poor of Neatishead show that from 1815 to 1875 the price per thousand remained surprisingly stable at five shillings, which seems to have been just the cost of labour for cutting the turves from the poor's allotment. Where turf had to be bought in by the Trustees it could cost as much a twelve shillings per thousand.[13]

Not all the fuel consumed in the cottages was either brushwood peat from the deeper deposits or the *phragmites* peat that lay close to the surface. Some of it was no more than the parings of the surface vegetation, the roots and vegetable matter of the rough fen growth, known to past generations as 'flag' or 'hover'. It must have been a relatively poor material for burning, giving out more smoke than heat even when thoroughly dried, unlike the best peat which burned with little smoke. But those suffering from an extreme of poverty during the agricultural depressions that followed the end of the Napoleonic Wars were probably thankful for any warmth, however meagre.

'Hover' was dug with a heart-shaped paring spade that was also used for clearing the surface layers of vegetation when pits were prepared for the extraction of the underlying peat with a becket. The 1801 Enclosure Act for Potter Heigham contained a clause ordaining that if anybody 'cut, dig, pare, grave, flay, or carry away any Rushes, Fodder, Reed, Turf, or Flags in, upon, or from the said Commons, Fens, and Waste Grounds ... without licence' they should be fined not more than £5, which money should be applied to paying the costs of obtaining the Act. Such a wide-ranging prohibition was certain to be resented by poor people who had been cutting turves or flag before the passing of the Act, with or without the licence of the lord of the manor.

The cutting of turves or hovers was, Dutt says, to some extent controlled by local custom or common land trustees, who fixed the maximum number of hovers to be cut by a household, and he quotes the Revd M.C.H. Bird as recording that at East Ruston 5,000 hovers was the maximum allowed per household.[14] As an instance of this control Dutt sets down the memories of an old grey-bearded marshman from the lower Waveney valley who had, as a young man, cut turves in the fen that had once been the site of Barnby Broad, one of those former broads that grew up and became bog rather than open water.

Peat had been the only fuel burnt in his father's cottage, old Ben told Dutt, as it was in all the cottages along the edge of the marshes, where the fires were kept burning day and night all through the year. The old man recalled for Dutt the annual 'peat-running', at which the men of the village decided where their turves were to be cut during the year to come. It took place every 10 May, all the men who wished to cut turves meeting in the village street in front of an inn; the rest of the villagers turned out to see the fun.[15]

> 'For th' way on it wor like this,' said old Ben. 'A line wor marked acrost th' road, and every man what wanted ter run had ter toe th' line jist as in a boys' race at a skule treat, ony each on 'em carried a spade in his hand. Th' parish constable wor th' starter, and as sune as he gin th' wud, they all started a-runnin' down th' driftway to th' fen as hard as they could put fut ter th' ground. When they got there, every man had ter stick his spade inter th' middle o' th' place where he wanted ter cut his turves, and a-course him as got there fust got fust chyce. Widders, owd maids, and owd men wor 'lowed to hev young chaps run for 'em. I can mind as how I used ter run for owd Betty Woodrow, what lived agin th' pound. It wor a fare sight ter see us a-runnin' wi' half the' willage at our haals – sich a sight as can't be seen nowadays nowhere.'

A rather similar race took place at Fleggburgh in connection with the rush mowing on the poor's allotment in the early years of the 20th century, as recorded by Barbara Cornford. While the Trustees of the Poor were responsible for the management of the common, the day-to-day supervision lay with the Fender (or Defender) of the common, and it was he who fired the gun that started the rush mowing at six in the morning on the first Tuesday in July each year. The widow of the Fender told Mrs Cornford that about twenty men went and selected the areas they wanted to mow; the cutting all had to be done in the one day, though the men could come back later to heap, turn and cart their mowings. Those men who had no livestock of their own would sell the rough hay to local farmers.[16]

The digging of turves was by no means confined to a single day, yet there were strict rules in some places as to the season during which this occupation was allowed. At East Ruston in 1832, according to the Revd M.C.H. Bird, naturalist and for nearly 40 years parson of the adjoining parish of Brumstead, digging was forbidden until two in the afternoon of 8 May, and was then allowed to go on until 15 July.[17] As the demand for peat declined in the course of the 19th century these limits were relaxed.

It is interesting to see from the Neatishead accounts how the numbers of turves cut rose slowly from some 5,000 in 1815 to a peak of around 15,000 in the mid-1830s, perhaps as a result of increasing poverty in the countryside. Production plunged dramatically to about 6,000 turves a year in 1843 and continued at that level for a few years before beginning what seems to have been a terminal decline.[18] It was probably a decline that would be reflected in the production figures for other villages, if we had them.

Six

FARMING AND DRAINING

In the early Middle Ages, with the land having reached its highest level since the waters of the Great Estuary receded, flocks of sheep grazed the saltmarshes along the lower reaches of the Broadland rivers as well as the fresh marshes of the river valleys further inland. We know from Domesday Book that there were large numbers of sheep in East Anglia in the 11th century, and it is likely that the saltmarshes served at least in summer as communal sheep walks, with the sheep being taken off the marshes on to higher ground at times when spring tides covered the grazing.

Sheep continued to be a significant part of the local economy for some hundreds of years, the abbot of St Benet's having more than 1,500 in 1343. The abbot of the cathedral priory in Norwich sent both sheep and cattle to be grazed on the marshes belonging to the outlying priory of Aldeby, and in the 13th century the priory kept a flock of sheep on Fulholm, which lay on the Yarmouth side of the Halvergate marshes between Breydon Water and the Bure; the sheep remained there almost the year round, except for ten weeks after harvest when they were fed and folded on the stubbles at Martham. Entries in the Martham manor account rolls include 'carrying dung from Fulholm to Martham by water 13s. 6d.' (1272/3) and 'in carriage of the foldcote from Fulholm to Martham 3d.' (1299/1300).[1]

Barbara Cornford's work on manor rolls of the Flegg parishes has revealed a good deal about the state of the countryside in the Middle Ages. Land at Martham called 'Dunsyng' at Dungeon Corner, between the Hundred Stream and the dyke leading to Somerton, was described as scythable meadow in a 1292 survey, was regularly used for pasturing cattle in the 14th century and was called a pasture in the early sixteenth. Today it is reed bed and fen. It is a little surprising to find what appears to be saltmarsh as far upriver as Burgh St Margaret (Fleggburgh), but names found in 16th-century records include 'Saltffen' and 'ffreshffen', which seem to be indicative of the state of the respective marshes.

Flooding from the sea has always been a serious matter on the low-lying coasts of Norfolk and Suffolk. Many lives have been lost when storms have sent the waves crashing on to the beaches, washing gaps in the dunes and breaking down the cliffs, and high tides have spilled through the gaps to

32 *Widespread flooding struck the region after heavy rainfall in August 1912, causing great damage to bridges and waterways and inundating parts of many towns and villages and the city of Norwich. This was the scene in Westwick Street on 17 August of that year.*

flood great areas of countryside. The situation became steadily more threatening as the land dropped from the 11th century onwards and sea levels became correspondingly higher.

The earliest serious flooding of which there is any written record occurred in the 13th century, during what seems to have been an unusually wet and tempestuous period. Popular attention has concentrated on the gradual overthrow of the town of Dunwich in Suffolk, but erosion and destruction was by no means confined to just one part of the coast. John of Oxnead, a monk of St Benet's who towards the end of the 13th century set down a chronicle of the times in small, neat lettering with coloured capitals that is now in the British Library,[2] relates how in 1251 'the sea flowing and swelling dreadfully, crossed its usual boundaries by claiming further shores' and how in 1257 very wet weather destroyed crops and caused disease.

Worse was to come in 1287, when John of Oxnead reported how the sea broke through in the area between Waxham and Winterton where the River Thurne had entered the sea before its waters were diverted into the Bure. Enormous damage was caused over a wide area of eastern England, and flooding also occurred on the other side of the North Sea in Friesland.

This storm seems to have been accompanied by a tidal surge sweeping down the North Sea that must have been similar to the one which wreaked such havoc not only on Britain's east coast but in Holland on the night of

31 January/1 February 1953. John tells us in graphic terms how the sea broke with huge force through its accustomed bounds, flooding places which nobody remembered ever having been covered with seawater before. 'For about midnight, climbing up in its approach, it suffocated or drowned men and women sleeping in their beds and babies in their cots, all kinds of draught animals and fresh water fishes; houses with their contents were ripped entirely from their foundations and carried away and with irrecoverable loss hurled into the sea,' the monk tells us. That, surely, is a description of a tidal surge that advances across the countryside like a wall of water, a term that was used by so many witnesses of the 1953 disaster.

Some of those who found themselves surrounded by water tried to reach a place of refuge or climbed into trees, but they were overcome by the cold, fell into the water and drowned with the rest. In the village of Hickling alone 180 men and women perished as the floodwater rose, submerging the high altar in Hickling priory and forcing the Augustinian canons to flee in a boat. Two of the black canons who chose to remain in the priory saved the horses from the water by putting them in their dormitory, which was presumably on an upper floor.

St Benet's Abbey was an island in the midst of the flood. The salt water flooded into all the houses and offices on the lower ground, leaving the church on its island just above water level. 'In that time of pressing need the church of Saint Benedict was a stable for the horses,' says the chronicler, telling for the first time a tale that has been retold time and time again down the centuries of how the monks took their horses into the nave of the church to save them from the waters.

John of Oxnead tells of further coastal flooding in 1292, and there were many later instances of the sea breaking through and inundating the marshes. Possibly it was one of the storm surges that blocked the outfall of the Thurne and resulted in the river's reversal of course. No evidence has come to light of remedial work in the Middle Ages, but we do know that in 1564 a Commission of Sewers was granted to deal with flooding in the river valleys behind Yarmouth.[3] The passing of the Statute of Sewers in 1531 had established the principle that owners and occupiers of property could be taxed to pay for services provided by such agencies as the Commission.

Then in 1601 the sea broke in both at Eccles and at the point at which the Hundred Stream (formerly the lower reaches of the Thurne) approaches the sea, where a half-mile-wide breach allowed the salt water to enter the river and flood all the low-lying land behind the coastal dunes. Seven years later there was even worse flooding, and an Act was passed 'for the speedye recoverye of many thousand Acres of marsh grounds within the Counties of Norfolk and Suffolk'[4] by which a Commission of 11 or more J.P.s from Norfolk and six from Suffolk was appointed with similar powers to those of a Commission of Sewers.

The inrush of the sea had flooded the marshes of the Ant valley up to Stalham, up the Bure to Coltishall, up the Yare nearly to Norwich, and up the

Waveney as far as St Olave's, contaminating the grazing marshes which were a necessary complement to the arable farming of the upland areas and destroying the fisheries on which many poor fishermen depended.

The Sea Breach Commission did its best to restore the defences, financed by a rate on owners of low-lying land in the 92 places affected. It met from time to time in reaction to renewed threats, as in 1617 after winter storms had destroyed much of the earlier repair work and made four large breaches in the dunes. A jury that travelled down from Wroxham Bridge in two wherries to inspect the damage and to make a list of the landowners who should be rated to pay for the necessary work found themselves unable to fulfil the latter function because of the number of owners and occupiers, and because 'the persons there be so untoward and unwilling to discover the same'. Nonetheless, £1,288 13s. 4d. was spent on building up the dunes, using timber and faggots of gorse, broom, thorns or holly, stones and clay being rammed in to make a firm bank. The members of the Commission thought their work was done.

Alas, by 1622 the sea had again breached the dunes, and the Commissioners were again called together. One of them suggested that 'some skilful, experienced Ingeneer of the Low Countries, whereof one is lately come to Lynn' should be invited over to advise them; Cornelius Vermuyden had not long before been invited by King James I to advise on the draining of the Fens. Truth to tell, the Dutch had been called in long before to help drain the marshes and to stabilise Yarmouth harbour, though the evidence for this is scarce and hard to find. The work of Joas Jansen (soon Anglicised to Joyce Johnson) in creating a new harbour mouth at Gorleston in 1566 is well known, but what of the Peter Peterson whose wife is commemorated on a floorstone in the nave of Haddiscoe church? The somewhat worn inscription is in old Dutch, but the accepted translation is

> Here lies buried Mistress Bele, daughter of John, wife to Peter, son of Peter, the Dike reeve, who died 2nd December 1525.[5]

Son of 'den Dyckgrave', Peter might well have been brought in to assist with embanking and draining the Waveney marshes, and the likelihood is that he was not alone in coming to an area that had definite affinities with his homeland. It is worth noting that when special 'subsidies' or taxes were levied on aliens in 1436 and 1440 there were aliens, most of them probably from the Low Countries, residing in Stalham, Catfield, Hickling, Ludham, Horning, Rollesby, Filby, Acle, Burlingham, Loddon, Langley and other Broadland villages as well as in Yarmouth and Norwich.[6]

Try as they might the Sea Breach Commissioners could not keep the sea out, and in 1625 the banks were broken and extensive flooding occurred again. What was to be done? One suggestion was that the causeway leading to Bastwick (Potter Heigham) Bridge should be raised to provide a flood barrier, a sluice should be constructed beneath the bridge to stop the flow of water, and the marshland to the north-east of the bridge should be abandoned to the sea.[7]

Both that and another scheme for a drainage system to carry water out to the sea through a sluice at Horsey were rejected by a Mr Briggs, Reader of Mathematics at Oxford, who pointed out that if the bridge were blocked all the countryside east of Potter Heigham to the coast would become a drowned land, 'utterly unprofittable, and at length a very sea ...'. Constant vigilance and careful repair of the sea banks was the only answer, though if the sea banks were carefully maintained it might be desirable to stop up Potter Heigham bridge and to pump the water from the east into the River Thurne by 'wyndmills or horsemills'. It is the first suggestion that we know of for pumping water in this way.

Which way was the Thurne flowing at this time? It is tempting to suggest that flood prevention measures taken at this time were responsible for the reversing of the flow, but there is no evidence to support this hypothesis.

Problems continued into the 18th century and it was necessary to maintain the banks to try to prevent the water overtopping them, as it did in 1717, 1718 and 1720, but the Sea Breach Commission seems to have proved unequal to the task. One might have thought that property owners would have seen the necessity for expenditure on such work, but as is so often the case few landowners were willing to pay up. To give just one instance, in 1620 the Commissioners complained that they were £200 out of pocket because some of the bigger landowners – probably those who could best afford to contribute – had refused to pay the tax, and 'their commission is spoken of as a foul business'. When in 1743 more than 200 ratepayers had failed to pay and some of them threatened to bring an action against the Commission, alleging that the rate was unlawful, the Commissioners simply gave up.[8]

The sea, of course, did not. A map printed in 1797 shows 'Breaches filled up' at Sea Common, Palling, and nine 'Gaps or Breaches made by the Sea in the Marum Hills prior to Summer 1792' between Waxham and Horsey, the widest of them 120 yards wide.[9] So bad had been the flooding that in 1784 the curate of Horsey complained to the Bishop that he had several times narrowly escaped drowning as he rode from Winterton to Horsey. One might suspect him of exaggeration but for the evidence of William Marshall, who wrote in 1795 of an excursion into the marshes between Halvergate and Yarmouth during which 'for nearly the first mile, we rode to our horses knees in water'. That was in June, and after 'a number of windmills have been erected, which throw the water into main drains, formed for the purpose'.

'By this means the principal part of the marshes are freed from surface-water early in the spring,' he wrote, 'so that cattle may now be turned into them about the beginning of May, and are kept free long enough to permit them, in general, to remain there until near Christmas.'[10]

Among the people Marshall met as he made his enquiries into Norfolk farming in the 1790s was Sir Berney Brograve, Bart, of Worstead House and Waxham Hall, who was at that time seeking to improve his estate and urging action to protect the Waxham-Horsey area from the sea. 'The character of this man is so extraordinary, that I cannot refrain from sketching some of its principal features,' Marshall wrote of Sir Berney.

He was, I believe, bred in the army; served some time in the militia; has fought two or three duels; quarrelled with most gentlemen of the county; and, coming to a good paternal estate, discharged his tenants and commenced farmer. His person is gross, and his appearance Bacchanalian – his dress that of a slovenly gentleman. There is a politeness in his manner; and his conversation bespeaks a sensible intelligent mind; borne away, however, by a wildness and ferocity which is obvious in his countenance and discovers itself in every word and action.

The tales told of him bear out Marshall's opinion. One popular legend credits Sir Berney with outwitting the devil himself. Always prepared to do for himself work that most men in his position left to their servants, Sir Berney was one day mowing alongside his farmhands and boasting of his skill; he would, he said, mow the devil a match for his soul. Who should turn up at that moment but Old Nick himself, and a match was arranged. The wily baronet made sure that the devil's chosen acre was well strewn with stones before the match, and it is said that the evil one, sharpening his scythe for the umpteenth time, eventually conceded defeat with the words 'Barney, bor, these stones do cut damned hard'.

Sir Berney might outwit the devil, but there were others who bested him. It is said that he sent for a sweep to clean the chimneys of Waxham Hall, and that when the job was done he immediately challenged the sweep to fight for his money, double or quits. The sweep demurred, but was eventually forced to accept the challenge, which seemed likely to result in the loss of his hardearned money and a good beating. Indeed, the poor sweep took some awful punishment, but then he managed to land two heavy punches into Sir Berney's stomach that caused him to double up in pain. He got his double pay, and lived to boast for many years that he had beaten 'Owd Sir Barney'.[11]

Somewhere about 1770 Sir Berney undertook the improvement of his Waxham estate, digging drainage dykes and building a windmill to lift the water into a cut that communicated with Horsey Mere. That mill perhaps bears witness to the defects in Sir Berney's character, for almost as soon as the bricklayers began work the tower began to lean, and, though they attempted to rectify the fault as they went, the tower is not merely out of plumb but also sadly deformed. Yet it has stood in that state for more than 200 years. It was either Sir Berney or his son that was responsible for making the Waxham Cut navigable.

On his death in 1797 Sir Berney was succeeded by his son Sir George Berney Brograve, who six years later sold the Horsey estate to Robert Rising. The Horsey Enclosure Act of 1812[12] describes how parts of the parish were 'frequently overflowed with Water, and in their present state and condition, for want of sufficient Drainage, yield but little Profit to the Persons interested therein', but the new owner energetically repaired the sea bank and set about draining the marshes, planted quickthorn hedges and also built a road from Somerton to Horsey, making it 'one of the most fertile estates in the county'.[13]

The Enclosure Act specifically empowered the Commissioner appointed to 'make and erect all such Drains, Dams, Banks, Mills, Dikes, Sluices, Engines,

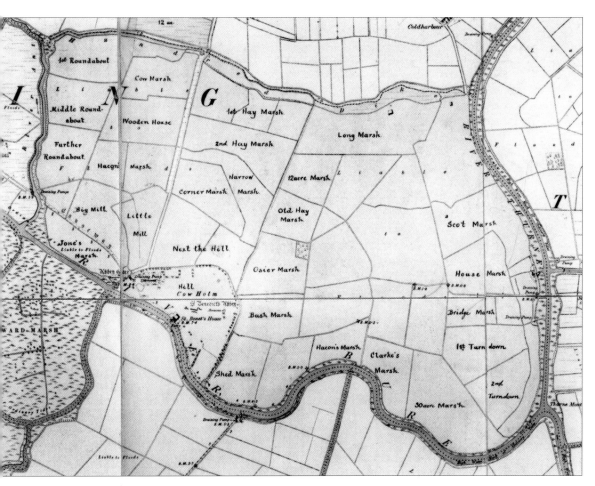

33 *This 19th-century map of the St Benet-at-Holm area clearly shows the network of drainage dykes leading water towards the drainage mill built in the ruins of the abbey gate, which had become disused when a gale in 1863 wrecked the sails. At the top of the map is the Hundred Stream, the former course of the River Ant, and at bottom is the River Bure. The section from the confluence of Ant and Bure to the abbey gate is a man-made cut enabling river traffic to avoid the loop around Ward Marsh.*

Bridges, and other works … as he the said Commissioner shall judge proper and expedient for effectually draining such parts of the said Lands and Grounds as in his opinion shall require to be drained and be preserved and protected from Inundations of the Sea'. Interestingly, it also forbade the planting of trees or erection of buildings, stacks or ricks less than 200 yards from any 'Mill or Engine'.

Horsemills and Windmills
Horsemills as well as windmills were used for marsh drainage. One of the last of the horsemills, built of timber and with a steep pyramidal reed-thatched

34 *The St Benet's Abbey mill before the storm of 1863. This early photograph shows that the mill had two shuttered sails and a pair of common sails; the canvas is furled. It also shows that the stage around the mill is as rickety as it appears in Cotman's print, proving that this was neither artistic licence nor exaggeration.*

roof, stood until the 1930s at Woodbastwick. It was said to have been one of three built by a member of the Cator family in the late 18th century in an endeavour to drain a tract of marsh, an attempt that failed because the earth and clay banks proved ineffective in keeping out water which seeped back through the underlying peat.[14] In the mill two horses operated a scoopwheel similar to those used in the windmills and in some of the early steam drainage pumping stations.

It would seem that the first drainage windmills in the area of the Broads were not built until early in the 18th century, though 'engines to drawe waters above their naturall Levill and to drayne waterishe and moorishe grounds' had certainly been in use in the Cambridgeshire Fens by the end of the sixteenth. William Faden's map of Norfolk of 1797 shows some fifteen drainage windmills on the Acle, Tunstall, Halvergate and Wickhampton marshes, confirming the evidence of paintings by members of the Norwich School portraying rather rickety windmills that had apparently been in existence for many years.

The earliest surviving drainage mill which can be dated is Oby Mill on the Bure above Acle bridge, which used to bear the date 1753 in copper figures on the tower. Brograve

35 *Still surviving into the 1920s, this octagonal shed housed a two-horse gear operating a scoop wheel to drain marshes at Woodbastwick, on the Bure. This 18th-century drainage scheme failed because the earth and clay banks proved ineffective in keeping out water which seeped back through the underlying peat.*

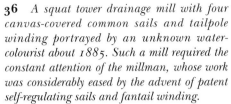

36 *A squat tower drainage mill with four canvas-covered common sails and tailpole winding portrayed by an unknown water-colourist about 1885. Such a mill required the constant attention of the millman, whose work was considerably eased by the advent of patent self-regulating sails and fantail winding.*

Mill, already mentioned above, is dated 1771. At that date the mills, whether of brick or timber, had four common sails that had to be individually spread with canvas before they could be put to work; the mills had to be relatively low so that the sails reached near the ground to enable the millman to set the canvas. The cap bearing the sails, windshaft and brake wheel was turned into wind by means of a long tailpole, the fantail being introduced later to turn the cap into wind automatically.

Early gearing was entirely of wood, but in the 19th century the ironfounder increasingly came to the aid of the millwright by producing cast-iron wheels, sometimes with integral teeth and sometimes with mortices for the fitting of wooden teeth, made normally of close-grained fruit wood or beech; Rex Wailes records that Dan England also used holly.[15] Wailes also lists seven drainage mills that had old-fashioned trundle gears with pegs instead of cogs: Lake's Mill, Acle; Six Mile House Mill, Cantley Marsh; Gilbert's Mill, Halvergate Marsh; Swim Coots Mill, Hickling; Old Hall Mill, Stokesby; Pettingell's Mill, Toft Monks; and Tunstall Mill. Gears of this kind can be seen in the Nether-lands, but they are somewhat uncommon in East Anglia, where mills tended to be rebuilt from time to time to keep them up-to-date.

Some mills with common (cloth) sails and tailpole winding were modern-ised in the 19th century, being given patent sails of the kind invented in 1807 by William Cubitt, the famous engineer son of a Norfolk miller, who was born at Dilham in 1785. These sails contained vanes which were opened and closed all together by a 'striking rod' passing through the windshaft and usually operated by an endless chain passing over a wheel at the rear of the cap. As it was unnecessary to set the sails individually from the ground in these mills the towers could be higher, and in some cases the mill towers were raised, or in Norfolk parlance 'hained', by adding a vertical section to the top of the tower; an example of this can be seen in Thurne White Mill. With the patent sails many drainage mills adopted the fantail, which turned the cap and sails into wind automatically and so greatly reduced the work of the millman, who previously had had to attend to the mill whenever the wind direction changed. The advent of self-regulating sails and fantail winding must have eased the lot of the millman more than a little.

The normal way of raising water, usually from a marsh drain into the river but sometimes from one dyke to another, was a scoop wheel with anything from 24 to 36 paddles set at an angle to the diameter of the wheel. It has been said that a scoop wheel would lift water three-eighths of the wheel's diameter, a 16ft. wheel having a lift of six feet, but this might be on the high side. Usually there was a single wheel working in a brick channel on one side of the mill, though Turf Fen Mill on the River Ant had two wheels, one on each side of the tower. Turf Fen Mill is possibly unique in having a pit wheel with two sets of gear so that the millman could 'change gear' according to the strength of the wind and whether he was driving one or both scoop wheels; there is a simple clutch enabling one scoop wheel to be disengaged. The mill had to be stopped to 'change gear' and to operate the clutch.

The scoop wheel was normally covered with a wooden 'hoodway' which was either tarred or painted white. In most cases the wheel and hoodway were set close to the mill tower. Only in the case of Berney Arms Mill was the wheel as much as 25 feet from the tower, and this 24ft. scoop wheel was operated by a pinion driving on an internally geared ring attached to the cast-iron arms of the scoop wheel, an arrangement more usually seen on steam pumping stations using a scoop wheel. Five Mile House Mill on the Bure had its wheel slightly away from the tower, possibly an alteration made when the tower began to settle. In a few instances the scoop wheel was placed within the tower; four mills, Mutton's Mill on Halvergate Marshes, Runham Commission Mill, Cadge's Mill at Seven Mile House and Swim Coots Mill, Hickling, all had internal wheels.[16]

The invention of the centrifugal pump by J.C. Appold about 1850 provided the millwrights with an alternative to the scoop wheel. In the horizontal 'turbine', as it was always called in Norfolk, an impeller fitted with curved blades was spun within a casing, creating an outward radial pressure and a partial vacuum at the centre. It has been said that the effect of the turbine is similar to that of stirring a cup of tea, which causes the tea to rise at the periphery of the cup and, if the cup be full, to spill over the rim. When turbines were placed outside the mill tower they were driven from the crown wheel, the driving wheel at the bottom of the upright shaft, through a bevel pinion called the 'counter wheel' on a horizontal shaft; at the other end of this shaft was another bevel wheel known as the 'pit wheel' which drove the 'pump wheel' on top of the vertical shaft driving the 'turbine' itself. Some mills had the 'turbine' placed within the tower, and in that case the drive could be direct from the crown wheel to the pump wheel.

Advertisements published in the 1830s indicate that a new generation of windmills was at that time being built and that the drainage was being greatly improved in some places. In 1832 an advertisement for the letting of 'A Level of Marshes, of about 200 acres, situate in the parish of Fritton, Suffolk' mentioned that 'A New Mill, capable of draining double that quantity, having been recently erected upon this Level, and a new embankment raised round it, it is capable of being kept dry all the year.'[17]

Another advertisement concerned a meeting held at the *Hare and Hound* at Halvergate one day in June 1833 to consider the best means of improving the drainage of marshes known as Crowe's Level, Fisher's Level, Howard's Level, Shuckford's Level, Hewitt's Level and Walpole's Level. A brick tower drainage mill 'with all its Going Gears, Water Works, and Appurtenances' was advertised to be sold by auction at the *Hare and Hound* at the same time. Quite clearly changes were being made that would in time alter the appearance of the area,[18] yet even in 1879 the village of Horning was said to be 'nearly surrounded by fen or marshland, where numerous windmills are constantly employed in pumping the water from the low lands, which, at certain seasons, are completely inundated.'[19]

As well as the tower mills there were small hollow post mills and skeleton mills used to drain smaller areas of marsh. A good example of the larger variety of hollow post mill, with patent sails and fantail winding, can be seen at How Hill, where it has been rebuilt by millwright Richard Seago. It formerly stood at Ranworth; a similar mill stood at Irstead Street, little more than half a mile as the crow flies from where the Ranworth mill has been re-erected.

37 *A small hollow-post mill operating a reciprocating pump on the Breydon marshes in the late 19th century. With single-sided automatic sails and kept to the wind by twin tails, it bears a distinct similarity to a windpump by the Suffolk millwrights Whitmore & Binyon, and might be another of their products. There were other small mills of somewhat similar design in other parts of the Broads area, but almost all have long since disappeared.*

Both these mills operated small scoop wheels, but other hollow post mills had reciprocating plunger pumps.

The men who operated the marsh mills often led a solitary life distant from the communities to which they might be thought to have belonged. Some mills had a millman's cottage only yards from the mill, but others were

38 *High's Mill at Potter Heigham, photographed in the 1950s after it had ceased to operate; the vanes have been removed from the sails and the fantail is disintegrating. Typical of the brick tower mills built by Norfolk millwrights, High's Mill drained an area of marshland on the west side of the Thurne just above Potter Heigham bridge. It has now been converted to a house.*

situated several fields away from the millman's home; to get from one to the other sometimes involved not just a tramp across the grazing marshes but the crossing of four or five or more 'liggers', as the planks spanning the dykes were known.

When it was necessary for the mill to be pumping day and night to clear floodwater from the marshes, the millman would sometimes take up temporary residence in the mill. He would sleep on a makeshift bed or a settle, and many mills had a fireplace in the wall so that he could have a fire to keep him warm and to boil up a kettle for his tea; the water would come out of the dyke.

Besides keeping an eye on the mill to ensure that it ran safely and was not tail-winded by a squall, the millman had to pay attention to the greasing of the bearings. A bearing running hot in a gale could easily result in the destruction of the mill by fire. He would need to see to it that a section of reedhover or a piece of wood did not block the run of water to the scoop wheel or the pump, or worse still get into the culvert and damage the scoop wheel. In addition, he might have to keep his eye on cattle on the marsh and watch for damage to the river walls which could threaten the low-lying ground behind.

The Millwrights

Most of the millwrights who built and maintained these drainage mills were based in the area. Among them were Daniel Rust at Martham and William Rust at Stalham, and in later years Benjamin Paine at Sutton. In an 1854 directory Dan Rust was listed simply as joiner and wheelwright, but four years later he was said to be millwright and agricultural implement maker, a sensible enough combination of trades. Several drainage mills, including at least two on the Waveney, are credited to Robert Martin of Beccles, who appears in White's Suffolk directories of 1844 and 1855 as a millwright in Ingate Street.

Then there was James Barnes at Reedham, a member of a local family, another of whose members operated the sawmills there. It was probably James

39 *The internal machinery of a drainage mill is relatively simple in most cases. This is the great spur wheel of High's Mill, with the drive to the external turbine pump on the right.*

40 *The other end of the drive shaft with a spur wheel driving the vertical turbine shaft. This turbine replaced the scoop wheel at Thurne Dyke Mill when that mill was rebuilt about 1885 with patent sails and a fantail.*

Barnes who in about 1830 built the little black-boarded mill at Herringfleet, with four canvas-covered common sails and a winch on the tailpole from which a chain is run out to one of a circle of posts to wind the cap and sails into the wind. The last smock drainage mill on the Broads to survive in working order, this mill is fortunately preserved by Suffolk County Council and is put to work occasionally by members of the Suffolk Mills Group.

Another member of the Barnes family, Richard, operated as a millwright at Yarmouth; Richard's premises at Bridge Foot were ablaze in 1867 and he then moved to premises near Southtown station.[20] It is possible that one or other of these was the iron foundry advertised for sale in 1852, with 'an Agricultural, Mill, and Ship-work Trade attached, and the Patterns required for the same'.[21] By 1879 he had moved further down the road to Southtown Ironworks, which was later taken over by Crabtrees. In 1880 Richard Barnes built a single-cylinder horizontal engine for a marsh pumping station at Reedham, where it drove a turbine pump through two pairs of bevel gears and a countershaft.

For the most part the early millwrights had little or no knowledge of the theory of mechanics, but they learnt from experience how to harness the wind to whatever task was required to be carried out, whether it be pumping water or grinding and crushing oil seed. It was this latter operation for which the brick tower mill was built into the gateway of St Benet's Abbey some time in the 18th century.[22] Why an oil mill should have been built in such an isolated position remains a mystery, but it was at least convenient for water transport, for wherries could have moored in the cut that reaches up to the mill. Whether this mill was built for dual use or was converted to marsh drainage is unknown, but it is said in several early 19th-century sources to be a drainage mill.

Berney Arms Mill was built in 1865 by Edmund Stolworthy, a Yarmouth millwright, who had his works in Northgate Street. This mill, more than 70 feet high and with an internal diameter of 28 feet at ground-floor level, replaced an earlier tower mill on the same site. Like its predecessor, its purpose was to grind cement clinker produced at the nearby works owned by T.T. Berney, one of the largest landowners in the parish of Reedham. It was the Berney family, of course, that gave its arms to the public house whose sign became the name of this isolated hamlet. The mill also processed cement clinker brought by wherry from the Burgh Castle cement works. The mill was conveyed to the Ministry of Works as a gift by the Lower Bure, Halvergate Fleet and Acle Marshes Internal Drainage Board in 1951, and it is now in the care of English Heritage.

The last of the Yarmouth millwrights to be associated with drainage mills was A.J. Thrower, of Lady Haven Road, Southtown, who recalled having fallen some 30 feet from the fly stage of a mill when removing the striking rod that passes through the windshaft to operate the vanes in the sails. He struck the forked wheel of the striking gear as he fell, but landed on his feet and was back on the fly stage within ten minutes with nothing worse than a cut eyebrow and 'a severe choking off from the guv'nor for being careless'.[23]

There are still many brick tower mills about the marshes, some of them restored in recent years by the Norfolk Windmills Trust. It is said that when building these towers the bricklayers confined their day's work to no more than four or five courses so as to avoid undue distortion of the tower resulting from settlement, yet some of the mills developed a distinct lean. In some cases the mill towers were built on piles; Rex Wailes records that Stracey Arms Mill, beside the Acle New Road at Tunstall, built by Richard Barnes in 1883, was founded on 40ft. piles topped with a pitchpine raft, and there are plans by William England showing mills constructed on piled foundations.

The last of these mills to be erected was Horsey Mill, built of Martham bricks in 1912 by Ludham millwright E.W.D. England on the foundations of an earlier mill. Horsey Mill was working until 1943, when it was struck by lightning which split the sail stocks from end to end. The work of draining the extensive level of marshes was then taken over by a diesel pump which had in 1939 superseded the earlier steam pump that worked hand-in-hand with the windmill. The mill was taken over by the National Trust when it acquired the Horsey estate in 1948, and it was eventually restored to working order, though it has not resumed work.

41 *Horsey Mill was rebuilt in 1912 using bricks brought from the Martham brickyard in Di Thaine's wherry I'll Try. When this photograph was taken repairs were being undertaken to the stand-by steam-driven pump in the shed to the left of the mill. The windmill remained at work until 1943 when it was struck by lightning and badly damaged. The auxiliary steam engine had been replaced by a diesel in 1939, and this continued in operation until replaced by an electric pump in 1957.*

42 *The millman clearing the reed screen at Norton Swing Bridge Mill on the south bank of the River Yare just downriver of Hardley Cross. The steam mill, which originally drove a scoop wheel and was converted to operate a turbine pump, was demolished in 1937 and replaced by an electric pump.*

The Englands were much involved with the construction of drainage mills, including a number of skeleton or trestle mills on the northern rivers. A William England was practising as a millwright at Ludham as early as 1845, and in 1858 he was one of 36 millwrights listed in a Norfolk directory. By 1879, when the number of millwrights had fallen to 22, Daniel England had taken the business over, and in the 20th century Edwin William Daniel England, builder of Horsey Mill, was running the business. A number of trestle mills were erected by E.W.D. England, a survivor of this type being Boardman's Mill at How Hill, which drove a turbine. Another of England's trestle mills stood at Barton Turf, but it was burnt down in a marsh fire about 1949. The firm, which claimed to have introduced the boat-shaped cap so typical of Norfolk, was still operating in the 1930s.

Another England, William Thomas, was operating as a millwright in Northgate Street, Yarmouth, possibly in the Stolworthys' old premises, in the early part of the 20th century. Rex Wailes in a Newcomen Society paper listed six drainage mills built by him, at Dilham, Fleggburgh, Runham, Upton, Fritton Warren and St Olave's. The last named was a small and very slender smock mill; it was really no more than a skeleton mill covered with boarding.

The last drainage mill actually to work was that on Ash Tree Level, north of the Acle New Road about a mile out of Yarmouth. Built by Thomas Smithdale and Sons for the Ecclesiastical Commissioners in 1910, it survived intact until the neck of the windshaft broke and the sails fell on to the marsh in the great gale of 31 January and 1 February 1953.

Longest lived of the Norfolk millwrighting firms and the last of the old businesses to operate, Smithdale's was established at Norwich in 1847 by Thomas Smithdale. The works was then beside the River Wensum, at St Ann's Ironworks, between St Ann's Staithe Lane and Synagogue Street. In the 1880s the firm built a new ironworks at Panxworth, some miles north of Norwich, and then in 1897 it moved to Acle, where it remained for the next 70 years until the closure in 1974.

The firm developed a particular interest in marsh and fen drainage, and in 1900 established a branch works at Ramsey St Mary's in Huntingdonshire to deal with the extensive business built up in connection with the drainage of the Fenland.

Steam Pumping Stations

Whereas windmills were of limited power and were dependent on a breeze, which even in such an area as east Norfolk could not be guaranteed, steam engines offered both power and reliability, though at a cost. As Anthony J. Ward has said, the windmill 'was a poor servant, a prima donna demanding constant attention and admiration. It was relatively cheap to install and used the power of the wind which came without charge, but it was fickle and would often fail when most needed. Often after rain came calm, thus making the windmill useless'.[24]

One of the first steam pumping engines in the area was installed by the local landowners at West Caister, probably at the instigation of the lord of the manor and one of the biggest owners of land, Thomas Clowes, in 1841.[25] It stood on the north bank of the Bure just upstream of Two Mile House and drained Bond's Level with a scoop wheel until 1936. At some time in the late 19th century another steam mill with a turbine pump was built just downstream of Three Mile House, and this drained Lacon's Level until 1946. This later mill took over the work of the 1841 engine in 1936 after a cut had been made in the dyke system, but because of the heavy rain both mills worked together for a time.[26] Another early steam pumping station with a small beam engine was built at Wheatacre for Sir Edward Kerrison by, it is said, William Garrood, who in 1884 went into partnership with William Elliott at Beccles. It is true that Garrood, son of the Haddiscoe blacksmith, was in business at Wheatacre as an engineer in the 1870s, but it seems a little unlikely he would have been in a position to build a steam engine in the 1840s.

Although the later steam pumping stations employed turbine pumps, many of the beam engines installed in early stations operated scoop wheels. William Thorold, of the Phoenix Ironworks in Norwich, was responsible for several early steam engines used in marsh drainage in the 1840s, including one driving a scoop wheel put in on the Cantley Level at that time; it was replaced in 1899 by an engine from Holmes & Sons, possibly the last they built. When Thorold retired from business in 1851 the stock-in-trade to be sold included a 'Cast-iron water wheel, 27 feet in diameter, for marsh draining'. Driven by a 20-hp steam engine that was probably made by Thorold, this wheel was used for draining the Thorpe Cut on the Yare when it was being made in 1843 as part of the

Norwich to Yarmouth railway project. Though a large wheel, it was probably by no means as wide as the scoop wheels of some of the Dutch steam pumping stations, the more powerful of which drove as many as six wheels side by side.

Three pumping stations, one near Beccles and the others at Haddiscoe and West Somerton, had engines built by the London firm of Easton & Amos between 1856 and 1866. These were of an interesting design, with two vertical cylinders at ground level on each side of a cast-iron tube containing the turbine pump, the crankshaft being carried by a pair of trunnions bolted to the top of the turbine tube.

As steam began to be used for marsh drainage the millwrights were quick to adapt to the demand for steam engines, Thomas Smithdale & Sons constructing a number of steam engines for drainage purposes. In 1867 Smithdale built a horizontal pumping engine which worked for many years at South Walsham driving a turbine pump. An advertisement from the beginning of the 20th century stressed that 'Scoop Wheels and Pumps for Fen Land Drainage' were a speciality of the firm, which had been awarded a silver medal for this class of work.

Another Norwich engineering firm which concerned itself with drainage machinery was Holmes & Sons, whose works were to the east of the cattle market. Besides building some pumping engines for the Fens, Holmes installed a two-cylinder crank overhead engine at Waxham to drive a turbine pump. It drained some 700 acres there. The same firm produced a double-crank compound horizontal engine about 1878 to drain the Calthorpe Level near Acle.

A similar engine by Holmes replaced an old beam engine and scoop wheel draining the Wheatacre marshes on the Waveney in 1882. The new engine drove a turbine pump capable of shifting 10,000 gallons a minute, and when the time came to set it to work friends of the landowner and neighbouring farmers were invited along to see the fun. The daughter of the tenant farmer renting the marshes

43 *The Easton & Amos engine installed in a wooden building beside the New Cut at Haddiscoe to drain the Haddiscoe marshes. The pumping unit consisted of a 'duplex' engine mounted on the top of a cast-iron well lining and driving an Appold turbine pump at the bottom of the well; there were two identical engines driving a single crankshaft through a crank at either side. The drawing, made by Anthony J. Ward in 1953, shows William Curtis standing at the throttle; to the left is the mahogany-lagged cylinder with the air pump of the condenser to its right. A similar engine is preserved at Westonzoyland in Somerset, appropriately as James Easton was a Somerset man.*

kindly consented to start the engine, and at the appointed time proceeded gently to open the valve admitting steam to the cylinders; the ponderous flywheel immediately began to move; life, power and speed quickly became developed in what a moment before seemed to be only a massive combination of iron, steel and metal. The turbine was quickly up to speed, and the delivery of water to the river ... was pronounced by all to be most satisfactory.[27]

The firm gave up the production of steam engines towards the end of the century and went into liquidation in 1902.

Although in 1890 there was resident at West Somerton a Henry Dyball, 'steam mill engineer',[28] who was presumably in charge of the Easton & Amos engine in the West Somerton pumping station, the operation of a drainage engine was usually left to the marshman employed on the 'level' that it drained. Some, no doubt, were excellent engineers, but others may have had little aptitude for this part of their work. Considerable care was needed when working a steam engine and boiler in order to get the best out of them, and this needed patience as well as muscle. The ideal procedure was to start a gentle fire in the firebox the night before the engine was to be worked, but during his researches into the drainage engines Anthony Ward heard criticism of some marshmen who would 'force' a locomotive boiler up from cold to full steam in a few hours, anxious to complete their 'stint' in one session.

Lacking the popular appeal of the windmill, the steam pumping stations have almost all disappeared since being replaced by diesel engines and then by electric pumps. Conservation volunteers were employed to demolish one 'eyesore', and not a single engine has been preserved in its engine house, though the Easton & Amos engine from Haddiscoe has found a home at the Strumpshaw steam museum. The Haddiscoe engine, along with the Holmes crank overhead engine at Waxham, was brought into use to clear floodwater after the 1953 storm, but that was the last use of steam for drainage in the Broads.

The Horsey Floods
Draining the marshes did not solve the problem of inundation by the sea, however. In November 1897 a storm that caused many casualties at

44 *This horizontal engine was built in 1880 by Richard Barnes, of Southtown Iron Works, for John William Rose, of Reedham Old Hall, and installed at Seven Mile House, Reedham; somewhat unusually, it was the owner's name and not the builder's that was cast into the engine bedplate. The engine drove a turbine pump in an adjoining turbine house.*

sea breached the sandhills and the sea poured through on to the Horsey marshes, as was recalled by a marshman whom William Dutt met when strolling along the marsh wall near Old Meadow Dyke. His account of the flooding and his criticism of the drainage authorities are alike of interest,

> 'If yow'd ha' sin th' sea come in,' he said, 'yow'd ha' thowt we wor all a-goin' to be drownded. It come in acrost th' Warren for nigh three hours – till th' tide went out; an' if it hadn't ha' bin for the deeks bein' pretty nigh empty at th' time, I don't know what would ha' happened. An' mind yow,' he went on, 'sich a thing never owght to ha' happened. There's th' Commish'ners; it's their bisness to luke arter th' merrimills, an' if they'd a-done it as they should ha' done, th' sea 'ud never ha' got tru. Kapin' th' sea out ain't a one-man-an'-a-boy job, as some o' th' Commish'ners fare to think 'tis. Why, there was one Commish'ner he say tu me, "What's wantin' is plenty o' faggots." Says I to him, "Sir, there wor faggots enow all riddy to be used long afore th' storm come, but no one was towd to use 'em." "Ah," he say, "that was werry wrong; it owght ter taach us a lesson." Says I, "Some folks take a daal o' taachin'," an' he larfed; but, thinks I, it ain't no larfin matter. But *he* didn't own no land out this way; *his* property wor all out Norwich way. Another man what come to hev a luke rouind when th' mills wor a-clearin' th' deeks fared a sight more consarned about th' fish bein' killed by th' salts than he did about anything else. "Shockin'," he say, "shockin!" "That 'tis, sir," says I, "some o' us mash folk stand a gude chance o' bein' drownded if suffin ain't done." "Ah," he say, "that 'ud be werry sad, but I wor a-thinkin' about th' fish"!'[29]

Much the same thing happened again in February 1938, when a northwesterly gale coinciding with full moon tore a half-mile breach in the sandhills. The sea poured through the gap and flooded almost 7,500 acres of land. Some people had to be rescued by boat from the upper windows of their house, while the village people were taken to safety in a lorry. The village of Horsey stood on an island in the midst of an inland sea stretching south to West Somerton and Martham Broad and west to Potter Heigham and Hickling Broad. It took three months to close the breach in the sandhills, and the effects of the saltwater lasted much longer, as Major Anthony Buxton, who was living at Horsey Hall at the time of the flood, remembered.

> An inland sea that turned into a desert was my general impression of the flood, and its worst feature was the resulting lack of life. There was some beauty in the scene, particularly at sunrise and sunset, while the water covered the land; there was none in the aftermath. The boundary line between flooded and unflooded area was during the spring and summer blatantly abrupt – from bright green life to red-brown death: it was reminiscent of an impressionist picture and a bad one at that, and over all hung the smell of a stale salting. Perhaps the worst feature of all was the dead timber, standing stark and bare of leaves, growing as time went on more skeleton-like as the bark stripped from the stems, and left them bare and glistening.[30]

The effect was to undo all the work that had been done by the enclosers and improvers years before. It was to be five years before the worst affected of the grazing marshes were returned to the same state they had been in before the sea swept over them.

I *The ruins of the abbey of St Benet-at-Holm, seen from the site of the abbey church, with the River Bure flowing right to left in the background.*

II *The Yare Valley grazing marshes, with Cantley sugar factory in the far distance.*

III   *Winter on the Broads: the River Thurne frozen up at Martham Ferry in January 1997.*

IV   *The former warehouse at Gay's Staithe, Irstead is now a holiday cottage. Wherries could be berthed under the arch so that cargo could be transferred direct through a hatch in the warehouse floor.*

V   *Flooding at Whiteslea Lodge, which was jacked up in 1928 after Lord Desborough had got out of bed and stepped into six inches of water.*

VI   *Trees and water, the view from the tower of St Helen's Church at Ranworth. The spread of alder carr and the growth of riverside trees have changed the landscape of the Broads in the past 150 years.*

VII *Wintry sunshine makes the reeds sparkle and glints on the tarred tower of Berney Arms Mill, tallest of the Broads drainage mills. When built by Stolworthy, the Yarmouth millwright, in 1865, the mill ground cement clinker as well as operating a large scoop wheel.*

VIII *The fantail of Berney Arms Mill kept the sails into wind automatically, while the chain hanging down by the light tailpole operated the striking gear and adjusted the angle of the shutters in the sails according to wind strength.*

IX *Eric Edwards tidying a bundle of reed that has been knocked up on the 'trouncing board' that lies on the ground in front of him. The very wet nature of the reedbed is apparent in this picture.*

X *Framed in a field boundary hedge, Turf Fen Mill on the River Ant can be seen across the riverside grazing marsh.*

XI *Inside the tower of Turf Fen Mill, looking up at the upright shaft.*

XII *At the foot of the upright shaft is a small spur wheel meshing with the pit wheel on the end of the scoop-wheel shaft. At Turf Fen the position of the spur wheel could be adjusted to drive either the outer section of the pit wheel or an inner gear ring, according to whether one scoop wheel was being operated or both; a dog clutch could be used to disconnect one of the scoop wheels.*

XIII *Broadland cloudscape: Potter Heigham bridge is silhouetted against the strongly lit sky.*

XIV *The northern Broads is the last stronghold of the swallowtail butterfly, a spectacular insect whose caterpillars feed on milk parsley growing in the marshes. This swallowtail caterpillar was photographed at Ranworth not far from the Norfolk Wildlife Trust conservation centre.*

XV *The green summer leaves of water soldier growing in a dyke at How Hill. In the winter this aquatic plant disappears to the bottom of the dyke. This plant has been lost from most of the Broads and their associated dykes, surviving only in isolated dykes that are free from pollution.*

XVI *Horsey Mere from the air, with the North Sea in the distance. The vulnerability of the northern Broads to flooding from the sea is apparent from this view, only a narrow strip of low-lying land separating the two.*

XVII *Water crowfoot and other aquatic plants in a dyke at How Hill.*

XVIII   *Mud dredging in progress at Barton Broad as part of the Barton Broad Clear Water 2000 project. The polluted mud was pumped from the dredger along a pipeline to the shore and deposited in settlement lagoons, which are now producing crops.*

XIX   *Heigham Sound and Whiteslea, looking towards Hickling Broad.*

Seven

RIVERS AND WATERWAYS

The Broadland river system divides neatly into three main sections: the northern rivers, Bure, Thurne and Ant; the Norwich River, as the old wherrymen termed the Yare and Wensum; and the Waveney, which for much of its length forms the boundary between the counties of Norfolk and Suffolk. These rivers have existed for many more years than the Broads themselves, and one might suppose that they have flowed in the same courses ever since the Great Estuary gave way to saltmarsh and fen. One would be wrong. There have been some quite startling changes, though the period at which some of them occurred and the factors responsible remain a matter of conjecture. Some changes were a result of deliberate action by man.

Perusal of a map suggests that at some period the Waveney might have found the sea by way of what is now Lowestoft harbour, perhaps until its mouth was blocked by sand and shingle brought down from beaches to the northward and deposited by the sea. If this is so, when the mouth became blocked the river made a new course across the flat lands west of the gravelly hills of Lothingland to a confluence with the Yare beneath the cliff of Burgh Castle, from where a joint approach was made to the sea through Breydon, that last relic of the Great Estuary, and Yarmouth harbour.

At what period this change occurred is unknown, but it is likely to have been in the very distant past. The legend that the change was effected in the 12th century when the people of Lowestoft were forced by their neighbours to the north to block their own harbour after a Yarmouth victory in the centuries-long conflict between the two towns is plausible, but unlikely.[1] A natural process is a much more probable cause of this major alteration in course.

The Waveney rises in Redgrave and Lopham Fen, only a very short distance from the source of the Little Ouse which runs westwards towards the Fens and a confluence with the Great Ouse at Brandon Creek. Flowing to the east, the river runs through a valley that was at one time a home of the linen trade, becoming navigable only beyond Bungay, one of the strongholds of the Bigod family whose castle, or the remains of it, still overlooks the great loop taken by the river around Bungay Common. When even sea-going ships were little more than single-masted boats Bungay might well have had a small maritime trade, though by the late 17th century it had become necessary to carry out works on the river between Beccles and Bungay to restore the navigation.

The Norwich River is in fact two rivers, the Yare and the Wensum, which join at Trowse Eye, a short distance below the city. It is the Wensum, which rises near Fakenham in the north of Norfolk, that flows through Norwich; the Yare rises near Shipdham, south-west of East Dereham, and flows to the south of the city before joining forces with the Wensum, after which the combined river is known as the Yare.

In commercial terms the Norwich River was the most important of all the rivers since it served the city of Norwich, once the second city of the kingdom and a major manufacturing and commercial centre. For some hundreds of years the river served as a highway of trade, carrying downstream to Yarmouth the city's manufactures and bringing in many of the necessities of life, including coal and even stone for the building of the cathedral. Such was the vital role that it played in the city's life that from an early period the city corporation took responsibility for maintaining navigation and ensuring that the condition of the river remained in a satisfactory state.

In 1422, for instance, the Assembly ordered that 'the King's River' should be cleansed from 'the mills called le Calkemyll to the gates called le Bishopesyates' by the inhabitants of that part of the city 'Over the Water', and that the river from Bishopsgate to Thorpe should be similarly dealt with by the inhabitants of the other wards, Conesford, Mancroft and Wymer. 'Over the Water' was the area north of the river, originally one of the several separate settlements that coalesced to form the city.[2]

The carrying of 'muck' by keels or boats on the river was strictly banned, but all sorts of 'mucke or other vile stuffe' was constantly finding its way into the river from the street drains, and it was necessary to repeat the 'cleansing' every so often. In 1543 there was 'a gret communicacion' in the city court about the 'ffeyeng' of the river. 'Fying' is a dialect word meaning cleaning or 'sorting out'. In the course of this discussion it was decided that a cofferdam of boards and posts should be made in the middle of the channel so that one side could be somehow drained, enabling carts to be driven into the river to carry 'oute of the rever the gravell and suche like that shalbe taken in makyng the rever depper wher shalow places are'.[3] What a clever idea! One wonders if it worked.

The corporation claimed jurisdiction over the river down to Breydon Water, according to a 15th-century copy of an earlier custumal, a record setting down the way in which the city was governed. In fact, Hardley Cross, the stone cross erected to mark the boundary of the city's jurisdiction, stands at the point where the River Chet enters the Yare and is now some five miles from the west end of Breydon.[4] Jurisdiction over the river from 'a certaine place of the northe parte of the Citie of Norwich called the Shepewashe unto a crosse called Hardly Crosse next Breydyng' was granted, or confirmed, by the second charter granted to the city by Edward IV in 1462.[5]

45 *Hardley Cross, standing at the boundary of Norwich Corporation's jurisdiction where the Chet flows into the Yare. This photograph was taken by H.C. Bolingbroke in 1880.*

The head of navigation was at the New Mills, in the west of the city, although to reach this point vessels had to negotiate a narrow channel which became increasingly congested as the city developed, with buildings rising directly from the river banks. They have been the New Mills ever since the first mill was set up on the site in the early 15th century. The ancient Quayside was in the heart of the city close to Tombland, the early market place, and to the site on which the cathedral arose; building materials for the cathedral were taken directly into the close by way of a short canal protected at its emergence from the river by a watergate. No doubt the same course was taken by the keels that brought turves to be burnt in the kitchens of the cathedral priory during the years the Broads were being formed by peat digging. In later centuries there were wharves and staithes scattered all along the length of river within the city and in particular along King Street, a prosperous and busy commercial quarter in the Middle Ages and later.

Alterations in the course of the Yare there may have been, but there is little evidence of changes earlier than the 19th century, when a scheme to bring sea-going vessels to Norwich resulted in a certain amount of minor manipulation of the river. On the northern rivers there are indications of much more radical changes.

46 *A conjectural map of the courses of the northern rivers in Saxon times. It is not known when changes were made to the courses of the Bure, Ant and Thurne, but it is suspected that they might have been in the Middle Ages, possibly by the monks of St Benet's, to alleviate flooding in the upper Thurne area.*

The River Bure rises near Melton Constable, known to students of the old Midland & Great Northern Joint Railway as 'the Crewe of Norfolk', and flows in a generally south-easterly direction through Aylsham, Wroxham and Acle to join the Yare at Great Yarmouth. It has two main tributaries, the Ant, which has its source not far from North Walsham, and the Thurne.

Strange things have indeed happened to this part of the river system, for the Thurne once flowed north to enter the sea between Horsey and Winterton. Those who have sailed down the Bure past St Benet's Abbey and then made a drastic alteration of course to starboard to follow the Bure south-eastwards towards Upton and Acle will not find it hard to believe that at one time the Bure and the Thurne were one river, the waters of the Bure/Thurne heading northwards to an estuary represented today by that low-lying area south-east of Horsey through which the sea has more than once broken in quite recent times. The original course of the river to the sea is represented today by the Hundred Stream, a minor waterway that gained its name from the fact that it formed the boundary between the hundreds of Happing and West Flegg.

It seems likely that the Hundred Stream could in storm conditions discharge into the sea right up to the 19th century, for a 'Floodgate' is shown at its seaward end on the 1st edition O.S. one-inch map, printed in 1838. The remains of this sluice were sometimes revealed on the beach even in the 20th century.[6]

Flood Prevention

How, then, did the Bure come to change direction and flow southwards towards Acle? Could it be that a new straight channel was dug to carry the waters of the Bure/Thurne into an existing waterway which carried the drainage of East Flegg eastwards to the sea? The reach below Thurne Mouth, known to the watermen of old as Thurne Reach or Long Thurne, is surprisingly straight, in contrast to those stretches of river above Thurne Mouth and below Acle Bridge, and it could well be an artificial cut. That such a cut might have been made by the monks of St Benet's, or others, to cure flooding in the Potter Heigham and Martham area seems a distinct possibility.

There have been other changes over the centuries in that part of the river below Acle. It seems that at an early period the Bure flowed into the sea between Caister and Yarmouth until diverted southwards by a sandspit deposited across its mouth, just as the sandbank on which Yarmouth arose forced the waters of the Yare to find a new outlet to the sea to the south.

The Ant, too, has changed its course at some time. It now flows into the Bure to the west of St Benet's Abbey, cutting the causeway that once provided access to the abbey from Horning; it formerly flowed west to east along the line of what is now named the Hundred Dyke – so called because it formed the boundary between Happing and Tunstead hundreds – to enter the Thurne almost a mile north of Thurne Mouth.

Hundred and parish boundaries provide many indications of changes in river courses, for they often follow river channels. Having become established, the boundary was sometimes left unchanged when a new channel was dug to divert a waterway for the benefit of navigation or for any other reason.

Tom Williamson has suggested

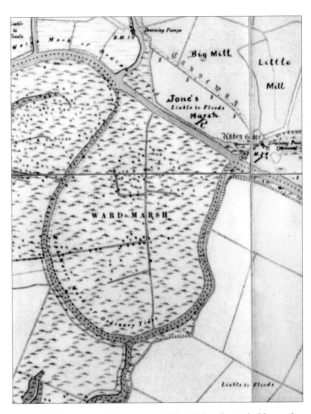

47 *The man-made cut across Ward Marsh, probably made in the 16th century to provide a short cut for commercial river traffic, can be seen in this section of a 19th-century map. From the evidence of this map it would appear that the old loop around Ward Marsh might still have been navigable in the 19th century; while the eastern section still provides access to Ranworth staithe, the western arm has since grown up and become blocked.*

that there might have been links between the changes to the Thurne and Ant.[7] Pointing out that the blocking of the Thurne outfall by an accumulation of sand would have been likely to cause severe flooding in the Thurne valley, he speculates on the possibility that the monks of St Benet's might have diverted the flow of the Ant southwards into the Bure in an endeavour to reduce the amount of water flowing into the Thurne and so relieve flooding of abbey property in Martham and elsewhere.

When the abbey was built on the island in the marshes known as Cow Holm, there was a large loop of the River Bure to the south-west of the site around Ward Marsh, a loop which, significantly, continued to form the boundary between the hundreds of Tunstead and South Walsham. It is still followed by the local authority boundary. At some time, probably about the

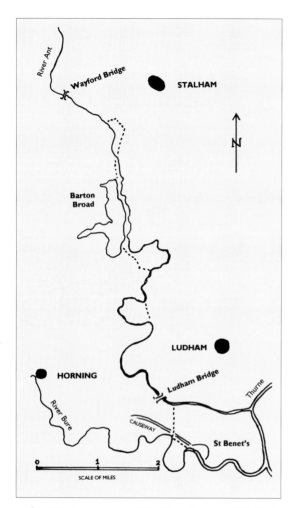

48 *The former course of the River Ant below Wayford Bridge and in the region of Barton Broad, as indicated largely by parish and hundred boundaries. The present course of the river is shown by the dotted lines.*

16th century, a broad straight cut was made from the new mouth of the Ant to near the abbey gateway, cutting off the loop and providing a much improved channel for navigation.

Naturally enough, the construction of the North Walsham & Dilham Canal in the 1820s entailed much straightening of the sinuous channel of the River Ant. The parish boundary of Honing and Worstead did not change with the alterations to the waterway, however, and there are several places where it preserves the old wanderings of the river.

The Barton Turf parish boundary follows the old course of the Ant below Wayford Bridge, where the present course makes a detour to the east. The reason for this diversion is unclear, but it seems to have been a 19th-century alteration since neither Faden in 1797 nor Bryant in 1826 shows the new course.

A similar example of this phenomenon, from an earlier period, is to be found lower down the River Ant, where the Tunstead-Happing hundred boundary preserves the former course of the river to the east of the peat diggings that now form Barton Broad and the considerable loop formerly made by the river around the eastern edge of Catfield Fen. It is clear that at some time after the flooding of the Barton Broad peat pits some of the merchants and watermen trading on the rivers decided it would be expedient to divert the water highway into the upper end of the broad and out at the lower end, cutting off the loop. A little further downriver the original course of the river was to the west of Reedham Marsh, a fact that was first pointed out to me by David Holmes as he navigated the network of dykes opposite the How Hill environmental centre that still follow more or less the old course of the Ant.

Unlike the later schemes for bringing waterborne trade to Bungay, Aylsham and North Walsham, these improvements did not require parliamentary approval and there appears to be no record of their being carried out. When proposals were put forward in the 17th century for making the Waveney

49 *Burgh Mills were still at work when this photograph was taken in 1928.*

navigable from Beccles up to Bungay an Act of Parliament was needed to put the scheme into effect.[8]

Bungay Navigation

The preamble to this Act made the point that the river had been navigable in former times for lighters, keels and other boats of considerable burthen, but that it was at that time so obstructed as to be unnavigable above Beccles, causing great poverty to the inhabitants of the surrounding district. Passed on 17 March 1670, the act empowered five Bungay men, Thomas Walcott, William Barker, Robert London, John Gouche and John Girling, and John Saverie of Downham Market, to improve the river so as to restore trade to Bungay staithe.

Four locks were built, the lowest of them at Shipmeadow/Geldeston, the second between Geldeston and Ellingham, and the others at Ellingham and Wainford. The second lock was dispensed with some time in the 19th century, but the 1:25000 O.S. map still shows a split in the channel where it once was. These were relatively spacious locks, capable of passing vessels 70ft. long and of 16ft. beam, which meant that most wherries could trade to Bungay.[9]

Geldeston/Shipmeadow lock lies in a somewhat secluded position, approached by the narrow Lock Lane from the village of Geldeston, which is reached along a navigable dyke branching off the river some 700 yards below the lock. In the 18th and 19th centuries it seems to have been a busy place, with a number of malthouses and a brewery as well as a watermill beside the lock, and in the 1790s a fleet of six wherries, four of them upwards of 30 tons burthen, quite large craft for that period. An 1855 directory lists Benjamin Utting Dowson & Sons, maltsters, corn and coal merchants, Edward Utting and Septimus Dowson, merchants, Henry Gibson Dowson, brewer, maltster and spirit merchant, and two shopkeepers, making it sound like a thriving industrial village at that time. There were also mills at Ellingham, a mill and later maltings at Wainford, and more maltings and a brewery at Ditchingham, where there was also an important silk mill, so there would have been plenty of trade for the navigation quite apart from that arising at Bungay.

The Aylsham Scheme

The Bungay Navigation had been operating with considerable success for just about a century when the people of Aylsham decided to take steps to improve the trade of their town by making the Bure navigable onwards from Horstead. In the early 18th century corn for the weekly market at Aylsham as well as other commodities were landed from sea-going ships at Cromer or unloaded from wherries at Coltishall and brought to the town by waggon, but in the 1770s news of the building of canals in other parts of the country persuaded the millers and merchants of Aylsham to formulate a scheme to bring wherries to their town.

On 27 January 1773, Parliament was petitioned for a Bill to extend the navigation of the Bure, otherwise the North River, to Aylsham, and there being no opposition the Bill had an unusually rapid passage through Parliament, being passed on 7 April.[10] The route was surveyed by a Mr Biedermann, of whom little or nothing seems to be known. John Adey, who was later to become Clerk to the Commissioners of the navigation, estimated that the work would cost £6,000, of which £1,300 was already available by voluntary gifts, with a further £200 or £300 expected. A subscription was to be raised to find the remainder. It turned out that a considerable amount of excavation was required and the Commissioners ran out of money before construction was completed. The project reached fruition only after 'many difficulties and interruptions', as William White put it in his 1845 county directory.

Work began on 29 June 1774 at the lower end of the proposed navigation, and the first boat, Mr Ansell's *Crampus*, passed through Horstead lock on 16 March the following year, followed three days later by a Yarmouth keel with a cargo of bricks, pavements, coals, cinders and salt. A resident of Coltishall, Mrs William Hardy, recorded in her diary on 29 November 1774:

> Tuesday, Mr Mrs and Miss Smith went with us to the new river to see the lock; carried the men 2 bottles of gin. Mrs Ives gave the men a barell of beer at J. Neaves and he forced them to drink it abroad.

It is unlikely that such 'treats' held up the work significantly, but the fact is that progress on the locks at Buxton, Oxnead, Burgh and Aylsham progressed only very slowly, and it was far from complete when in October 1777 the engineer, John Smith, reported that some £3,600 had already been spent and

50   *The lock at Burgh-next-Aylsham, derelict but still intact in 1928.*

that another £2,951 was needed to finish the project. Eighteen of the local landowners and tradesmen came to the rescue, lending sums of between £50 and £150 each, and the work went on.

There were further problems ahead, however. At Burgh the navigation was carried on an embankment leading off from the original river just above the mill, with the lock standing at one end of the embankment, and it was probably this work that proved so costly and caused financial problems. It also resulted in John Smith decamping. A mile above Burgh bridge the navigation left the river altogether, a new channel being dug alongside the river to reach the basin at Aylsham.

In March 1779, John Green of Wroxham was appointed joint engineer, and the navigation opened throughout in the October of that year. That was by no means the end of the work, however, because it was soon found that shoals forming in the channel were reducing the depth and dredging operations needed to be carried out. Horstead lock could accommodate wherries 54ft. long by 13ft. 9in. beam, but the other four locks could take vessels with a beam of no more than 12ft. 8in.[12] In spite of such a restriction the navigation played a significant part in the mercantile life of Aylsham, as many as 26 wherries trading to the town at one time. *White's Directory* of 1855 speaks of 'a considerable business in coal, corn and timber' and lists five wherry owners operating from 'the Canal basin' to Yarmouth.

51 *Buxton mills, with the entrance to the lock at right.*

No doubt aided by the trading activities centring on the staithe at Millgate, the town of Aylsham entered on a period of economic prosperity that saw the population grow from 1,667 in 1801 to 2,741 fifty years later. In mid-century there were five coal dealers in the town, two of them at the Basin, four timber merchants, and a millwright and agricultural machine maker, among many lesser tradesmen in business there, indicating a thriving centre of commercial activity.[13]

The coming of the railways took away some of the trade from the navigation, but did not render it entirely redundant. The Great Eastern's Wroxham-Dereham line crossed the navigation on an ugly steel bridge on a bend close to where the tail race of Buxton Mill joined the navigable river, arousing the indignation of wherrymen who declared that the bridge had been sited there deliberately to make difficulties for them.

The navigation continued to be well used until flooding caused by heavy and sustained rainfall in August 1912 created havoc on the river and wrecked Buxton lock. The Aylsham wherry *Zulu*, which had passed into the ownership of Barclay, Pallett & Co. when that company took over Benjamin Cook's Dunkirk roller mills at Aylsham in 1908, was trapped above the lock when the flood occurred. She was hauled out by workers from a Coltishall boatyard, dragged on rollers across the road and launched into the river below the lock.

Damage to the navigation would have cost an estimated £4,000 to repair, and the Commissioners, with their diminished income, had no resources from

52 *A wherry lying at Bacton Wood Bridge, on the North Walsham and Dilham Canal, on 24 June 1928. The* Ella *took the last cargo from here just over six years later.*

which to meet that expenditure. An appeal to the government for assistance fell on deaf ears, so that was the end of the Aylsham Navigation, though it was not until 1928 that it was formally abandoned.

The 1912 floods also did serious damage to another Norfolk waterway, the North Walsham & Dilham Canal.

Wherries to North Walsham

The story of this waterway had begun little more than 100 years earlier, in 1810, when the suggestion was put forward that the River Ant be made navigable to near North Walsham, which was then a busy little market town of some 2,000 with a free grammar school at which Nelson had been a pupil. Coal, timber and other commodities were landed on the beach at Mundesley or Bacton and carried the five miles or so to the town by road, but the added cost of that road transport persuaded some that a canal would be a particular convenience to a growing commercial centre like theirs.

Two plans were prepared, one by William Youard and the other by John Millington, both of which were presented in January 1811. Millington, a civil engineer who had not been involved in inland waterways earlier in his career, made a second report in September the same year, and following submission of that report a meeting was called at the *King's Arms* in North Walsham on 14 September. Those attending the meeting decided to apply to Parliament for leave to bring in a Bill to make 'a cut or canal for boats … from the River Ant … at or near a place called Wayford Bridge near Dilham to the towns of

53 *Two wherries on the North Walsham and Dilham Canal at Briggate Mill, Worstead, in 1928, in a photogaph by Horace Bolingbroke.*

North Walsham and Antingham'. The latter place, far from being a town in any real sense, was a parish of some 250 inhabitants, but within its boundaries were two lakes known as Antingham Ponds which formed the source of the River Ant.

The old head of navigation on the Ant had been at Dilham, where a dyke about a mile long led to a private staithe owned by Isaac Harris Lewis, who carried on business there as a coal, corn and oilcake merchant and also derived some profit from shipping corn and flour for the millers on the upper Ant. There were sufficient people in the adjoining parishes of Dilham and Worstead whose livelihoods seem to have depended on the trade through this staithe for there to be spirited opposition to the canal proposal.

In spite of this opposition, however, the Bill received royal assent on 5 May 1812. The Act[14] empowered the undertakers of the canal to raise £33,000, plus a further £10,000 by mortgage of the rates and dues, but the money was slow to come in. The fact that a new plan was made by Millington in 1815 hints at some lack of resolve on the part of those responsible, and it was more than ten years after the passing of the Act before anything was done towards building the canal.

Possibly the opposition from Dilham and Worstead was partly at least to blame for this delay. Lewis brought a claim for damages for possible loss of trade which was heard before a jury at the Quarter Sessions in April 1825.[15]

Having listened to all the evidence, 'the Jury (who were very respectable) after a deliberation of about twenty minutes, assessed the damages at £1,500'. By then the proprietors had, on 15 December 1824, given authority for the work to start. It began formally under Mr Millington's direction on 5 April 1825, when about sixty workmen assembled in North Walsham market place and marched behind a band to Austin Bridge, where the first flag of turf was cut by William Youard, who was described in a newspaper report as 'clerk of the sub-committee'.[16]

The actual construction of the canal was delegated to a contractor, Thomas Hughes, who had been involved with the Caledonian Canal and other waterways in Scotland. The work was by no means easy, difficulty being caused by the marshy nature of the ground through which the channel had to be dug.

Thousands of people are said to have gathered to watch the first laden wherries sail up to Mr Cubitt's mill at North Walsham in June 1826, and 'the day finished with a plentiful treat to the workmen of Mr Sharpe's strong ale and Barclay's brown stout'.[17] The canal was formally opened on 29 August that year, having cost £32,000, but only wherries less than 50ft. long and 12ft. 4in. beam and drawing no more than 3ft. 6in. could use it.[18]

In spite of a reduction of the rates at the beginning of 1830[19] the dues on coal were considered so unduly expensive that the old trade to the beaches at Mundesley and Bacton continued, and the average annual receipts between the opening of the canal and 1844 seem to have been only about £360. The canal company's shaky finances led the proprietors to obtain a private Act in 1866 enabling them to sell off the canal. Edward Press, who farmed at Spa Common and was a partner in Press Bros., which ran the mill at Ebridge as well as a windmill in Yarmouth, bought the undertaking for £600. A capital dividend of 28s. per share was declared on the 446 shares whose owners were known, but the principal clerk had paid out only 55 of those shares when he absconded with the remaining money.

In the wake of this scandal the proprietors appointed Walter Rye, the Norwich solicitor and antiquary, their new principal clerk. With characteristic energy he looked into the company's affairs, and pointed out 'great irregularities in the management and direction of the company'. The affair might have resulted in an even greater scandal, but this was avoided by letting the matter drop as quietly as possible.

In 1874 the canal was deepened at Dilham and East Ruston by emptying the canal between the locks, damming it top and bottom in 300-yard sections and barrowing out the gravel bed of the canal with a large labour force from nearby farms. The trade continued to decline, however, and in 1893 the upper part of the canal between the locks at Swafield and Antingham was abandoned. On Edward Press's death in 1906 the canal was bought by a London company for £2,250, and it was sold again in 1921 to E.G. Cubitt and G. Walker for £1,500. These two men, who were partners in the milling firm of Cubitt & Walker, of North Walsham, immediately sold it on to a new company which they formed, the North Walsham Canal Co. Ltd., for the same price.

54   *Opened in January 1833, the Haddiscoe New Cut formed a vital part of the Norwich and Lowestoft Navigation. The Norwich-Yarmouth road crossed the New Cut at Haddiscoe by means of a small lift bridge, seen here in a postcard of about 1910, with the* Queen's Head *close beside it. Forty years later the little bridge was becoming decidedly ramshackle but was still in operation.*

Three years later the canal was dredged from Wayford Bridge to Bacton Wood lock by a small pontoon dredger, but traffic was still dwindling. It is said that the last wherry to make use of the canal was Barclay, Pallett's *Ella*, built on Allen's yard at Coltishall in 1912 – the last trading wherry to be built; she took the final cargo from Bacton Wood in December 1934.

'Norwich a Port'

These three schemes pale into insignificance beside the great campaign of the 1820s and 1830s to make 'Norwich a Port', the slogan that was trumpeted so loudly by supporters of the project that resulted in the construction of Lowestoft harbour and the excavation of the Haddiscoe-Reedham New Cut. The leading voice in the 'Norwich a Port' lobby was that of Crisp Brown, an alderman of Norwich and one of the city's leading maltsters, who devoted his considerable energies to promoting the improvement of the city's maritime trade in the early years of the 19th century. Crisp Brown had begun his career with Matthias Kerrison at Bungay, moving to Norwich in 1795 to set up in business on his own account. He was elected sheriff in 1814 and mayor in 1817.

One of the reasons he and other Norwich merchants put forward for bringing sea-going ships upriver was the need to prevent the theft of coal and other cargoes on the river. It was all too easy for a wherryman to lay his craft alongside the bank in some secluded spot and put a few sacks of coal ashore, to be picked up later by a willing accomplice, or to sell a sack or two of corn to someone who needed feed for his poultry. It was said in 1820 that depredations on the River Yare during the preceding five years had amounted to £25,000, an enormous sum when one considers the change in the value of money between then and now.[20]

A local newspaper made an interesting comment on these robberies when in May 1820 it was announced that a number of men had been lodged in Norwich Castle accused of theft:

> Long practised and extensive as these depredations have been, few instances have occurred which have been followed by the detection of the offenders. – The fact is, this nefarious system has generally been pursued on those parts of the navigable stream, from this City to Yarmouth, which are situated at a distance from any house, road or path, and where the plunderers have consequently regarded themselves as secure from discovery, when in the act of transferring the property from one wherry to another.

It was only when the merchants hid men on board the wherry *Betsy*, with

55 *Wherries lying in a narrow part of the Wensum in the heart of Norwich, two of them unloading deals into a timber yard. It will be noticed that the nearer of the wherries on the left, which belongs to Yarmouth, lacks the white quadrant on the bows; in wherryman's parlance it has a black snout. The throat block has been hooked to the top of the spen block to hold the gaff horizontally and the gaff has been swung over the bows to clear the hold for unloading.*

the connivance and co-operation of the skipper, William Buttle, that the thieves were observed at their work. As a result of that piece of undercover observation more than a score of watermen and others were charged with stealing or receiving coal from a number of wherries. Not surprisingly attempts were made at the subsequent trial to hide the identity both of Buttle and of his wherry, but they were unsuccessful and the story came out. Buttle had been employed by the city's corn and coal merchants as a 'watch', in effect an early river policeman. Naturally his success in detecting their operations made him

56 *A high sternsheets wherry lying on the Fishergate side of the river close to Fye Bridge, in the middle of Norwich. It is loaded 'down to the binns', but there is no way of telling what cargo is stored beneath the hatches.*

most unpopular with the criminal element among the watermen, and on one occasion he was put to flight with a shower of brickbats when some of them found him concealed under a tarpaulin in a small boat.

The battle of wits between the merchants and the criminal fraternity went on, with the success of the merchants proving to be short-lived. When he gave evidence to a House of Commons committee on the Norwich & Lowestoft Navigation Bill in 1826, Crisp Brown, estimating his loss by plunder in the preceding year at more than £840, said, 'We cannot detect the thieves now, they keep so good a lookout'.

Crisp Brown said that he exported between 900 and 1,000 quarters of corn every eight or nine days and bought three to four thousand chaldrons of coal a year at Yarmouth for resale in Norwich. These goods were, of course, carried between the two places by wherry, and he found that the loss from transhipment and pilferage was between one and a half and two per cent. Within the preceding month he had found a deficiency of nearly five quarters in a cargo of 126 quarters of barley he had sent to Yarmouth.

Pilferage was only one of the disadvantages faced by the manufacturers, merchants and exporters of Norwich as a result of their dependence on Yarmouth, and in 1814 a group of these men asked William Cubitt, the Norfolk-born civil engineer who was at that period working with the Ransomes at Ipswich, for advice on the best way of countering what was increasingly being seen as a Yarmouth stranglehold on the trade of the city. He suggested that the simplest way of overcoming their problems was to dredge a channel to the south of Breydon Water, bypassing the shallows there that prevented deep-draughted vessels from proceeding upriver, and to improve the river generally; the cost would be little more than £35,000.

His idea provoked fury in Yarmouth, whose corporation called in the celebrated engineer John Rennie. In his report to the corporation he expressed the view that the cutting of a new channel would reduce the scour resulting from the tidal stream from Breydon Water flowing down the harbour and would thus result in silting of the harbour. With such eminent opinion on their side the Yarmouth men were in an excellent position to oppose the Norwich plan.

Faced with the implacable opposition of the corporation of Yarmouth, Cubitt drew up an alternative scheme for making an entry to the sea at Lowestoft and bringing ships up to the city from there by way of Oulton Broad and a ship canal across the marshes from Haddiscoe to Reedham. It would cost more than double the original envisaged cost of the Breydon bypass scheme, but the promoters decided to go ahead with the Lowestoft scheme.

Both sides brought in the country's top engineers to advise on the pros and cons of the Norwich proposals. Thomas Telford, who had worked on waterways and harbours both in the United Kingdom and abroad and was then at the height of his fame, reported favourably. 'I am led to hope for the desirable co-operation of Yarmouth and Norwich, because, as an Engineer, I can foresee no injury to the Harbour or Port of Yarmouth, from the New River Channel,' he said. The Scots engineer James Walker was equally diplomatic when he reported to Yarmouth Corporation in 1826:

> The general result of all my consideration is, that the natural Port of Norwich is
> by Yarmouth, to separate them, were it possible, would be injurious to both, and
> both parties are, I am convinced, blind to their own interests if they either desire
> a separation or refuse to each other those facilities which each has the means of
> offering to the other ...

The Yarmouth lobby, adamantly opposed to any proposal that threatened their perceived interests as the port for Norwich, received support from the proprietors of the Aylsham Navigation and the North Walsham & Dilham Canal. These two bodies feared that any diversion of traffic from Yarmouth to Lowestoft would lead to the neglect of Breydon and consequent injury to the navigation of the Bure and Ant. With this support, the corporation of Yarmouth declared that it would do everything in its power to oppose an

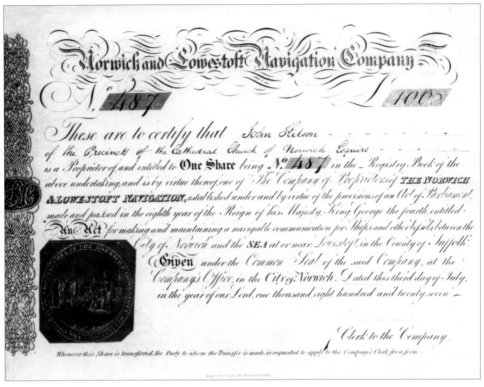

57 *Share no.487 in the Norwich and Lowestoft Navigation Company, belonging to John Kitson 'of the Precincts of the Cathedral Church of Norwich Esquire', was issued on 3 July 1827.*

undertaking 'which was pregnant with the most ruinous consequences to the interests of the town and neighbourhood'.

When in 1826 a Bill was brought forward in Parliament by the Norwich party to enable the Norwich & Lowestoft Navigation Company to embark on the Lowestoft scheme it was indeed stoutly opposed by the Yarmouth interests, and some of the evidence given before a committee of the House of Commons revealed the diehard nature of the opposition. Yarmouth harbourmaster John Bracey argued that the cost of towing vessels up to Norwich against a contrary wind would be prohibitive. Asked how they would be towed up when no towpath was planned, he answered with all the confidence of a seaman brought up in sail: 'They would track them up by those steamboats while they last – but they are going out.' Called by the promoters of the Bill, the masters of several Leith and Berwick smacks said how useful a harbour at Lowestoft would be to those taking part in the coasting trade, but their evidence was countered by a Yarmouth pilot who was certain that the proposed harbour pier would cause a bar to grow up and stop up Lowestoft Roads altogether. Great was the rejoicing at Yarmouth when the Bill was thrown out.

A similar Bill was introduced in the 1827 session, and in spite of Yarmouth spending some £8,000 to oppose it this Bill passed safely through all its stages. The promoters travelled back to Norwich in triumph by the *Times* coach, which was met at Harford Bridges by a joyful procession. The horses were removed from the coach at St Stephen's Gates, and a gang of men dragged it triumphantly through the city. 'Norwich a Port!' was the exultant cry as wooden palings and watch boxes fed the celebratory bonfire in Norwich market place – and when the ringleaders of the mob were lodged in clink, their comrades rescued them and added the clink doors to the fire.

That autumn, on 4 September to be precise, Crisp Brown dug the first spadeful of earth somewhere near Mutford Bridge, and the great project was under way. A lively view of the celebration at Mutford Bridge can be seen in the publication that was produced to commemorate this ambitious scheme: James Stark depicts a gathering of wherries and pleasure boats, including the *Rob Roy*, with a gentleman aboard one of the boats firing his pistol in what was presumably a *feu de joie*, and people on the old bridge waving their hats in the air.[21]

As work proceeded on the Norwich & Lowestoft Navigation the 120-ton steam packet *Thames* arrived at Norwich in May 1828, to be hailed as the first seaborne vessel to sail from London to Norwich direct. The odd thing is that she must have come through the bridge at Yarmouth and have used that shallow channel over Breydon, because Lowestoft harbour and the navigation were by no means ready to receive any kind of shipping.

The new Mutford Bridge, a swing bridge, and the lock linking Oulton Broad and Lake Lothing were completed towards the end of 1828, and it was by way of Yarmouth harbour, the Waveney and Mutford Lock that the little sloop *Rose* arrived at Lowestoft, at the end of March 1830, with the heel posts for the gates of the sea lock and parts for the bridge which was to cross it. That summer the same route across Oulton Broad and through the lock was used by a number of pleasure boats that came to Lowestoft regatta.

The sea lock was completed in 1831, and the harbour piers the following year. The first ships entered the harbour in June 1831, and the first load of goods brought by way of Lowestoft reached Norwich by wherry on 14 July, though the wherries had to sail all the way down the Waveney, under St Olave's Bridge, and then all the way up the Yare because the ship canal across the marshes had not even been started at that stage. It was not until June 1832 that a local newspaper carried an advertisement relating to the New Cut:

> To Contractors, Excavators, and Others.
>
> Such Persons as may wish to Contract for the New Cut or Ship Canal, to connect the Rivers Yare and Waveney, may obtain a Plan, Section and Specification of the same (after Monday, the 4th instant) on application either to William Cubitt, Esq., No.2, Derby Street, Westminster; Mr George Edwards, New Harbour Works, Lowestoft; or at the Company's Offices, Surry Street, Norwich.[22]

By mid-August between two and three hundred men were engaged in cutting the canal across the marshes, and a very rough lot they were. These navvies were imported from other parts of the country, and they cared not how they behaved, entering people's houses and taking whatever provisions they pleased from the larder 'without any fear of contradiction'; nobody dared argue with them. It was only in November that they met their match in a parish constable who was sent for when some of the navvies attacked a licensee after a drinking session in a village alehouse. In spite of being assaulted himself, the constable pursued two of the men, Thomas Mott and his brother, as they ran off. In their efforts to escape the two jumped into the river and attempted to swim across; Thomas drowned and his brother also very nearly lost his life.

It must have been with great relief that local people saw the water admitted at each end of the New Cut in January 1833; the navvies would quickly be on their way to another job somewhere else. On 29 January the wherry *Friendship* became the first vessel to pass along the New Cut from the south, while the *Henry*, owned by Thomas Geldart, a Norwich merchant, was the first to enter it from the River Yare.

The people of Beccles had meantime risen to the challenge and had made arrangements for their town to be linked to the Norwich & Lowestoft Navigation. In 1831 Beccles Corporation played a leading part in obtaining an Act of Parliament for deepening the Waveney from the town down to Oulton Dyke, thus making it possible for sea-going vessels to use Lowestoft harbour and the Norwich & Lowestoft Navigation to reach Beccles. Money was spent on improving the river, and in July 1831 there appeared an advertisement for the London, Lowestoft, Norwich and Beccles Shipping Company. For the time being, the advertisement announced, it was proposed that one vessel a week should sail between London and Lowestoft, and that wherries should be provided to carry the goods on to Beccles, Bungay, Norwich and other places. However, the advertisement promised that 'as soon as the Navigation to Norwich and Beccles is completed, the Vessels will proceed direct to those places'.[23]

In March 1832 Captain John Moon took his aptly named vessel the *Luna* upriver to Beccles with the first cargo of coal to reach the town without having to be transhipped at Lowestoft. By 1834 several ships were coming to Beccles each week with coal from Goole in Yorkshire, goods from London, tiles from Hull and timber and deals from London and elsewhere. A common outward cargo was ale and grain, or ale and malt. Yet in spite of the apparently thriving trade, we are told by William White's directory of 1854 that the Beccles navigation 'proved an unprofitable speculation to the original proprietors' and was sold in the 1840s.

As for the navigation to Norwich, the date on which Norwich is traditionally said to have become a port was 30 September 1833, when the schooner *City of Norwich* and the sloop *Squire* became the first vessels to enter the Norwich River direct from sea by way of the New Cut. The *City of Norwich* had been built for the London, Lowestoft, Norwich & Beccles Shipping Co. by John Korff the year before on a yard at Lowestoft leased from the Norwich & Lowestoft Navigation Co., while the *Squire* had been built at Carrow by Thomas Batley in 1831, the second sea-going vessel to be 'raised' on his yard.

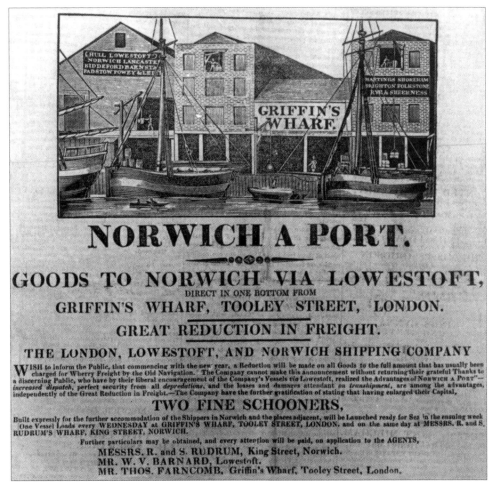

58 *An advertisement from the* Norwich Mercury *of 18 January 1834 for the London, Lowestoft and Norwich Shipping Company's service between London and Norwich.*

That was a day of farce and tragedy as well as of triumph. Customs officials at Yarmouth had raised objections when Captain Moon took the *Luna* to Norwich in March, but these had been overcome; now the harbour officials were determined to spoil the Norwich fun. Arrangements had been made for the steamer *Jarrow* to tow the *City of Norwich* and the *Squire* from Lowestoft to Norwich, but she happened to be in Yarmouth at the time. Harbour officials refused to open the bridge for her to pass through, making the excuse that it was a Sunday, and the bridge was never opened on Sundays. As the tide ebbed away Captain Wilkinson of the *Jarrow* unbolted the funnel and squeezed his vessel under the firmly shut bridge, but he had lost his tide and was forced to wait on Breydon for the next flood.

The non-arrival of the *Jarrow* caused consternation at Lowestoft. There was no hope that the two sailing vessels could proceed under sail because the wind was against them, and in the narrow Oulton Dyke there was no room for them to tack. There was a little steamer, the *Susannah*, at Lowestoft, but with her 7hp engine she was hardly powerful enough to tow two vessels. Nonetheless, the procession set off behind the *Susannah*. Progress was painfully slow until the *Jarrow* was met with at Haddiscoe and the towrope of the *City of Norwich* was transferred to the larger steamer.

All might yet have been well for a triumphal entry into the city had not the cardinal sin of pride intervened. The crew of the little *Susannah* somehow heard that the *Jarrow* and the *City of Norwich* were to be given the honour of being the first ships into the city, and in a fit of pique they cast off the towrope. Captain Allerton of the *City of Norwich* sent his son across in the ship's boat to carry a new towrope to the *Squire*; the young seaman drowned when he fell overboard.

It was a rather solemn little procession that made its way into the new port of Norwich. Crisp Brown was not there to see the fulfilment of his dream, either. He had died in 1830 on board the *Lyra* while on an Atlantic voyage, taken for the benefit of his health.

Later in 1833 the London, Lowestoft, Norwich & Beccles Shipping and Trading Company advertised the establishment of a regular weekly service between London and Norwich. Besides the *Squire* and the *City of Norwich* the company owned two schooners, the *Sally*, bought from King's Lynn in 1831, and the *Orion*. In 1834 it had the 80-ton schooners *Lowestoft Merchant* and *Norwich Trader* built at Yarmouth by Thomas Branford and sold the *Orion* to Wells, replacing her with the schooner *Sarah*, built at Wells the previous year. In addition the company owned another *Sarah*, a sloop, and the Wells-built sloop *Ocean*, which it bought in 1838.

The local shipping company played a considerable role for a number of years, even though it found itself in competition with the New and Direct Beccles and London Shipping and Trading Company in the autumn of 1832. For a time it seemed that both Norwich and Beccles would become thriving ports; in the three-month period between August and October 1834, some 170 vessels entered the harbour with cargo, and about half of them went on upriver either to Norwich or to Beccles.

In 1834, however, the Norwich & Lowestoft Navigation Company found the money running out and had to apply for a further Act enabling it to borrow more. In the end it owed the Public Works Loan Commissioners some £54,000, and even with the harbour in operation and vessels proceeding to Norwich and Beccles by way of the navigation the income was insufficient to pay back the borrowed money. When the undertaking was put up for sale no purchaser came forward.

It was a sad ending for those who had bought shares in the company, believing that they had invested in the future of their city. The city and the shareholders saw little real benefit from the £100,000 that had been sunk into the scheme. Not that Norwich ceased to be an inland port – far from it. In 1846, for instance, one reads of a 70-ton Dutch-built Norwich-owned vessel bringing coal to the city, and of no fewer than 18 vessels with cargoes arriving in the city in one week.

These sea-going vessels had to berth at staithes in King Street Reach, for they could not pass under Foundry Bridge, even after the original wooden bridge of 1810 had been replaced by an iron one in 1844 to improve access to the newly built railway station. Wherries, on the other hand, lowered their masts and passed beneath not only Foundry Bridge but Bishop's Bridge, Whitefriars Bridge and others to reach timber yards, maltings and mills, and all kinds of other business premises further upriver. They traded right up into the pool below the New Mills, and when the sluices there were opened to let floodwater through after heavy rain they had to be moved out of harm's way or they ran a risk of being swamped. Before the widening of the river channel in the wake of the very serious flood-ing of August 1912, some parts of

59 *The Yarmouth-built spritsail barge* Alf Everard *towing upriver to Norwich in the 1930s. Such vessels traded to the city throughout the Second World War and continued to do so with coal and grain until about 1960.*

the river within the city were very narrow, and even at the beginning of the 20th century it could be a difficult job to get a wherry up to R.J. Read's City Flour Mills in Westwick Street or to George Jewson's timber yard in Colegate.

When the ebb tide was backed up by fresh water coming down through the New Mills wherrymen would face a gruelling task. It was impossible to quant against such a current, and the usual method of progressing upstream was to take a line to one of a series of posts set in the river for the purpose. If it was possible to raise the mast the line could be put on to the winch; otherwise the sheet blocks and mainsheet would be used to haul the wherry ahead. Such work put a great strain on the winch, and the *Tiger*'s winch was once strained in 'bowsing' her through a narrow reach.

It seems unbelievable that it once took a whole day to move two wherries from the *Adam and Eve*, the little old public house in Bishopgate, up to Quayside

60   *The motor coaster* Apricity, *belonging to F.T. Everard & Sons, proceeding up the Yare with coal for Norwich electricity power station on 18 March 1948. At that time Norwich was quite a busy inland port, with regular cargoes of coal, grain and timber arriving both coastwise and from the Baltic.*

and to Jewson's timber yard just above Fye Bridge, a distance of no more than a quarter of a mile or so. It is said that in the 1830s it was not unknown for a wherry to take three days to move a mile and a half from Bishop's Bridge to the New Mills. That was after alterations to the haven mouth at Yarmouth had lowered the water level in the city by 1ft. 6in. or 2ft.

Engineer George Edwards, who had been resident engineer on the Norwich & Lowestoft Navigation, reported to the Yarmouth Port and Haven Commissioners in 1838 that the narrowest part of the river in Norwich was only 25 feet wide. His comment on this is worth quoting:

> The name which this part of the river has obtained (Hell Hole) is scarcely severe enough to convey a just idea of the excessive nuisance that here exists to the navigation, it is a disgrace to the city.[24]

A considerable amount of business was, he said, carried on in this section of the river, wherries even lying there to retail coal. Sometimes when a wherry needed to pass, all the craft lying there had to drop down to the wider part of the river, and then be heaved back to their berths after it had gone by.

Edwards had been asked by the Port and Haven Commissioners to recommend an appropriate place to build a lock which would retain a sufficient depth of water in the river at Norwich. The political motives behind the Commissioners considering the construction of a lock at Norwich at this time are unfathomable. Pointing out that the watermen using the river would undoubtedly consider a lock to be a nuisance to their trade, he considered that a cut across the Hospital Meadow close to the 15th-century Cow Tower incorporating a lock would be the best option, but for whatever reason the proposal was never proceeded with.[25]

Nor, happily, were ideas of replacing the inconvenient and ancient Bishop's Bridge put into effect. Until 1791 the bridge had a gate on the city end, but this had to be removed when its weight threatened to destroy the bridge, which provided an approach to the cathedral precincts from the east as well as a way into the city from that direction. There were moves to widen the bridge in 1923 to make it more suitable for 20th-century traffic, but these were scotched by a group of residents who banded together to form what became the Norwich Society.

Built between 1337 and 1341 by Richard Spynk and the first of the city's bridges to be of stone, Bishop's Bridge survives as an historic monument and a memorial to those citizens who fought to preserve the city's past at a time when much of its history was being swept away in the cause of progress. It is now closed to road traffic but small vessels can still pass beneath to reach the heart of the city.

Ironically, the need for the Norwich & Lowestoft Navigation was removed when in 1849 their Lordships of the Admiralty insisted that the Port and Haven Commissioners should deepen the channel over Breydon and across Burgh Flats as a condition of their assent to the Great Yarmouth Haven, Bridge and Navigation Bill then before Parliament. By dredging the channel to give a depth of not less than ten feet at low water at this point the Norwich River was opened up to sea-going ships using Yarmouth harbour, providing the city with a more convenient access to the sea than by way of Lowestoft. It was only the opposition of Yarmouth that had prevented such a relatively inexpensive scheme being carried out in the 1820s.

Railway Competition

Increasingly in the course of the 19th century railways took over the carriage of freight from water transport. The first line in the area was the Yarmouth and Norwich Railway, opened between Norwich and Yarmouth in 1844, many other lines being built over the following twenty years. The Yarmouth and Norwich Railway crossed the River Yare twice at Thorpe on a pair of fixed bridges, and a new cut was made alongside the railway track to enable wherries and other vessels to proceed to Norwich without having to negotiate the two bridges. It was near one of these bridges that the up mail train from Yarmouth and Lowestoft was in head-on collision with a down express in 1874, resulting in the deaths of 25 people.

Trade did continue, however, to towns like Loddon that were not on the railway network. As late as 1886 Wood, Sadd & Moore found it worthwhile to have the River Chet dug out by hand to enable wherries to reach the firm's premises just below Loddon mill.

By the second decade of the 20th century the wherry traffic was in sharp decline in the face of rail competition, yet there was a resurgence of seaborne trade to Norwich in the 1920s and 1930s, when small steam and motor coasters began sailing upriver from Yarmouth mainly with grain, timber and coal. The establishment of an electricity generating station beside the river at Thorpe boosted the coal trade, a telpher railway being installed to take fuel from the ship's hold into the power station.

Throughout the Second World War and for some years afterwards sailing barges and motor coasters were to be seen berthed alongside R.J. Read's flour mill just above Carrow Bridge or at Moy's coal yard; auxiliary sailing vessels and later motorships from the Baltic unloaded timber a little further upriver. In the late '30s a turning basin was formed by dredging out the inside of the bend by St Ann's Staithe to enable the larger ships to turn before proceeding downriver. Tankers brought petrol to a distribution depot at Trowse Eye.

In the 1950s the trade of the port of Norwich was expanded when a local scrap merchant began exporting scrap metal to Belgium, for a time using his own small fleet of motor coasters, but the general trend was downwards. When a southern by-pass was constructed to carry road traffic towards the coast around the city instead of through it, the possibility of providing a swing or lift bridge over the river at Postwick was discounted on grounds of cost; instead a fixed bridge was provided that was of insufficient height for most sea-going ships to pass under. Norwich is no longer a port.

Eight

KEEL AND WHERRY

When the Broads were being formed by the cutting of peat turves it was water transport that carried those turves to the cathedral priory in Norwich, and it was the river that was used to bring stone to the city for the building of the cathedral. Travel by sea and river was the normal, and places that we now consider difficult of access were well served by the relatively simple craft of medieval times.

We know little of the type of craft used on the rivers in the 12th and 13th centuries, but it is probably safe to assume that the square-sailed keel was already assuming the purely local form that it had in later centuries, quite different in hull form from the keels of the Yorkshire and Lincolnshire waterways and from those of the Tyne. It need not surprise us that craft so different in design should have the same name, for the word is descended from the Anglo-Saxon *ceol* and the Old Norse *kjoll*, both of which are synonyms for 'boat'.

The fact that passengers as well as goods travelled by water in the 14th century is made obvious by the inquest on the victims of a disaster that occurred on 19 October 1343, when a boat called the *Blitheburghesbot* sank in a storm near Cantley when on its way from Yarmouth to Norwich. Besides the sea coal worth 10s., salt worth 12d., three barrels of iron and various other goods with which it was laden, the vessel was apparently carrying passengers, for 38 men and women lost their lives as a result of the sinking, which was caused by 'a great rain that fell that night and the darkness of the night and the great and strong wind and the immoderate loading of goods and people which the boat could not bear'. Only two men escaped with their lives.[1]

One might expect from the name that this was perhaps a small coaster that had come from the River Blyth, but this was not necessarily so. A member of the inquest jury was a William de Blitheburgh, a resident of Conesford, one of the Norwich leets. There is nothing in the record to tell us what kind of vessel the *Blitheburghesbot* was.

The early keels were small and somewhat simple craft with a mast more or less amidships setting a single square sail, not greatly different from those to be seen in 17th- and 18th-century prints of the city of Norwich. The men who operated them did not make an appearance in official

61   *A delightful engraving of 1825 by Joseph Stannard showing a hay-laden wherry crossing Breydon in light airs. The mainsail has been boomed out with a boathook and a small squaresail has been set; a small boat alongside is rigged with a spritsail and jib, the latter being boomed out to starboard to catch every puff, though nobody seems to be paying much attention to making the best of the wind.*

documents until the 16th century, when some of them purchased their freedom of the city.

The city corporation was always concerned to control the use of the river, for it was a vital commercial link with the port of Yarmouth and thus with the outside world. And in order to control the river they had to exercise control over the watermen who used it, as they sought to do in 1570 when the Assembly set out to regulate the 'passage boats' and the watermen who operated them.[2] It was enacted that the mayor should license three boats, and that the people operating them should obey certain instructions regarding the carriage of people and merchandise. It was found necessary to reinforce the rules governing the use of boats on the river from time to time, as in 1616 when the Assembly passed 'A Law to be observed by watermen':

> Forasmuch as the transportacion of goods by the Ryver from this Citty to the Towne of Great Yermouth and to other places and the bringinge of goods from the said towne of Great Yermouth and other places to this Citty and the passage and repassage of merchants ffactors and other persons in wherryes to and from this Citty ys very behovefull and comodious not only for the freemen of this Citty but for all the kings subjects whom it concerneth,

62 *A keel, laden with bundles of reed, seen in a drawing by an artist of the Norwich School.*

63 *The stern and rudder of a keel.*

64 *The keelman's wife, with her baby, in the scuttle of the cabin in the bows of a keel.*

it was decreed that no waterman should use any keel, boat or wherry on the Sabbath day, that every waterman should enter bond for the safe keeping of goods committed to him, and that the indentures of apprentices taken by keelmen and wherrymen should be enrolled by the Town Clerk. 'And that no keleman wherryman or other waterman usinge passage upon the said Ryver shall willingly or wittyngly cary or suffer to passe in any their keles wherryes or boates any common Rogue, harlott, ffelon or other person notoriously knowne or suspected to have committed any such cryme ....'

The coming and going of petty criminals by river continued to worry the city officials, for in 1667 there were complaints that a house on the Common

Staithe in King Street '(being a publick-house) harboured dissolute persons, who put off from thence at unseasonable times', whereupon the mayor ordered that the boom across the river should be shut between 10p.m. and 4a.m. in summer and 9p.m. and 6a.m. in winter.[3]

All this makes it perfectly clear that in the 16th and 17th centuries the river was a highway not only for goods consigned to city merchants and for merchandise produced in Norwich for export but also for passengers, both lawful and illegal. Indeed, there is a supposition that the wherry originated not as a cargo vessel but as a passenger craft such as that seen on Corbridge's prospect of Yarmouth. Whether this craft, seen under oars, was in truth the forebear of the sailing wherry has to be open to some doubt, for the wherry had already made its appearance on the river by the 18th century, and a detailed depiction of the *Happy Return* on a horn cup dated 1789 in the Castle Museum at Norwich shows that the 18th-century wherry was surprisingly similar to later craft, though smaller. On one side of the cup is 'Success to the Happy Return' and on the other is 'Robert and Mary Adkins, Irstead. September 12th, 1789'. Intriguingly, six years later Robert Adkins is recorded as master of another wherry, the *Beeston* of Barton.

There is simply not sufficient evidence to prove the lineage of the wherry, though we do know that in the 17th century craft bearing this description were engaged in a regular service between Norwich and Yarmouth.[4] C.J. Palmer, the Yarmouth historian, says that before the days of the stage coach the most commodious conveyance from Yarmouth to Norwich was by 'a barge or wherry' and tells how when, in 1725, a coach was advertised to run every Tuesday and Friday the innovation was resented by supporters of the barge. To combat the switch to road transport they 'caused a complete barge to be built, fitted with suitable conveniences for the reception of gentlemen and ladies and others, to pass from Yarmouth to Norwich every Monday and return Tuesday, and so to pass and repass every day as occasion should require'.[5]

The journey was not without its dangers in the 18th century. The same historian records how in 1712 a wherry carrying passengers to Norwich was upset on Breydon and 20 people were drowned, and in 1782 the *Royal Charlotte* barge on its way from Yarmouth to Norwich was sunk by a sudden squall, six people losing their lives.[6] Less than three years later 'the barge' carrying passengers and goods upriver was overset on Breydon by a sudden gust of wind, but the 18 passengers were picked up by two passing keels and no lives were lost.[7]

In the 18th century keels carried the products of the Norwich textile industry downriver to Yarmouth, there to be loaded into sea-going ships that would take them to Russia, Spain, India and a host of other countries whose populations were anxious to avail themselves of exports from the city that was then one of Britain's foremost manufacturing centres. 'Nearly the whole of the continent of Europe, together with China, South America, and the Cape of Good Hope, were supplied by Norwich with a variety of worsted goods, such as calimancoes, tabinets, brocaded satins, satinets, florettes, brilliants, damasks, and battlings … Spain likewise took large quantities of camlets for the use of the religious orders,' a 19th-century writer tells us.

Information on 18th-century trade on the waterways is hard to come by, but a register drawn up by the Town Clerk of Yarmouth pursuant to an Act of 1795 requiring all inland waterways craft to be registered sheds a sudden, unsustained light on the vessels working on the Norfolk and Suffolk waterways. Between July and December 1795 no fewer than 149 vessels were registered; the following year the Town Clerk registered four more, and in 1797 he re-registered just one vessel, the Yarmouth keel *Flora*, since Robert Kett had taken over as master from Roger Page. Then, it seems, his enthusiasm ran out, for in 1798 he added just two more vessels, and the rest of the register book consists of uncompleted forms.[8]

Included in this register are 34 keels varying in size from a little craft carrying no more than 20 tons, the *Venture* of Panxworth, to the Yarmouth keel *Success*, of 97 tons burthen. Twenty of those 34 keels belonged to Yarmouth and nine to Norwich. It is apparent that the day of the keels was already passing, for there were 118 wherries in the register: eight belonged to Yarmouth, 15 to Norwich, seven to other places on the Norwich River, 64 to places on the northern rivers and 24 to places on the Waveney.

It is no more than a snapshot, comprising little more than a list of those keels and wherries trading to and from Yarmouth in the year 1795. It certainly does not supply evidence of the last-ditch fight of the Yarmouth keel owners described by Roy Clarke in his book *Black Sailed Traders*, but it does supply a few bare facts to illuminate what is otherwise a very shadowy period, even if it prompts more questions than it answers. For instance, how does it come about that the only two keels from the North River, the 40-ton *Trial* and the 20-ton *Venture*, belong to Panxworth, a parish which does not lie on any waterway, even though in earlier centuries there were strong links with Ranworth?

The importance of the waterborne trade can be seen from the statement of John Greaves Nall in 1866 that 'before the opening of railways, 230,000 quarters of wheat, barley and malt, and 150,000 sacks of flour were forwarded by the rivers Wensum, Bure, Yare, and Waveney, from Norwich, North Walsham, Bungay, Beccles, &c., to Yarmouth, to be shipped thence to London, Liverpool, Scotland, Newcastle, &c. The average export of the three years ending 1785 was 270,000 quarters; from 1810 to 1819 it averaged 310,000 quarters; from 1839 to 1843 it exceeded 400,000 quarters yearly; and in 1840 the export of grain from Yarmouth was 480,363 quarters.'[9]

After remarking that the textile exports from Norwich by way of Yarmouth at one time amounted to £1 million a year, Nall added that, 'Prior to 1826, two-fifths of the coals and goods imported into Yarmouth were sent up the Yare to Norwich, and more than half the imports and exports to and from Yarmouth belonged to that city.'

By the beginning of the 19th century the wherry was fast taking over the waterways. *A General History of the County of Norfolk* published in 1829 says that 'the general navigation from Norwich to Yarmouth is performed by keels and wherries; the former are chiefly restricted to the freightage of timber, and are far less numerous than formerly …'. Although several of these craft were still in trade, and one was to remain at work for another half-century or more, the predominant type on the waterways of Norfolk and north-east Suffolk was by that time the wherry, with its single mast set right up forward carrying a big gaff sail.

Those keels that did survive into the 19th century were for the most part relegated to rough work such as the carrying of heavy timber, leading to the misleading statement so often made that the hold of the keel was open, without any hatch covers. It is clear from the description in *The Norfolk Tour* and from other evidence that until their relegation to the timber trade keels did have hatch covers of much the same form as those of the wherries; silken textiles for export would hardly have been carried in an unprotected hold. An advertisement that appeared in the local newspapers in 1779 relating to the sale at Coltishall of the *John and Joseph* was specific in referring to her as a 'hatch keel'.[10]

Besides carrying cargoes between Norwich and Yarmouth and along the other rivers the keels were taken out into Yarmouth Roads to lighten sea-going ships which were too deeply laden to negotiate the troublesome bar at the mouth of Yarmouth harbour. It is recorded that in 1782 a keel engaged in taking coals from a collier in the roads suddenly sank 'with upwards of thirty chaldron'; the crew seem to have escaped with a wetting.

Illustrations of keels at this period are not easy to find, but a series of pen-and-ink sketches by an artist of the Norwich School, possibly one of the Stannards, depicts both keels and wherries in some detail. The hull of the keel is clinker-built, with a round bottom, and there is a transom; the cabin is in the bows – wherries had theirs aft. On the small foredeck is a winch for raising the comparatively light mast, which was not counterbalanced like that of the wherry; a similar winch on the after deck served to hoist the sail on its long yard.

It is commonly said that the keel could not go to windward; certainly it would be unable to point as close to the wind as the wherry, but the limitations of square rig are often accentuated by those who have no experience of its use. Having discussed the merits and demerits of square rig with Captain Fred Schofield, owner and master of the Humber keel *Comrade*, I am by no means sure that it is true to say that a Norfolk keel could only blow along before a following wind.

James Stark's striking picture of a keel on the Wensum by the Devil's Tower at Norwich shows a timber-laden keel close-hauled on the starboard tack. The yard is braced round and the lee sheet has been brought aft, while the wind-ward sheet is belayed somewhere in the bows, and so she sails placidly on as the keelman holds her up into the wind with a casual lean on the tiller.

It could almost be 'Tiger' Smith's old keel in which he is said to have brought logs up to Blyth's timber yard opposite Hospital Meadow at Norwich.

65 *The last Norfolk keel, in use by J.S. Hobrough to support a railway line designed to dump spoil from a dredger on to the bank. The bow cabin is well seen in this photograph. Note the newspaper reporter taking down details of Mr Hobrough's latest innovation.*

Her name is said to have been *'Dee-dar'*, obviously a phonetic rendering of a name unfamiliar to the tongue of the speaker; perhaps it was *Deodar*, the Himalayan cedar. Her dimensions were not very different from those of a wherry, 54½ feet long overall, 52 feet on the keel, with a breadth of 14½ feet and a depth amidships of a little over four feet.[11] A wherry of similar size would have had a depth of no more than 3½ feet. The last keel to survive in trade, she was sold to James Hobrough, a dredging contractor with premises by Bishop Bridge in Norwich and a dockyard at Thorpe St Andrew, not many miles downriver from Norwich, who used her in connection with his dredging operations. At one stage she supported a contrivance for transferring mud from the dredger's grab to the shore, where it was deposited to build up the banks, and in this guise she was photographed – almost certainly the only Norfolk keel to be recorded by the camera.

When she was no longer robust enough for this work she was taken downriver and sunk opposite Postwick Grove to support the bank. It was there that in 1912 William Hall, a member of the Reedham family that had built so many fine wherries, with four helpers took measurements of this venerable craft from which to make a model for the Bridewell Museum in Norwich; in 1928 he made a similar model for the Science Museum, South Kensington.

66   *Another view of the keel working with a steam dredger. It is thought that these photographs were taken by J.S. Hobrough himself.*

In 1985 she was raised from her riverbank grave by a team of sub-aqua enthusiasts who brought her up to Norwich supported on a steel framework and given bouyancy by oil drums so that she could be lifted from the river by crane and taken away for preservation. The idea was that she should form a major exhibit at a proposed Broads museum. Sadly, the museum did not materialise at that time, and for nearly twenty years the timbers of the keel have been deteriorating, aided by vandalism and neglect. Offers of grants from the Heritage Lottery Fund and the Science Museum were dependent on a permanent home being found for the vessel, and nobody has been able to find a suitable place for her.

Wherries varied greatly in size, the largest of them, the *Wonder*, being a relative monster that was built primarily for loading from ships in Yarmouth Roads. Built in 1878 for William 'Dilly' Smith, she was later operated by T.M. Read, a Norwich miller, but she proved too big even for the Norwich River. The smaller wherries, possibly little more than 25 feet long, might very likely have been handled by one man; larger wherries were sailed by two men, or a man and a boy, and sometimes by a man and wife team.

The rig was an unusual one, with a stout mast, unsupported by shrouds, set in a tabernacle forward of the hold; the mast was weighted with lead or iron at the foot, and the forestay had a tackle consisting of a single block on a long iron and a double block on the stay by which the mast could be

67 *This old wherry had been converted to a dredger when it was photographed by Thomas Ayers in the late 1880s. With its raking stem and transom stern, it is similar to wherries depicted in Norwich School paintings of the early 19th century, and was probably built about 1820. The stern cabin is so small that one wonders how any man ever slept in it.*

lowered and raised. There was a single loose-footed gaff sail with a bonnet – a laced-on extension to the sail – at the foot. In place of the throat and peak halyards normal in other fore-and-aft-rigged craft, the wherry had but a single halyard, which in later 19th-century craft was rove to a winch either on brackets on the tabernacle or on two wooden stanchions rising through the deck just ahead of the mast.

Before the winch came into common use a series of single whip purchases was attached to the standing end of the halyard to enable the gaff to be sweated up after the running end of the halyard had been made fast; this device can be seen on a small model of the *Norfolk Hero* in the maritime museum on Yarmouth promenade. The last wherry remembered to have been rigged in this way was the *Emma*, said to have been built by Allen of Coltishall and owned about the 1880s by John Gay of Irstead.

68 *The stern of a wherry sketched at Horning Ferry in 1883 by an unknown artist. Like a sizeable minority, this wherry has a transom stern, which is as usual painted white to make it the more visible after dark.*

Like the keel, the wherry had a clinker-built hull fashioned of oak, but her lines were somewhat sweeter than those of the keel. It has been said that a major difference between the two types was that the keel had a transom while the wherry was double-ended, but pictures by artists of the Norwich School suggest that some keels had a stern similar to that of the normal wherry, while it is known that quite a number of wherries had transom sterns. Latter-day wherrymen could name half a dozen, the *Bertha*, *Elizabeth*, *Maria*, *Rachel*, *George* and *Heron*, and in the 19th century there had been many more. The transom of the latter-day wherries was normally painted white, doubtless like the white eyes on the bows to render them more easily seen when sailing at night.

The 'white snout', as it was known by wherrymen, was by no means universal, for the big Norwich River wherries in which the helmsman stood on deck did not have this feature. Far from being, as sometimes claimed, a survival of the oculus on the bows of Mediterranean craft, the white quadrant on the bows appears to have been introduced only around 1800, if one is to judge from evidence provided by the Norwich School of artists.

The wherry was no flat-bottomed barge. In cross section it was somewhat saucer-shaped, like the smaller reed lighter and the marshman's punt, with which it possibly shares a common ancestry, and an external keel was added to provide good sailing qualities. Wherries sailing to such upriver places as Aylsham, Bungay and North Walsham were able to slip their keels by unscrewing three bolts and plugging the bolt-holes, leaving the keel moored beside the bank until their return downriver; it was not lifted out on to the bank to avoid it becoming warped. There were irons that fitted either side of the stem and ropes to manoeuvre it under the wherry; knots in the handling ropes assisted the wherrymen to judge when the keel was in the correct position for the bolts to be inserted. Wherries trading into shallow waterways like Waxham Cut, which strikes northward from Horsey Mere, often towed a reed lighter into which cargo could be lightened if the wherry ran aground.

All kinds of cargoes were carried, including coal loaded in Yarmouth harbour from sea-going colliers that had brought it from the Tyne and the Wear, and in later days from the Humber. Some of the coal went to supply the steam pumping stations that helped drain the marshes, and some went to village staithes, consigned to local coal merchants. Timber was also loaded from ships in Yarmouth and Lowestoft and carried upriver to the timberyards along the river in Norwich, deals being loaded into the hold until that was full and then being stacked so that the cargo was sponsored out on either side of the wherry. Bricks, tiles, cement, grain, flour, malt, reeds, hay, were all carried, and so in the smuggling days were less legitimate cargoes. Contraband run ashore on the coast at a place like Horsey could easily be taken inland by a seemingly innocent wherry, but one learns only of the occasional capture, as when a reed barge with a contraband cargo was seized on Hickling Broad. Of the successful runs it was a case of 'dun't you know nuthin', they can't git uvver that!'

While there were many skipper-owners who would carry any cargo that was offered, there were also merchants and tradesmen who owned small fleets which they used to transport their own goods, their raw materials and their products. Timber merchant Isaac Wales, of Reedham, had some of the very fin-

69 *Cargoes of deals destined for the Norwich timber yards were stacked above the hatches after the hold had been filled, a layer of deals being laid across the rightups so that they extended out on each side. Further deals were then stacked on top of them, as seen in this picture. It will be seen that one reef point has been tied up so that the wherryman can see under the sail to leeward.*

est wherries on the rivers, including the *Fawn*, which had the most consistent success of any wherry in the racing at local regattas. Wales took great pride in her achievements, and her skipper, 'Ophir' Powley, used to carry a basket of homing pigeons with him when racing at sea; a pigeon would be sent off at the end of each round with a message for the owner, waiting at home at Reedham.

Many old wherries eventually joined the fleet of James Hobrough & Son, dredging and piling contractors, whose dockyard at Thorpe St Andrew was one of the last places where wherries could be seen at work right into the 1950s, albeit under power rather than sail. The firm is said to have been founded in 1854, when James Hobrough became licensee of the *Bishops Bridge Inn* at Norwich, from which base he ran the contracting business. There was also a 'dockyard' at Thorpe. James died in 1901 and was succeeded in the business by his son, James Samuel Hobrough.

As the older craft became too decrepit for further use they were sunk wherever the river bank required protection and buttressing, or else they

70 *A wherry hauled out at 'Petch's Dock', a boatyard opposite the Cow Tower at Norwich that was operated by William Murrell Petch, who combined his boatbuilding activities with running the* Horse Barracks *public house in Barrack Street. Earlier it had been occupied by William Petch, perhaps his father, and then by Mrs Hannah Petch, possibly his widowed mother. The yard had been in existence at least as early as 1812, when John Thirtle painted a watercolour of a wherry hauled out for repair. From this yard came, among others, the wherries* Jenny Morgan, Jessie *and* Caroline.

were moored in dykes at the Thorpe dockyard and allowed to rot away. In 1930 a number of old wherries were sunk in a line across Surlingham Broad on either side of the channel dredged across the broad.

In the 1930s the *Caroline*, a big Norwich River wherry built by William Murrell Petch on his yard opposite the Cow Tower in Norwich, was fitted up as a steam-operated suction dredger to combat the spread of a floating weed that threatened to choke Hickling Broad each summer. With a steam engine from the old towing launch *Terrible* in the hold driving a large centrifugal pump, the weed was to be sucked up through a pipe held by a gantry over the bows and pumped through a floating pipeline on to the marshes, but the equipment does not seem to have been put into operation at Hickling.

In 1940 J.S. Hobrough retired at the age of 75 and the firm was taken over by May, Gurney & Co. Ltd. of Trowse, a firm which has since grown considerably in the field of civil engineering. In the late 1940s and 1950s

71 *This wherry is hoisting sail, and the mate is just finding the winch hard to crank; he will probably change the winch handle to the lower gear position as the luff becomes taut and the peak begins to rise. The gaff line is led aft so that the helmsman can control the peak of the gaff, which does not begin to rise off the hatches until the jaws have risen up the mast and the luff is taut.*

the foreman and his men in the big corrugated-iron boatshed at Thorpe were busy rebuilding some of the fleet, including the *Primus*, *Secunda* and *Maud*. Even at that stage a good deal of money and effort was being expended in extending the life of these craft, which were playing a useful if humdrum role in keeping the rivers open to navigation. In spite of that work the wooden craft were all eventually replaced by rather ugly steel lighters that, in a concession to tradition, carried on their bows the white quadrant of the old wherries.

72   *Lowering sail to pass under Acle bridge; the mate is lowering the gaff carefully with the winch while the helmsman hauls in the gaff line to ensure that the peak drops on to the hatches. When the sail is down the parrel line will be cast off and the gaff jaws moved clear of the mast, the winch barrel will be swung aside and the mast will be dropped.*

73 *Two of the wherries lying alongside the quay at the North End of Yarmouth have transom sterns, a feature that was by no means as uncommon as some writers have suggested. Many cargoes were landed here by wherries that had brought timber, bricks or other commodities for the Yarmouth merchants. In the background can be seen the north-west Tower, at the end of the town wall.*

74 *A wherry hauled out at Robert Harrison's boatyard at Ludham, in a watercolour sketch of 1887 by an unknown artist. Harrison combined boatbuilding with farming from about 1850 to the end of the 19th century.*

It was the culmination of a process that had started a century earlier when the first 'steam wherries' were put into service. Steam had come early to the Norfolk rivers, one of the earliest steam passenger services in Britain having commenced operation on the Yare between Norwich and Yarmouth in 1813, employing a vessel that had begun life as a French privateer and had been converted to steam by Fenton, Murray and Wood at Leeds.[12] In spite of a disastrous boiler explosion at Norwich in 1817 that led to one of the packets being converted from steam to horse propulsion, employing a number of horses walking round and round on a circular platform and operating the

75 *The wherry* Cornucopia *unloading at Stalham on 24 May 1934. The mast has been partly lowered and a single block suspended from the crane iron at the masthead; through this block is rove a line led down to the wherry's winch so that the winch can be used to hoist sacks from the hold. Often the gaff and sail was swung aside to clear the hold, but this has not been done in this case.*

paddle wheels through a system of gears, a long succession of steam packets operated on the Yare and also between Beccles and Yarmouth.

One of the best-remembered steamers was the *Jenny Lind*, named after the 'Swedish Nightingale' and built on the Hall yard at Reedham in 1883. A clinker-built steamer with a length of 81 feet, the *Jenny Lind* operated mainly between Norwich and the riverside resort of Bramerton Woods End under the command of William Crowe, who had begun his career on the water as a boy of nine on the steamer *Alpha*, owned by the Norwich firm of Clarke & Reeve and skippered by his uncle Richard. Though he never learnt to read and write, William Crowe certainly could swim, and during his years on the river he saved a number of people from drowning, including a Norwich leather merchant who subsequently provided Crowe with a regular supply of boots.

These were passenger steamers, but by the 1860s steam was invading the world of the cargo wherry. One of the earliest steam wherries was the *Wensum*, built by Petch on his Norwich yard and fitted with a steam engine by an unknown builder. I have the particulars of the sale by auction of 'The well known Steam Wherry the "Wensum" with the Steam Engine, Boiler & Stores

76 *George Rump, owner of the wherry* Dispatch, *on right, and his mate, seen as the* Dispatch *passes through the New Cut at Thorpe St Andrew under motor on 25 April 1940. The mast has been lowered to reduce windage. The* Dispatch *was acquired by May, Gurney in 1948 and broken up four years later.*

therein' on 30 May 1879. She was knocked down for £75 to James Hobrough, who took the engine out of her and no doubt used it for some other purpose while putting the *Wensum* into his little fleet of unpowered wherries.

The largest wherries carried a cargo of no more than 50 tons, making it difficult for them to compete with the railways which towards the end of the 19th century were increasingly taking over business from the coasting trade. One man who realised the need for change was Henry Newhouse, who founded the ABC line of steamers working between Hull, Yarmouth and London about 1892, eventually taking over the long-established Norwich firm of Clarke & Reeve. ABC stood for Accelerated Boat Communication. Setting up the Yare & Waveney Lighter Co. Ltd. in 1903, Newhouse built up a fleet of steel barges capable of carrying much larger cargoes, though still able to get through the Norwich bridges and right up to the New Mills.

The first of the fleet was the steam barge *Active*, which was probably a Clyde puffer as she was built at Kirkintilloch, on the Forth & Clyde Canal, and she was followed by the *Busy, Commerce, Despatch, Expedition* and so on through

77   *The wherry* Hilda *after sinking in a dyke near Horning Ferry during a severe frost in 1939. She was frozen in and filled with water when the ice furthest from the bank melted, causing her to cant over; she was never refloated. The photograph was taken by Horace Bolingbroke in March 1940.*

78   *The wherry* Plane *in 1948 when she was owned by Colman's, the manufacturers of mustard; some of the firm's steel lighters can be seen in the background. The only carvel-built trading wherry, she had been built by William Brighton for W.D. & A.E. Walker, the Bungay maltsters and merchants; in 1949 she was acquired by the Norfolk Wherry Trust, which restored her to sail and continues to operate her.*

the alphabet to *Quickness, Readiness* and *Speediness*, most if not all of them built at Gainsborough on the Trent. Whether the end of the alphabet was ever reached is uncertain, but in 1916 the fleet was commandeered for war service on the French canals. With the departure of the lighters and their associated tugs the lighter company's wherries *Bell, Dora, Gertrude, Maud* and *Shamrock* went to other owners, all except the *Gertrude* being acquired by Hobrough.

That was not, however, the end of the lighter story, for the Great Yarmouth Shipping Company, formed in 1923 and from 1931 a subsidiary of the General Steam Navigation Company, which had in 1906 taken over the shipping operations of John Crisp & Sons, of Beccles and Lowestoft,

79 *A motor wherry, probably Thaine's* I'll Try, *on the Thurne at Potter Heigham in 1960 towing a reed lighter. In this case the wherry appears to be light, but it was common practice for wherries taking cargo to places such as Somerton to tow a reed barge into which some cargo could be placed if the depth of water proved inadequate for a fully laden wherry.*

built up a large fleet of steel lighters all named after trees and semi-precious stones. Some, including the steam lighter *Opal*, were old vessels built at Gainsborough, while others were built at Yarmouth in the 1920s and 1930s. The dumb lighters were towed by two little steam tugs, the *Gensteam*, built at Yarmouth in 1924, and the *Royal Sovereign*, built in the same yard six years later, both of which had hinged funnels to enable them to go through the Norwich bridges. When the General Steam Navigation Company required the name for a new excursion motor vessel in 1937 the *Royal Sovereign* was renamed *Cypress*.

Steam engines and boilers took up a good deal of space and so restricted the amount of cargo that could be carried, but the arrival of the internal combustion engine provided an economical power unit that could be fitted in the cabin of a wherry. One of the first wherries to be converted to power was the *Bell*, which had a two-cylinder petrol-paraffin motor fitted about 1915. Bought by J. Hobrough & Son about three years later, she was strengthened and had her original engine replaced by a 20-hp single-cylinder Kromhout crude oil engine which gave her sufficient power to tow two other wherries. Since the engine took up the space originally given over to the crew a new cabin was built into the forepeak.

Other wherries were also fitted with motors, including some of those used by Hobrough for carrying spoil from the dredgers, and when the *Hilda* sank at Horning in 1940 she was almost the last wherry trading under sail.

Nine

EXPLOITING A WETLAND

The Broads area has often been described in promotional literature and in the less accurate guidebooks as a natural wilderness, but it is nothing of the kind. Far from being a natural wilderness, the landscape of the region is almost entirely the result of human exploitation in one way or another.

From the earliest days there were fishermen who exploited the well-stocked rivers as well as wildfowlers who used various methods of harvesting the many wild birds who visited and bred in the region. Eggs of some species were collected in large numbers for human consumption, in some cases to the serious detriment of the species concerned. In the 19th century great quantities of lapwing eggs were being collected, arousing the concern of the Revd Richard Lubbock, for this bird was, he said, 'greatly reduced in numbers'. Lubbock noted that 'in 1821 a single egger, resident at Potter Heigham, took an hundred and sixty dozen' peewits' eggs 'in the adjacent marshes'. And Thomas Southwell added in a note to the 1879 edition of *The Fauna of Norfolk* that 'the indiscriminate plunder of the eggs of this bird is slowly but steadily tending towards its extermination. A gentleman informed me that in 1861 he took 254 eggs of this bird on the marshes near one of the broads not many miles from Norwich; and that in 1862, he took 338 eggs in the same place.'

80 *Workers on their way home from the marshes, as pictured by Peter Emerson in the 1880s. The two men are carrying meaks, straight-handled cutting tools used for reed-cutting and for harvesting bolder and gladdon.*

Another cause of decline of certain species was shooting. Many men in the region were occupied in wildfowling, for the Norwich and Yarmouth poulterers were always keen to obtain supplies from those who spent the early hours of each day afloat in search of fowl. Arthur Patterson has written at length of the Breydon men and their doings in his book *Wildfowlers and Poachers* (1929), but there were many others elsewhere in the region who took to their

81 *Marsh crops stacked on Rockland Staithe at the beginning of the 20th century. The* New Inn *can be seen in the right background.*

punts at hours when other men were still abed. Their bread-and-butter was the ducks that went to the poulterers, but they were always on the alert for some rarity that could be sold to wealthy naturalist-collectors. T.E. Gunn and his son Frederick in the shop they ran in St Giles's, Norwich, stuffed many a specimen shot by the likes of 'Scientific' Fuller and 'Tough' Parker of Rockland.

'Old Scientific' was a well-known character of whom many tales were told. It is said that, when Rockland Broad was frozen for several weeks, one of the skaters taking advantage of the hard weather challenged 'Scientific' to shoot a black-headed gull while skating at full speed across the broad. Holding his gun in both hands, Fuller waited until the gull wheeled above him, then skated after it, brought the gun to his shoulder and fired, the gull dropping almost at his feet.

Shooting was not the only way of acquiring duck for the table. Several Broadland estates once had their decoys into which wild duck were enticed by tame ducks swimming on the surface of a pond or small broad. A curving dyke led along a netting pipe up which the duck were led by the decoyman's dog and their own curiosity, until they reached a point of no return. G.C. Davies tells how 'so silently and skilfully … is the decoying practised, that, while half a hundred ducks are having their necks wrung by the decoy-man within fifty yards of the water's edge, hundreds more may be sitting on the water close by, all unconscious of the tragedy which is being enacted'.

82 *The pipe of Fritton Decoy, into which wildfowl would be attracted by the use of tame ducks and a well-trained dog. During the winter of 1879-80 no fewer than 2,400 ducks were killed at this decoy, one of several operating in the region during the 19th century. Although such numbers were killed, these decoy ponds attracted wildfowl to the Broads and when that at Ranworth closed down the wildfowl largely deserted the Ranworth area.*

In the mid-17th century Sir Thomas Browne observed that there were very many decoys in Norfolk, 'especially between Norwich and the sea, making this place very much to abound in wild fowl'. His point was that the attraction of the decoy pond was its absolute seclusion, which brought fowl to the area; when the decoy at Ranworth closed down wildfowl largely deserted that part of the Broads. Besides the Ranworth decoy there were others at Acle, Fritton and Flixton in Lothingland, Gunton, Hemsby, Hempstead, Mautby, Waxham, Winterton and Woodbastwick, most of which lapsed into disuse during the 19th century.

Considerable numbers of ducks were taken at these decoys. In 1864 no fewer than 877 mallard, 70 teal, eight wigeon, three shovellers, a pintail, a tufted duck and a goosander were taken at the Ranworth decoy, while during the winter of 1879-80 the number captured at the Fritton decoy was an amazing 2,218 mallard, 123 teal and 70 wigeon.

In the Middle Ages there was no free-for-all on the rivers so far as fishing was concerned, for fisheries were strictly controlled by the owners, including monastic houses such as St Benet's that depended on them for supplies of fish for Fridays and other fast days. Several different kinds of net were used, including trammel nets – double nets, one with a large mesh and the other with a smaller mesh which combined to trap fish swimming into them – peter

83 *By the nature of their occupation eel catchers were solitary men, and photographs of them at work are difficult to come by. This photograph entitled 'The Eel-catcher's Home' is from* Life and Landscape on the Norfolk Broads *by P.H. Emerson and T.F. Goodall, published in 1887, and shows an old ship's boat with a cabin built on top that served as a home for the fisherman while he tended his eel sett.*

nets, into which fish were driven by beating the water with an oar, and bow nets, stretched over a series of hoops and used for catching tench.

Even as far back as 1545 concern was being expressed at the need for conservation, the company of fishermen expressing to Norwich Corporation the opinion that the Yare was being overfished. They complained that 'One or two fishermen inhabiting this citie seeking rather the destruccion of the comon river than the maynteyning of the same doo daylye so overcharge the seid river with so many and sondry tramelye nettes' that other fishermen were unable to maintain their families. There was, they said, also the problem of otters depleting the stock of fish, and they sought a ruling from the mayor that every fisherman should be obliged to keep a dog 'to kill otters etc.'.

Besides the small nets set from fishermen's boats there were setts at various places on the rivers used for catching eels, particularly in the autumn when these fish were running downriver towards the sea on the way to their distant breeding grounds in the Sargasso Sea – though the strange life cycle of the eel was quite unknown to medieval fishermen, some of whom believed that eels grew from horsehairs shed by animals grazing on the marshes. These setts were arrangements of nets stretched across the river or dyke with the head of the nets facing upstream; the eels swam into the 'bossom' and were

84 *Another photograph from* Life and Landscape on the Norfolk Broads *shows the operation of taking up the pod to remove the night's catch. The boat in use is a typical marshman's double-ended punt.*

trapped in the 'pod', from which they would be removed periodically into floating boxes or trunks for storage.

Blomefield records that there were once 19 setts between Norwich and Hardley Cross, two wardens of the Fishermen's Company being appointed in 1620 to inspect the setts and to ensure that small fish were not taken. These setts had names such as The Panne and Carrow Dyke (the first two downstream from Norwich), Dames End, Middle Trayle and Rowghflete or Fayerflete. There were many others on the northern rivers, only one of which is still in operation.

In relatively modern times the eel fisherman operating a sett kept watch from his houseboat, usually an old fish-carrier from a North Sea smack or some other ship's boat with a cabin built on to it. He had to be ready to lower his net to the river bed if a wherry came sailing through the darkness.

Before the marshes were drained, and for many years afterwards, the Broads were indeed a haunt of fish and fowl second to none. The Revd Richard Lubbock wrote in 1845 of 90 pike, many of them large, being taken in a day by two fishermen in a single boat using trimmers, hooked lines wound on a floating bundle of reeds the size of a rolling pin so that they unwound as the fish was hooked, and George Christopher Davies has written of Surlingham Broad being so choked with bream and roach at spawning time that the water seemed to be a moving mass of fish, whose backs could be seen breaking the water in every direction. Not only eels and freshwater fish used to be taken in the Yare, for there was a time when smelts migrated into the river and were taken in draw-nets or by the use of cast nets as far up as Norwich itself, and even in the pool below the New Mills.

85 *A marshman's punt, a local type of boat that was used for fishing and for general transport on rivers and dykes in the region. Like the larger reed lighter, it is flat-bottomed with clinker-built sides.*

86 *Sketch plan and profile of a 30ft. marshman's lighter, with a pump amidships to clear any water that might accumulate inside its flat bottom.*

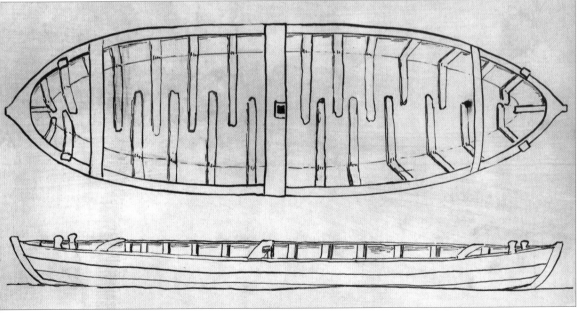

87 *A marshman in a full-load reed lighter at Hunsett Mill on the River Ant. Like the punt, the reed lighter has a flat bottom, in this case covered by bottom boards. There are hefty beams fore and aft with boards forming bulkheads to prevent the cargo from straying into the head and sternsheets. The name Hunsett is thought to derive from an eel sett kept by a man named Hunn.*

Considerable changes were made as drainage of the marshes proceeded and farming was improved. For a picture of the marshes before the enclo-sures of the early 19th century one can turn to the pages of Nathaniel Kent's *General View of the Agriculture of Norfolk*, published in 1796, which refer to the marshes lying between Norwich and Yarmouth as being largely under water for much of the winter. Though those areas were drained mainly by windmills in the spring so that cattle could spend the summer on them there were, he said, many areas that were almost totally unproductive because of lack of effective drainage.

> There are many large tracts of swampy ground, particularly in the neighbourhood of Ludham, which produce little more at present than sedge and reed. Perhaps the intermixed state of these lands may be the principal cause of their drainage being neglected; but their loss to the public is very much to be lamented, as there is no doubt but they would very well answer the expence of improvement.

Where the marshes were improved, as in the Halvergate marshes north of the Yare and in the Haddiscoe area between the Yare and the Waveney, they were used in summer for fattening cattle. These cattle, and the marshes on which they grazed, were looked after by the marshmen whose homes were deep within the marshes. Their work took them out in every weather, for it was their responsibility to look after a large area of marsh and the dykes that drained it, and often in later days also to operate the windmill or the steam plant that cleared the water from those dykes into a main drain or into the river. The dykes had to be cleaned out each year; 'bottom fying' and 'drawing' them was a task that could not be neglected if the water were to be cleared and the marshes made available in the spring for grazing cattle, many of them belted Galloways and other Scots breeds that had been driven south by Scots drovers and bought by the local farmers at St Faith's fair. This fair just to the north of Norwich was held each year 'on the 17th of October, and continuing during the three following weeks'. Nathaniel Kent tells us that it was one of the greatest of cattle fairs, 'to which are brought a vast number of Scotch and Irish cattle'. On the wall of the Mid Steeple at Dumfries is a cast-iron plate that records the mileage to, among other places, Huntingdon, 272 miles; that was the point on the Great North Road from which the drovers struck off into East Anglia.

The marshmen would also turn their hands to reed-cutting in winter and sedge mowing in summer, and to wildfowling to supply the shops in Norwich and Yarmouth. To the mind of an agricultural improver like Nathaniel Kent reed and sedge were not agricultural crops, but they were nevertheless valuable products, and so was the marsh hay that was harvested from the marshes. Good reeds were, and are, much in demand for thatching buildings, since reed thatch has a much longer life than straw. Churches as well as houses and barns in the Broads area were commonly thatched, and there was in the 19th century a thatcher in many villages; in 1890 *White's Directory* listed thatchers in 19 places in the region of the Broads.

Five of those thatchers were named Farman, a family name that became almost synonymous with thatching and basketmaking over a long period. Alban Farman at Upton, Robert Farman at North Walsham and his namesakes at Great Hautbois and Rockland all combined the two trades around 1890, and some thirty years later Farman Brothers at Salhouse, Robert Farman at Claxton, Robert William Farman at North Walsham and William Farman at Horsham St Faith's were still engaged in both.

88 *Two men setting up a bow-net, used for trapping fish in the dykes and reedbeds. Peter Emerson tells us that one of the men was 84 and the other not much younger; the photograph is from* Life and Landscape on the Norfolk Broads.

Robert William, who proudly appended 'plain and fancy reed thatching' to his entry in *Kelly's Directory*, gained a nationwide reputation as a fashion for reed thatch spread throughout the country in the 1930s. A job that is said to have given him particular satisfaction was the thatching of a dolls' house presented to Princess Elizabeth by the Welsh people; he was the first thatcher to be granted the Royal Warrant. He died in 1961 at the age of seventy-one.

Reeds grow best on land that is covered with a foot or so of water, and are harvested in winter, after the frost has trimmed off the leaves and left the tough stems standing bare. When growing on flooded land the reeds are cut with a scythe, but when growing in water they were cut from a boat using an implement called a 'meak' or 'meag', with a short blade not unlike that of a reap hook set at right angles to the straight handle. The reed is gathered up and tied into bundles using bands of roughly spun rushes, the butt ends being knocked up on a board and the reeds carefully cleaned of loose stuff to produce a tidy bundle. Sedge cut from the marshes was used to form the ridge of a reed-thatched roof.

The standard measure of reeds is a fathom, that is a quantity of reed six feet in girth a foot from the stub end. The size of bunch and the number of bunches to the fathom varies according to the district: Barton, Stalham and Hickling put 600 bundles, 120 fathoms, to the long hundred; while in the Rollesby, Ormesby and Filby area the long hundred consists of 120 fathoms each of six bundles, making 720 bundles to the long hundred. On the rivers, at places such as Reedham, Stokesby, Fritton and St Olaves, the tally is five score fathoms of six bunches to a fathom, namely a short hundred.

It is not only the fact of standing in water in mid-winter that makes reed-cutting an uncomfortable job. Ted Ellis, the naturalist, tried his hand at it and discovered some of the occupational hazards, one of which arose from the flinty texture of the reeds. 'After grasping a few hundred swathes firmly while cutting the stalks with a sickle, I noticed a tingling of the skin on my hands rather like "pins and needles", and this persisted for 24 hours,' he said. The reeds are so abrasive that they even wear down the finger nails of those who handle them regularly, and they reduce jackets to tatters very quickly through the carrying of bundles. 'I am not greatly surprised that experienced reed cutters are scarce these days', Ted said in one of the letters that he contributed to the *Eastern Daily Press* over so many years. There are compensations, however. Marshman Eric Edwards, of Ludham, has told me of how those elusive little birds, the bearded tits, will come close to the reed-cutters as they are working and feed on the insects they disturb.

The bundles of reed used to be carried to the nearest staithe in large flat-bottomed boats known as reed lighters, which could be either quanted or rowed by a man in the bows using a pair of oars. They were categorised according to the amount they were able to carry, a large one being known as a full-load boat and having a length of some 25 feet and a beam of about nine feet; smaller ones were classified as three-quarter load or half-load boats, the latter size being able to hold all the reeds a single man could cut in a day. Following the Second World War some reed cutters adopted ex-Army bridging pontoons for the purpose, and few of the distinctive reed lighters survive today.

Basketmakers also made full use of products from the fens and marshes; not only willow wands but also rushes that were split and used to make frail baskets in which many workers carried their 'dockey' or dinner. In a number of Broadland parishes there were osier beds supplying the rods used both by local basketmakers and by the basketmakers of Yarmouth who made the peculiar swills in which herring were landed at that port. Such was the scale of the herring fishery that there was an almost insatiable demand for willow rods, and it has been said that osier beds were probably more numerous in the Flegg than anywhere else in Britain.

The soft rush (*Juncus effusus*), which grew in the wetter fens and marshes, was much used at one time for making the rushlights that provided illumination in many a cottage. After being well steeped in water to soften the outer rind the rushes were peeled to expose the pithy core while leaving a continuous thin length of rind to provide strength. The pith was then allowed to dry and weather before being dipped into melted fat collected from the cooking utensils, to which a small amount of beeswax had been added.

Rushes were also used for the making of horse collars; in 1890 there were three separate tradesmen making rush collars at Neatishead alone, and others in Norwich and at Stalham and Upton. Earlier in the century there had also been a rush mat and collar maker at Clippesby. The making of rush mats is a trade that still survives at Oulton Broad, where Waveney Rush Industry, a business which started up in 1947, is exporting woven rush mats to Mexico, the USA and a number of European countries.

The material used for the making of such mats, and for horse collars, is known in Norfolk as bolder; it is the true bulrush (*Scirpus lacustris*). Bolder was also used by the cooper for caulking in between the staves of barrels. Another product of the Broads was what is locally known as gladdon, by

89 *A gamekeeper landing a four-pound pike, photographed by Peter Emerson. 'Our keeper has been snapping,' Emerson says. 'That is, he has strung a small dead roach on to a piece of wire armed with hooks and weighted with leads; he then paddles gently up to an opening in the lilies or the rush, and drops in the bait, pulling it this way or that towards the surface, thus often attracting the hungry fish.'*

which is meant lesser reedmace (*Typha augustifolia*) and yellow flag (*Iris pseudacorus*), which was also used for horse collars and frail baskets. Cut from shallow water in summer, gladdon was carted to the nearest staithe by boat and there stacked to weather before being sold. Somewhat confusingly, while always calling the true bulrush by the name of bolder, the East Anglian uses the name 'bulrush' for the greater reedmace (*Typha latifolia*).

The dialect used in the Broads area can prove a stumbling block for visitors who do not know the local language, which contains many a survival from the English of Chaucer and also many words and grammatical peculiarities adopted from Scandinavian and Dutch settlers who have been assimilated into the local population at diverse periods. The local usage sometimes, as in 'loping' and 'crowding', approximates to the original usage in the language from which the words have been adopted, but in some cases it has been changed; the Dutch *dijk*, an earthen bank, has become a ditch in eastern Norfolk, where drainage dykes bisect the drained marshes, though in other parts of East Anglia the word *is* used for a bank, as in the Devil's Dyke. An upraised earthen bank in the Broads is a wall.

East Anglian dialect has its own grammar, quite different from the English grammar that used to be taught in schools, and these variations can all be traced back to particular influences. Not only do many dialect variations stem from a form of English that was spoken in Chaucer's time but has since changed, but instances of similar variations can be found in certain foreign languages that provide clues to the origin of East Anglian dialect.

The separable prefix that is so striking a feature of our dialect is found also in Dutch and German, and is likely to have been introduced by incoming travellers who settled on the East Coast perhaps a thousand years ago. As in German, so do we tell someone 'Push the door to!', and as the door is opened by somebody else, we might ask 'Where are you a-going to?' The double demonstrative 'that there' is demonstrably of Scandinavian origin. Often used by speakers of East Anglian dialect, it is considered incorrect English; it is popular Danish, and correct Swedish.

Then there is the double negative that has proved a challenge to generations of schoolteachers; it was once common in many languages, including everyday English. The countryman who is heard to say that 'he hin't seen naathin'' is making use of a form of speech that has passed out of use in ordinary English, yet still survives in Afrikaans, a derivative of the Dutch language spoken in South Africa.

Not so often heard now is the peculiar half-cough given by a Norfolk man instead of the 'T' in words such as butter and water, which seems comparable with the 'glottal stop' of Danish speech, and is probably a survival of it. In the past fifty years the name of one Broadland village has changed from Po'er Ham to Potter Hayham and even Potter Higham, a mark of how the old dialect usage has been diluted and even extinguished by an influx of newcomers and by the influence of radio and television as well as education.

Our dialect has not always been understood even by those scholars who were of a kindly disposition towards it. An amusing instance concerns the use of the word 'sammodithee', which was supposed by the Revd Robert Forby, who found it mentioned by Sir Thomas Browne, the 17th-century philosopher and physician, to be a word of great antiquity. Another philologist, referred to by Forby in his long and learned note, interpreted it as 'Say me how dost thou', pointing to the Saxon 'saeg me hu dest thu'. The derivation of the expression turned out to be more down to earth than the antiquaries and philologists expected. The Revd W.T. Spurdens, who with John Deere made the collection that was the basis of Forby's book, came upon the real meaning of the expression by accident:

> The first time I ever heard it, or of it, was from Mr W. Hooker, now Sir W.H., who breakfasted with Mr Deere and myself at his cottage at Brundall. He was just come from Mr D. Turner's at Yarmouth, where he also had first heard of it, and inquired if we knew anything about it. A day or two after Mr D. and I went to visit the site of St Benet's Abbey; and, sitting on the staging of the mill upon the ancient gate there, I poured out two glasses of ale, one of which I took for myself, and handed the other to the well-known Peter Pike, of South Walsham, who had conveyed us thither in his boat. 'A health to you, Peter,' said I. 'Sammodithee,' replied he.
>
> An explanation ensued; and the result was that the cabalistic expression was not a mode of salutation, but a reply to one; and being interpreted, was merely, 'Same unto thee'. Amid the bogs and fens, which surround the old Abbey's mouldering fragments, we had ample opportunity, before the day was closed, of testing the matter. 'Good evening', said to a ploughman on his way home from labour or to a boatman gliding past us on the river, brought out, more frequently than any other expression, the mysterious 'Sammodithee, sir!'.

It might be wondered how such a curious dialect, so different from received English, should have survived even into the 20th century until one
reads the account by the Revd Richard Lubbock of the secluded life of a
marshman in the 18th and early 19th centuries. He paints a picture in words
of a man whose knowledge and whose aspirations did not extend beyond the
confined area of his daily activities:

> When I first visited the broads, I found here and there an occupant, squatted down,
> as the Americans would call it, on the verge of a pool, who relied almost entirely
> on shooting and fishing for the support of himself and family, and lived in a truly
> primitive manner. I particularly remember one hero of this description. 'Our
> broad', as he always called the extensive pool by which his cottage stood, was his
> microcosm – his world; the islands in it were his gardens of the Hesperides – its
> opposite extremity his *ultima Thule.* Wherever his thoughts wandered, they could
> not get beyond the circle of his beloved lake; indeed, I never knew them aberrant
> but once, when he informed me, with a doubting air, that he had sent his wife and
> his two eldest children to a fair at a country village two miles off, that their ideas
> might expand by travel; as he sagely observed, they had never been away from 'our
> broad'. I went into his house at the dinner hour, and found the whole party going
> to fall to most thankfully upon a roasted Herring Gull, killed of course on 'our
> broad'. His life presented no vicissitudes but an alternation of marsh employment.
> In winter, after his day's reed-cutting, he might be regularly found posted at
> nightfall, waiting for the flight of fowl, or paddling after them on the open water.
> With the first warm days of February, he launched his fleet of trimmers, pike
> finding a ready sale at his own door to those who bought them to sell again in the
> Norwich market. As soon as the pike had spawned, and were out of season, the eels
> began to occupy his attention, and lapwings' eggs to be diligently sought for. In the
> end of April, the island in his watery domain was frequently visited for the sake of
> shooting the ruffs which resorted thither, on their first arrival. As the days grew
> longer and hotter, he might be found searching, in some smaller pools near his
> house, for the shoals of tench as they commenced spawning. Yet a little longer, and
> he began marsh mowing, his gun always laid ready upon his coat, in case flappers
> should be met with. By the middle of August, teal came to a wet corner near his
> cottage, snipes began to arrive, and he was often called upon to exercise his vocal
> powers on the curlews that passed to and fro. By the end of September, good snipe
> shooting was generally to be met with in his neighbourhood; and his accurate
> knowledge of the marshes, his unassuming good humour, and zeal in providing
> sport for those who employed him, made him very much sought after as a sporting
> guide, by snipe shots and fishermen; and his knowledge of the habits of different
> birds enabled him to give useful information to those who collected them.

Later generations of marshmen knew rather more of the outside world,
though they lived and worked in secluded places that were quite unknown to
the average resident of Norwich or Yarmouth. Their homes were solitary
houses often many miles from the nearest village, and their work bred in
them a self-reliance that might have been envied by the factory worker or
shop assistant of the town, had he known anything of it.

Ten

WATERY PLAYGROUND

It is debatable whether the entry in the records of the city of Norwich for 1367-8 of 20 pence being spent on the hire of the Prior's barge for conveying the Bishop to Thorpe is our earliest record of Broadland yachting or simply a mundane matter of transport by river, but as the Bishop travelled in company with the 20 aldermen of the city perhaps we can assume that he had a pleasurable journey down the river.[1]

Of course, it has always been possible to mix business and pleasure. However serious the annual trip made by the mayor of Norwich to Hardley Cross to impress on anyone who cared to watch the fact that the city claimed jurisdiction over the river down to that point, it was hardly to be expected that the opportunity to turn the voyage down the Yare into an occasion for junketing should be passed by.

Burgh Water Frolic was already an ancient institution by the end of the 18th century, when we are told how the mayor of Yarmouth and the corporation walked in procession from the Town Hall to the quay to embark in a wherry 'purposefully fitted up for their accommodation and plentifully stored'. Year by year the corporation 'barge' led the fleet across Breydon and over Burgh Flats, where sporting men raced their craft the more keenly, no doubt, for the wagers that were made on the results of the matches. One year we read of 'a sumptuous dinner, provided by the Mayor', being laid out in the hold of the mayor's wherry, while another year it was reported that there were in the procession 'wherries crammed with comestibles internally, the freights of innkeepers and others ... and externally loaded with human beings'.

Certainly by 1834, when James Stark produced a painting of Yarmouth Water Frolic, the old formalities had given way to a much more popular gathering. In a book published to commemorate the completion of the Norwich & Lowestoft Navigation, J.W. Robberds quoted William Taylor's description of the event:

> Annually in July the Mayors of Norwich and Yarmouth meet in their state barges
> on the River Yare, at Hardley Cross, which separates their respective jurisdictions,
> and in the afternoon fall down into Breydon ... All the many pleasure boats kept
> on these rivers assemble; the commercial craft is in requisition to stow spectators,

90 *This trade card issued by George Mason, proprietor of the* Wherry Inn *at Oulton Broad in the 1870s, refers to 'The Suffolk Rosherville', an allusion to well-known pleasure gardens in Kent. The story of Oulton Broad reflects the growth of the Broads holiday industry: when Mason took over the* Wherry Inn *from John Q. Stebbings the parish of Oulton had a population of some 800; Mason was still there in 1891 when the population of the parish topped 1,300; and when Oulton Broad was separated from Oulton and became an urban district in 1904 the new suburb had a population of 4,000. By then the* Wherry Hotel *had been 'entirely rebuilt' and was 'lighted throughout by Electricity'; it had also become the headquarters of the Waveney Sailing Club.*

to waft music, to vend refreshments; such of the shipping as ascends above the Yarmouth drawbridge is moored within ken; there are sailing matches, rowing matches, and spontaneous evolutions of vessels of all sorts, a dance of ships, their streamers flying and their canvas spread. It is a fair afloat, where the voice of revelry resounds from every gliding tent. And when the tide begins to fall, and to condense this various fleet into the narrower waters, and the bridge and quays and balconies and windows of Yarmouth are thronged with innumerable spectators – and boys have climbed the masts and rigging of the moored ships, adding to the crowd on shore a rocking crowd above – and the gathering boats mingle their separate concerts in one chorus of jollity – and guns fire – and loyalty and liberty shout with rival glee – and the setting sun inflames the whole lake – the scene becomes surpassingly impressive, exhilarating, and magnificent.[2]

Another of Stark's pictures showing the scene at Mutford Bridge on the morning of 4 September 1827, when Crisp Brown ceremonially inaugurated work on the Norwich & Lowestoft Navigation, features a considerable gathering of pleasure craft including the 'barge' *Rob Roy*, a substantial open boat with a mainsail having both gaff and boom. Some years later a rather similar cutter-rigged pleasure boat, the *Red Rover*, was for sale at Yarmouth, the advertisement in a local newspaper giving an excellent description of a yacht of the period.[3]

> To be sold by Mr B. Rix
>
> On the Quay, near the Bridge,
>
> the fast Cutter-Rigged Pleasure Boat Called the 'Red Rover', Twenty-six feet ram, 10 ft. 5 in. beam, drawing under 3 ft. water, fitted with commodious 9 ft. covered cabin and 8 ft. Stern Sheets with benches and lockers around and handsome copper rail, copper fastenings, copper bolts and bands throughout, with lead keel, about 1 ton of iron Ballast, 2 complete suits of Sails, Rigging, and Spars of the best quality.
>
> The 'Red Rover' is universally admitted to be the fastest and handsomest Boat on the Stream: her Cabin is fitted with sleeping berths and hair mattress, and has a mahogany dining table with additional leaves and drawers, painted floor cloth, copper cooking stove, and every requisite for a first-class Boat for the Season.

Also in the picture of Mutford Bridge is a smaller boat named the *Maria*, one of a type that became well established on the local rivers around that time. The *Maria* was a lateener.

How a rig that was indigenous to the Mediterranean and the Red Sea came to be employed on boats in Norfolk and Suffolk is something of a mystery. It could have been introduced by the master of some Yarmouth brigantine trading out to Naples with barrelled herring or bringing home dates and figs from Smyrna, who thought that the sail that served so well on tartanes and caiques would take a pleasure boat to the fore of any sailing match at home. The *Maria* was built in 1826-7 by a Yarmouth boatbuilder named Brown for Mr John Bellamy Plowman, who lived at Normanstone House on the Beccles road at Lowestoft; the house has gone, but it gave its name to Normanston Park.

91 *The last outing of the famous lateener* Maria, *sailing on Barton Broad on the eve of war in 1914. When built in 1827 she was lateen-rigged on both masts, but she later received the rig seen here with a gaffsail on the mizzen. After this excursion she was taken back to the thatched boatshed in which she was housed and never brought out again until her move to a museum 55 years later.*

The Customs Licence for the clench-built *Maria*, of Yarmouth, No. 84680, is dated 30 April 1827, providing indisputable evidence of her age. She was an instant success, beating five other boats at Lowestoft Regatta on 13 July 1827, and then a week later beating four craft to take the cup at Yarmouth Regatta. She also took first place in races at Wroxham and Oulton Broad in succeeding weeks, and went on to build up an impregnable reputation over the years.[4] According to Yarmouth sailmaker Robert Pike, when first built the *Maria* had lateen sails on both masts, the foresail being one reef larger than the mizzen. Later in her life she was rerigged, possibly when new sails were made in the 1860s, being given a lateen lug on the foremast and a gaff sail with a boom on her mizzen.

Her original owner died in 1834, and the *Maria* then passed to his daughter, Mrs Maris Gilbert, of Cantley. She sold her in 1837 to Sir Jacob Preston, of Beeston Hall, who kept her in a thatched boatshed off Barton Broad. Under Sir Jacob she continued her winning ways, gaining cups at all the principal regattas and water frolics in the area. Nicholas Everitt tells the story of a Wroxham Regatta at which all the other yachts present refused to compete with her because of her winning reputation; Sir Jacob withdrew from the match, and the other boats then battled it out for the cup, which went to the *Hornet*. However, the crew of the *Maria*, all professional watermen, were so angry at being deprived of their prize money that they boarded the *Hornet* and fought it out with the *Hornet*'s men. In the course of the battle the man holding the cup was knocked overboard, taking the cup with him.

> An obliging diver appeared on the scene, and in consideration of the sum of half-a-sovereign recovered the lost trophy, with which, safely stowed away in her lockers, the *Hornet* got up sail and made all haste towards Yarmouth. When the crew of the *Maria* heard of this their anger rekindled, and they also crowded on every stitch of canvas possible, with a view to overtaking the *Hornet* and renewing hostilities, but the latter boat had obtained such a good start that she was never overtaken, although she received some little damage from a few volleys of stones which the partizans of the *Maria* hurled at her when passing Horning Village on Sir Jacob Preston's estate. In those happy days of yore sport on the Broads hardly seems to have been confined to yacht-racing pure and simple.[5]

The *Red Rover* already mentioned, a much larger vessel known far and wide as a successful racer, was one of the *Maria*'s main rivals. The *Maria* beat her at Oulton Broad in 1839, at Wroxham in 1842 and at Yarmouth in 1843. Sir Jacob gave up racing her after about 1850, but he still took her to all the regattas.

In 1888 Dr W.A.S. Wynne, of Herringfleet, noted in his log that 'one of the sights of the day, I consider, was seeing old Sir Jacob Preston in the *Maria*, sailing his own boat all over the Broad just as I have seen him doing years ago. The same boat, the same rig, the same master, now 80 years of age. It was worth going up the North River to see such a reminder of old times …'. Sir Jacob died in 1894 and the *Maria* passed to his son, Sir Henry, and when he

92 *The epitome of Victorian yachting on the Broads: on the left is a cruising cutter, in the middle a racing cutter with huge jib and jackyard topsail, and on the right what is apparently a development of the lateener.*

died in 1897 she was handed on to his son, another Sir Jacob. Perhaps because of Sir Henry's death the *Maria* was absent from Wroxham Regatta in 1897 for the first time in 60 years.

The *Maria* was out sailing on Barton Broad on the day that Britain declared war on Germany in 1914. It has often been said that that fateful year was the end of an era; the *Maria* was taken back to her thatched boatshed, her spars were put aside and she never went afloat again. In fact she never left her boatshed until she was moved to the Maritime Museum for East Anglia at Yarmouth in 1969.

The lateeners under their original rig were impressive craft. Under the pull of that immense lateen sail

93 *The underwater lines of a Victorian Broads yacht are revealed in this picture of a St Olave's boatyard, probably that occupied by Arthur Brown. The deep hull would seem quite unsuitable for the shallow Broadland rivers, and this vessel is very different from the later shallow-draught yachts of the mid-20th century.*

they were fast if unwieldy craft. Beating into wind was the best point of sailing, but running before the wind could be extremely dangerous work as the towering foresail poised right over the bows forced the boat's head deep into the water. Sometimes, in spite of the whole crew being gathered on the counter to bring their weight as far aft as possible, a lateener would drive under, fill and sink. It was unfortunate that in fitting the foreign rig to local conditions the Norfolk builders not only placed the foremast right in the eyes of the boat but also raked it forward, for in this position the big sail tended to push the head of the craft down. The sail of the dhow on its aft-raking mast, on the other hand, was a lifting sail.

Nicholas Everitt mentions a number of lateeners in his *Broadland Sport*, including the *Waterwitch*, designed and built by a boatbuilder named Etheridge in 1818. The date of her building was identified by one of her owners, who narrated how an old shipwright at Etheridge's yard would fix all subsequent events from the day of her launching: 'Ter *Worterwitch* wor lornched the daay Painter' – a celebrated Norfolk pugilist – 'fought the Black on Mussel 'eath [Mousehold Heath].'[6]

One of the later examples of this rig, the *Ariel*, was built by William Brighton at Bungay in 1861 and, like the *Maria*, was still to be seen on the Broads in the first decade of the 20th century, receiving a new suit of sails in 1896. She had a waterline length of only 22 feet and a beam of 10 feet, but her overall length was increased by an 8ft. 8in. counter.

Long before the *Maria* and the *Ariel* had left the scene the cutters had taken over on the Broads. These craft hardly seemed well adapted for the narrow waterways on which they sailed, with their enormous gaff sails and long bowsprits carrying the very large foresail needed to balance so large a mainsail. An excellent description of such a yacht was given by well-known Norfolk yachtsman L.E. Bolingbroke:

> In the construction of yachts for these waters, the first thing to be thought of (on account of the shallowness and narrowness of the rivers in some parts) is to get stability with a small draught of water, and also handiness and quickness in tacking and coming about. The following are the dimensions of a ten-tonner:
>
> Length between forepart of stem and afterpart of main stern post, 25 ft.; counter, 9 ft., making a total length on deck of 34 ft.; extreme beam, 10 ft.; draught of water amidships, 4 ft. 6 in.; freeboard, 1 ft. 10 in.; with mast stepped 10 ft. 6 in. from fore part of stem. From the above it will be seen that the draught is comparatively small, therefore, to get stability, the beam is proportionately large, with a result that enables a great amount of sail to be carried ... and to give handiness in turning to windward in narrow waters, where quickness is of great importance, the keel is short, with a long overhanging counter, and this results in the boat carrying a very strong weather helm. The sails ordinarily carried by such a boat as the above are mainsail, jib, and topsail ... One big jib is always used in preference to foresail and jib, and it is undoubtedly far superior, so much greater power being obtained from the unbroken plane of sail.[7]

94 *Issued in the club's twentieth year, this list of officers and members of the Norfolk & Suffolk Yacht Club lists four regattas in 1879, at Cantley in June, Wroxham in July, and Oulton in August, with the Marine Regatta in Lowestoft Roads later the same month. A general meeting was held on the first Saturday in every month at the Club House, the* Royal Hotel *at Norwich.*

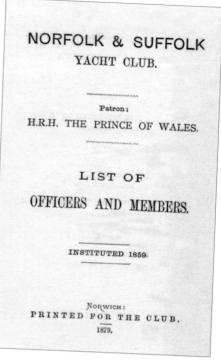

NORFOLK & SUFFOLK
YACHT CLUB.

Patron:
H.R.H. THE PRINCE OF WALES.

LIST OF
OFFICERS AND MEMBERS.

INSTITUTED 1859.

NORWICH:
PRINTED FOR THE CLUB.
1879.

Some time about 1860 a Norfolk parson and a Norfolk miller fitted out a wherry as a temporary floating home for a cruise on the Broads. The parson was the Revd T.A. Wheeler, father of the Dr Wheeler who became known to later generations as the headmaster of Bracondale School, Norwich, and the miller was Horace Gambling, of Buxton Mills, the owner of the wherry. After a cruise of three weeks or so the wherry reverted to trading. Another miller, William Cooke, is said to have carried out a similar conversion of a wherry for pleasure at about the same time.

While some 19th-century yachtsmen were content to cruise in a leisurely manner among the reedbeds and marshes, others constantly rebuilt their boats in search of greater speed and more prizes. Those who could afford it spent considerable amounts of money having new racing machines designed and built in the local yards, and Broads boatbuilders played a significant part in the development of such craft.

The formation in 1859 of what was to become the Royal Norfolk & Suffolk Yacht Club provided a boost to racing and resulted in a change of the rules of measurement. The old rules involved a time allowance that was calculated 'on the ram', that is, on the measurement from the top of the stem to the top of the sternpost, and this had encouraged the building of yachts with extreme counters such as the *Ariel*. The new club introduced fresh rules of measurement, and also sought to curb the activities of paid watermen, whose behaviour had proved disruptive, to say the least. Such altercations as that involving the crews of the *Maria* and the *Hornet* had occurred on a number of occasions: in 1858 the matter came to a head when the crews of two competing yachts at the Burgh Water Frolic lashed their craft together and resorted to a pitched battle.[8]

The club's rules stipulated that yachts of up to six tons should be allowed two watermen, those of six to ten tons were allowed three, and those over ten tons could carry four. Each yacht had to carry on board a club member who should ensure that the regulations were complied with – and to make sure

95 *Wroxham Regatta on 23 July 1880, a photograph taken by H.C. Bolingbroke, one of the leading members of the Yare Sailing Club at that time.*

that he was a properly responsible man his name had to be given to the secretary in writing before the match.

Fifteen craft took part in the club's first event at Cantley on 16 June 1859, and six of them were 'lateen or fore and mizzen'. The first four boats over the finishing line were all cutters, the winner being T.M. Read's *Belvidere*, which had been built by R. Harrod at Yarmouth only the previous year.

The club had considerable difficulty in choosing a suitable burgee and ensign, first selecting a white flag which bore too great a resemblance to the White Ensign, which only the Royal Yacht Squadron was entitled to wear – apart from the Royal Navy, of course. Having been told a white flag was inadmissible, the club wanted a Red Ensign with the Prince of Wales' feathers in the fly, but this brought a letter from their Lordships of the Admiralty stating that 'If the vessels of the Norfolk and Suffolk Y.C. are in the habit of wearing the colours My Lords will give directions to their officers to haul down and take possession of every such flag as is found flying on board any vessel of the club ...'. It was not until 1888, after their royal patron the Prince of Wales had apparently interceded on their behalf, that the club obtained a warrant allowing them to wear the defaced Red Ensign. Ten years later the club became the Royal Norfolk & Suffolk Yacht Club and was allowed to add a crown above the feathers on ensign and burgee.[9]

One imagines that no such thoughts pre-occupied the founders of the Yare Sailing Club, formed in 1876, for they seem to have been a very different bunch of men from the early members of the Norfolk & Suffolk Yacht Club. They sailed their own boats without the aid of paid watermen, and some of them were working men from Carrow Works, the Colman mustard manufactory beside the River Wensum at Norwich. It was, according to H.C. Bolingbroke, one of the founder members of the club, an offshoot of the Rovers Rowing Club, which had an eight-oar boat and about twenty members. 'We used to cycle down to King Street and row to Bramerton before breakfast, starting at six o'clock,' he remembered at the time of the club's golden jubilee.

> The first sailing race we had, I think, was in 1875, when we went from the Marl Staithe to Bramerton and back several times. About five boats started. There were certainly three boats from Carrow. After the race we had dinner at Thorpe Gardens, and it was on that occasion we agreed it would be a good thing to have a small sailing club of our own.

96 *George Christopher Davies, whose writings helped make the Broads a popular holiday area in the late Victorian period. His* Handbook to the Rivers and Broads of Norfolk and Suffolk *ran to no fewer than 50 editions, and another of his books,* The Swan and her Crew, *proved almost equally popular with the younger generation, or rather with several younger generations.*

One of those who joined the club was George Christopher Davies, the man who did so much to popularise the Broads holiday in the early days; he served as commodore of the club in 1885 – and his son served in the same position some forty years later, after the club had changed its name to the Yare and Bure Sailing Club. The secretary in the 1880s was the Revd George Buck, vicar of the Broadland village of Belaugh. On one occasion he sailed his yacht *Kittiwake* to Oulton Broad, where he left her in charge of members of his family while he returned to Belaugh to take the Sunday services. On the Saturday night some high-spirited young fellows in a yacht moored nearby were somewhat rowdy and were heard telling jokes that, in those days, were 'not fit for the parson'. Another local yachtsman, W.S. Everitt, partly in jest, let it be known the following day that he had received a complaint about the behaviour of these youngsters.[10] 'So impressed were these young bloods by the great pain they had inflicted on a high-minded clergyman that they wrote and severally signed an abject letter of apology to him, greatly to his mystification, for not one of the Buck family had the remotest idea there had been any breach of good taste,' recalled Bolingbroke with obvious relish many years later.

97 *This gathering beside the Yare at Bramerton c.1880 is thought to be members of the Yare Sailing Club enjoying what the Victorians called an alfresco meal. In the middle of the group with his back to the camera is probably the Revd G.P. Buck, who was secretary of the club for some years. One of the members has brought a servant (standing at back) to serve the wine.*

Members of the Yare Sailing Club were typical of the men – and women, for the members' wives sailed as well – who helped popularise the Broads as a place for out-of-the-ordinary holidays. Books and articles by Davies and others spread the word across the country, and before long people from far away were seeking to hire boats in which to explore the waterways.

The man who was later to be hailed as the pioneer of the boating holiday on the Broads was, surprisingly, not a boatbuilder by training. John Loynes, who by the time he died in 1939 had become a legendary figure in the area, was born at Woodton, between Norwich and Bungay. Early in life he obtained a job as a footman at Brooke Hall, not far from his birthplace, and it was during his time there that he learnt to sail on a large lake in the grounds of the hall. After leaving his job at Brooke Hall he became apprenticed to a carpenter at Bungay, and on coming out of his time went to work in London.

City life seems not to have suited him, however, and he returned to Norfolk, eventually settling in Norwich, in premises in Monastery Court, off Elm Hill, where he carried on trade as a master carpenter. While there he spent

98 *Not only were wherries converted, and later built, for pleasure use, but trading wherries were sometimes requisitioned for Sunday School outings and similar trips. This wherry is crowded with people, including two boys sitting on deck and dangling their legs towards the water, but we have no record of the occasion.*

99 *A medal that he had won at the National Fisheries Exhibition in 1881 for a model of a fishing boat for Norfolk and Suffolk waters formed a part of John Loynes' advertisement, the only one from a boatbuilder to appear in the first edition of G.C. Davies'* Handbook to the Rivers and Broads of Norfolk and Suffolk.

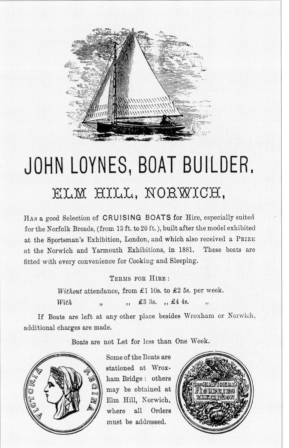

JOHN LOYNES, BOAT BUILDER,
ELM HILL, NORWICH,

Has a good Selection of **CRUISING BOATS** for Hire, especially suited for the Norfolk Broads, (from 13 ft. to 20 ft.), built after the model exhibited at the Sportsman's Exhibition, London, and which also received a Prize at the Norwich and Yarmouth Exhibitions, in 1881. These boats are fitted with every convenience for Cooking and Sleeping.

Terms for Hire:

Without attendance, from £1 10s. to £2 5s. per week.
With   „   „ £3 3s. „ £4 4s.   „

If Boats are left at any other place besides Wroxham or Norwich, additional charges are made.

Boats are not Let for less than One Week.

Some of the Boats are stationed at Wroxham Bridge: others may be obtained at Elm Hill, Norwich, where all Orders must be addressed.

his leisure hours boating on the Wensum and, finding the local boats too heavy to lift easily over the various obstructions on what Norwich people call the Back River, he built his own lighter craft.

Tiring of the Wensum, he put the boat on a handcart and with two friends trundled it off to Wroxham to spend some time exploring the northern rivers. Little is recorded about those early days when John was simply enjoying his spare-time trips on the rivers, but legend recounts how he eventually built himself a heavier cutter-rigged boat in which to continue his explorations. When friends asked him to hire the boat to them for holidays on the rivers the Broads boat-hire business was born.

That was in 1878, if later accounts of the progress of his business are to be believed. It is said that as his hiring business in Norwich prospered his clients repeatedly made for the prettier scenery of the North River and finished their voyaging at Wroxham, leaving John Loynes to collect the boats from there. Local folklore has it that they were put on a horse-drawn cart and

100 *John Loynes was in his thirties when he became one of the first men to establish a hire fleet on the Broads, and he was still helping to run the business when this photograph was taken of him at eighty.*

carried by road back to the Wensum, but the larger boats he was hiring out by that time had to be sailed back by way of Yarmouth and across Breydon.

Loynes seemed well aware of the advantages of good publicity, and made a series of models of the boats he offered for hire. In 1891 he exhibited at the National Fisheries Exhibition in Norwich a model of a fishing boat for Norfolk and Suffolk waters which gained him a bronze medal. That medal featured in Loynes' advertisement in the first edition of George Christopher Davies's *Handbook to the Rivers and Broads of Norfolk and Suffolk,* which appeared in 1882; he was the only boatbuilder to advertise in that book.

At the 1883 International Fisheries Exhibition in London Loynes won a gold medal for his models of yachts and boats for cruising on the Broads, and by 1888 he was advertising cabin yachts from three tons to 15 tons, 'fitted with every convenience for cooking and sleeping'. By that time he had moved his business from Norwich to Wroxham, where he set up a yard on the south side of the river just below the bridge. In *Boat Sailing for Amateurs,* published in 1886, George Christopher Davies describes Loynes' four-ton boats as having all the useful qualifications needed for cruising on the Broads, and thereby doubtless boosted not only Broads holidays generally but John Loynes' business in particular.

> They are beamy, of light draught – to enable them to visit the shallowest of the Broads – and they have centreboards. The latter is not inconveniently in the way in such a beamy boat, and is made use of as a support for table flaps, which, when set up, make a convenient table. The rig is one sail, Una fashion, and under this rig the boat is handy, and works well, while the simplicity of the rig is in its favour. The boat has a comfortable cabin, the special feature of which is, that it is collapsible. While a high cabin is of great comfort when at anchor, it is an impediment while sailing, as it catches the wind; therefore, Loynes's cabins are

101   *John Loynes' yard at Wroxham towards the end of the 19th century when, as recorded on the signboard, he was also operating yachts on the Friesland Meres and the Dutch waterways. Just visible on the extreme left of the picture is a pleasure wherry with a transom stern.*

designed to be raised up, or lie flat, as occasion is required. This is effected by making the cabin top and sides like a large lid overlapping the fixed coamings. This lid is supported by two levers on each side. To raise the cabin top, it is pulled towards you as you stand in the well, and so rises about a foot, and remains up; to lower it, it is simply pushed forward, when it falls into its place. There is a large open well, which is at night covered in with a waterproof awning, which goes right over both the cabin and the well. To set this awning, the boom is propped up on rather high crutches on the counter; and, to stretch the sides out, there are, on each side of the well, collapsible rails, which, when not in use, fold down inside the coamings.

As the Broads became more and more popular Loynes not only built up his fleet at home but set up a yachting station at Stavoren in Friesland for yachtsmen who wished to explore the Friesland meres. He sent over the yachts *Victoria, Enterprise, Puritan, Mayflower* and *Blanche,* the two first-named being sailed across the North Sea and the others consigned as cargo in trading ships. Youngest member of the crew of the *Enterprise* when she crossed the North Sea in 1893 was a certain George Colman Green, who

THE WHERRY-YACHTS

"Bertha," "Elsie," "Kate," "Diligent," & "Lucy,"

BELONGING TO

Messrs. PRESS BROTHERS,

NORTH WALSHAM,

Are fitted with every Convenience for the Enjoyment of Parties wishing to Visit the

Rivers and Broads of Norfolk.

They contain: Ladies' Cabin, 7 ft. long, 9 ft. wide, and 6 ft. high, to sleep 3 or 4 Ladies, and are fitted with Washstand, Looking-Glass, Lockers, &c., &c.

Gentlemen's Cabin, 14 ft. long, 9 ft. wide, and 6 ft. high, to sleep 4 or 6 Gentlemen; this Cabin is used in the day time for a Dining Saloon, and is fitted with a table down the centre, and sitting space for 8 or 10.

The Cabins throughout are furnished with Blinds, soft Cushions, plenty of Rugs, and are lighted at night by lamps; they are divided by a gangway leading from the Deck, and a W.C. entered from either the fore or aft Cabin, and private to each.

Two men are provided by the owners to look after and Sail the Yachts, and are under the direction of the Party hiring the Boat; they will attend to the cooking, cleaning, and washing up, and to the wants of the Party on board.

When sailing, a seat is provided on the fore deck of the Yacht, and a 'Jolly Boat' accompanies each.

The Yachts are provided with all necessary Glass, Crockery, Table Linen, Knives, Forks, Spoons, &c., &c., and the men's Cabin is fitted with a good Cooking Stove.

When required a Piano can be provided at an extra cost of 15 shillings per week.

The Yachts are so arranged as to be able to visit all the Norfolk and Suffolk Broads:—Barton, Wroxham, Hickling, South Walsham, Horsey Mere, Mutford, Oulton, and all places of interest on the Rivers.

Parties are required to go on board wherever the owners may desire, but can leave the Yachts at any place convenient to themselves by giving a week's notice.

For Terms and further particulars, apply—

PRESS BROTHERS,
North Walsham, Norfolk.

102 *Press Brothers' advertisement for their five wherries which were withdrawn from trading during the short summer season and converted into pleasure wherries. It appeared in 1888 in the 11th edition of G.C. Davies's* Handbook to the Rivers and Broads of Norfolk and Suffolk.

as a writer and artist was to make something of a name for himself in later years.

A Suffolk man, George Montague Doughty, took the pleasure wherry *Gipsy* to Stavoren in 1888 and sailed the Dutch waterways for two summers, then in 1890 went further afield, sailing by river and canal to within a few miles of Prague.[11] When the *Gipsy* eventually returned to England in 1902 the arrangements for her to be towed across the North Sea were made by John Loynes, whose Dutch enterprise was about to fall victim to anti-British feeling in the Netherlands as a result of the Boer War.

In 1888 John Loynes' brother George left his job as a coachman in London to join the Wroxham business, which by that time had plenty of rivals in the boat-hire business. The 11th edition of G.C. Davies's *Handbook* contains a number of advertisements from other boatbuilders who had yachts and boats for hire. It was not only small craft that could be hired; Press Brothers of North Walsham, millers and maltsters, had fitted out five of their wherries 'with every convenience for the enjoyment of parties wishing to visit the rivers and broads of Norfolk'. The holds had been scrubbed clean and partitions inserted to form two cabins, a lavatory was fitted, and everything necessary was provided; a piano could be provided at an extra 15 shillings a week.

The *Elsie* was lost in 1891 when she foundered under tow in the North Sea as she headed for the Friesland meres, where the charterer, who planned to follow the example of H.M. Doughty and the *Gipsy*, had planned a three-month shooting expedition. The place of the *Elsie* in the hire fleet was taken by the *Ethnie*.

John Loynes at Wroxham and Press Brothers were among no fewer than 37 boatbuilders and owners listed as having boats for hire in an 1891 edition of the *Handbook*. Some of those in the list became household names in the area.

Robert Collins had been involved in the carrying trade at Coltishall, where his son Ernest was born in 1869, but in 1886 he founded the boatbuilding business at Wroxham that was to grow to maturity under Ernest's name. At the Yachting and Fisheries Exhibition in Norwich in 1894 the firm won two prizes, one for a ten-ton cruiser and the other for a sailing dinghy best suited for the Broads. In 1899 R. Collins & Son were claiming to have 'the largest laying-up stores for yachts on the Broads' and were advertising a number of yachts including the *Florinda*, built 1890, the *Mayflower* (1891), the *Iverna* (1893), the *Cambria* and *Britannia* (1894) and the pleasure wherry *Victory*.[12] The Collins family not only built up one of the earliest and biggest hire fleets on the Broads but took a leading part in the development of yachts for the Norfolk rivers.

Though he never entered the boat-hire trade, George Mollett at Brundall played a leading part in developing small sailing boats for racing. In 1892 he built the *Castanet*, an early example of the 'skimming dish' type of yacht, for Russell J. Colman, the mustard manufacturer and keen yachtsman, and he was also involved in the development of racing dinghies. He later moved to Thorpe, on the outskirts of Norwich.

It was there that John Hart took over a boatbuilding business at Thorpe Gardens previously run by Stephen Field about 1880. It might be that he was more experienced in the licensing trade than in boatbuilding, for he was licensee of the *Three Tuns*, but in those days many a tradesman had more than one string to his bow. However, the third edition of Davies' *Handbook* contains an advertisement 'To Gentlemen about visiting the Norfolk waters' announcing that J. Hart & Son of Thorpe Gardens had for hire a good selection of yachts and boats.

The Harts soon moved on to the island lying between the old river at Thorpe and the New Cut made when the Norwich-Yarmouth railway was constructed in 1844. Their advertisement in 1888 listing the 12-ton cutter *Island Queen*, five-ton cutter *Belvedere*, the smaller cutter *Imogen* and the una-rigged boat *Florence* is flanked by another stating that B. Buck at Thorpe Gardens has yachts, sailing and fishing boats of all kinds to let.

John Hart's son George carried on the business, which eventually changed its title to G. Hart & Son. George died in 1927 and the business was built up by his son Geoffrey, who became a partner when in his late teens. During the Second World War Geoffrey Hart and his workmen were sent to Southampton, where they were engaged in the building of motor torpedo boats and similar craft, but they returned to Thorpe after the war. The business was, however, sold in 1948 to Ron Ashby, who changed the name to Hearts, the firm's motor cruisers being named *Ace of Hearts*, *Six of Hearts* and so on.

One of John Loynes' early advertisements recorded his business at Wroxham as being 'only three minutes from railway station', and both the Great Eastern

Railway and the Eastern and Midlands Railway, a constituent of the later Midland and Great Northern Joint Railway, were keen to develop the Broads for their own purposes.

The first railway in Norfolk, that between Norwich and Yarmouth, began the process of breaking down the isolation of the Broads. The line was laid across the marshes of the Yare valley, and when it opened in 1844 the railway soon made inroads into the traffic carried by wherries between Norwich and the port of Yarmouth. It was the beginning of a process that eventually brought about the demise of the sailing wherry as a means of local transport.

The building by Samuel Morton Peto of a branch from Lowestoft to the Norfolk Railway at Reedham and the eventual linking of the Norwich-Yarmouth line to the Norwich and Brandon Railway and then to the Eastern Union opened up Norfolk to a spreading network of lines stretching right across Britain. That was just a start. Work began in 1865 on a line to North Walsham by way of Wroxham, which was to become known as the capital of the Broads; by the time it was completed in 1877 the line had been extended to Cromer. And in 1883 the Norwich-Reedham-Yarmouth line was supplemented by the alternative route by way of Acle, which itself was by then involved in the infant Broads holiday trade.

In 1877 the Great Yarmouth and Stalham Light Railway began building a line from a terminus later known as Beach Station at Yarmouth to Martham and Stalham, in the heart of the Broads. Hardly had trains begun running before Parliamentary approval was obtained for an extension to North Walsham and a change of name to the Yarmouth and North Norfolk Light Railway. That, of course, later became part of the Eastern and Midlands Railway and then in 1893 of the Midland and Great Northern Joint Railway, which provided a route from Leicester and the industrial Midlands direct to the East Coast resorts and to the Broads.

There is no railway advertisement in the first edition of Davies' *Handbook*, but later editions carry advertisements inserted both by the Great Eastern Railway, signed by William Birt, and the Eastern and Midlands Railway, signed by C.L.C. Tait, their General Manager. The Eastern and Midlands advertisement mentioned that 'The New Direct Route from London and the Midland and Northern Counties to Norwich (City), Yarmouth (Beach Station), and vice-versa, via Peterborough, Sutton Bridge, Lynn and Fakenham, is now open for Traffic. This Railway forms the most direct means of access to the Broad district …'.

With firms like Press Brothers of North Walsham fitting out their trading wherries as pleasure craft for the summer and boatbuilders who had been used to constructing marshmen's punts and wherries turning their hands to yachts, the railways competed enthusiastically for the holidaymakers who began to seek out quiet spots in East Anglia each August. A.J. Wrottesley in his history of the M & GN points out that in spite of the extra length of both route and journey time the joint railway did have several advantages. King's Cross was regarded in those days as far more accessible from much of London,

103 *Links between the corporation of Norwich and recreation afloat continued into the 20th century, as may be seen from the programme of the 'Grand Water Carnival' held at Whitlingham to celebrate the Coronation of King Edward VII in 1903.*

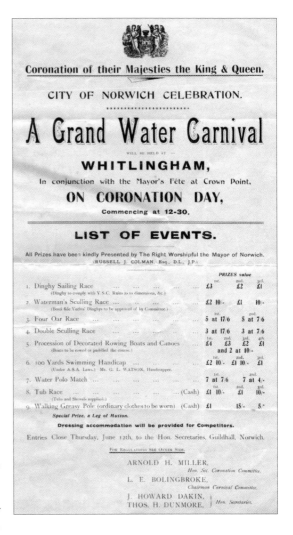

Coronation of their Majesties the King & Queen.

CITY OF NORWICH CELEBRATION.
. . . .
A Grand Water Carnival
WILL BE HELD AT

WHITLINGHAM,
In conjunction with the Mayor's Fête at Crown Point,
ON CORONATION DAY,
Commencing at 12-30.

LIST OF EVENTS.

All Prizes have been kindly Presented by The Right Worshipful the Mayor of Norwich.
(RUSSELL J. COLMAN, Esq., D.L., J.P.)

	PRIZES value		
	1st.	2nd.	3rd.
1. Dinghy Sailing Race	£3	£2	£1
(Dinghy to comply with V.S.C. Rules as to dimensions, &c.)			
2. Waterman's Sculling Race	£2 10/-	£1	10/-
(Bonâ fide Yachts' Dinghys to be approved of by Committee.)			
3. Four Oar Race	5 at 17/6	5 at 7/6	
4. Double Sculling Race	3 at 17/6	3 at 7/6	
5. Procession of Decorated Rowing Boats and Canoes	1st. £4	2nd. £3	3rd. £2 4th. £1
(Boats to be rowed or paddled the course.)		and 2 at 10/-	
6. 100 Yards Swimming Handicap	£2 10/-	£1 10/-	£1
(Under A.S.A. Laws.) Mr. G. L. WATSON, Handicapper.			
7. Water Polo Match	1st. 7 at 7/6	2nd. 7 at 4/-	
8. Tub Race ... ... (Cash)	1st. £1 10/-	2nd. £1	3rd. 10/-
(Tubs and Shovels supplied.)			
9. Walking Greasy Pole (ordinary clothes to be worn) (Cash)	£1	15/-	5/-

Special Prize, a Leg of Mutton.
Dressing accommodation will be provided for Competitors.

Entries Close Thursday, June 12th, to the Hon. Secretaries, Guildhall, Norwich.

FOR REGULATIONS SEE OTHER SIDE.

ARNOLD H. MILLER,
Hon. Sec. Coronation Committee.
L. E. BOLINGBROKE,
Chairman Carnival Committee.
J. HOWARD DAKIN, }
THOS. H. DUNMORE, } *Hon. Secretaries.*

including the West End, than Liverpool Street, tucked away as it was in the unfashionable East. Passengers heading for a Broads holiday and wanting to alight at Potter Heigham or Stalham could change trains at Melton Constable, merely crossing from one side of the platform to the other. Those using the Great Eastern route had to change from one station to another at North Walsham to reach stations on the former Eastern and Midlands line – and because of their keen sense of loyalty to their own respective employers neither M & GN nor Great Eastern porters were very willing to take passengers' luggage to the other company's station.

Once aware of the potential of the Broads holiday for boosting his passenger traffic, Mr Birt lost no opportunity to promote the region. In the later 1880s the railway company commissioned a photographer from Ashtead in Surrey, Payne Jennings, to produce a series of 'Artistic Photographs of the Rivers & Broads of Norfolk and Suffolk' for display in their carriages. Before long the demand for these 'Exquisite Examples of Photography' was such that Jarrolds were appointed agents, and it was announced in the 1888 edition of Davies's *Handbook* that, while single copies would be sent post free on receipt of 13 stamps, a complete set containing all hundred views, elegantly bound in one volume, could be had for four guineas. One wonders how many copies sold at that price; I have never seen one. Obviously something cheaper was needed, and in 1891 there appeared *Sun Pictures of the Norfolk Broads: One hundred photographs from nature of the Rivers and Broads of Norfolk and Suffolk*, printed at the Permanent Photo Printing Works, Ashtead, Surrey.

By the end of the century trading wherries were being converted permanently into pleasure craft and were no longer reverting to trading in the winter, and some builders were launching specially designed pleasure wherries. In 1899 H. Adcock of Beccles had the wherry *Zoe* for hire and stated, 'This well-known yacht, which has all the conveniences of a sumptuously-fitted Thames House-boat, together with the pleasures of a Sailing Yacht, is 37 tons burthen, oak built, and is not used at any period of the year for trading purposes.'

Those who took Broads holidays in the late Victorian period were either people of independent means who demanded some degree of service even when 'roughing it' or professional men who delighted in looking after their own affairs. Few working men could afford even the £2 10s. for a 26ft. yacht out of season.

All wherries and large yachts, and not a few of the smaller craft as well, were let with watermen in charge to work the boat and to prepare meals. The largest of the yachts and the pleasure wherries had a professional crew of two, a skipper to sail the vessel and a steward to cook and serve the meals.

One holidaymaker from Middlesex wrote to the hirer 'my companions and myself wish to express our entire satisfaction with both the Cutter *Lotus* and her skipper and steward. We found the two men, John Woodrow (skipper) and Sam Newstead (steward) most obliging and attentive, and always anxious to meet our wishes and do anything for our comfort.' Happy the party that could write such a testimonial. Some watermen gained a reputation for belligerence rather than any wish to give good service. Many are the stories of skippers who persistently frustrated the wishes of their hirers in order to ensure that they could slip away to a convenient hostelry as soon as possible.

'No one wants, for the sake of a few shillings, to have a cruise spoiled by defective gear, a dirty boat, a surly or a drunken skipper,' said one hire company in its brochure, setting forth the advantages of using their boats and their paid hands in preference to others. 'There are antiquated boats on the water; and there are unreliable skippers. They may both be had cheap sometimes; but it is not worth the risk. Attention, civility, a reliable boat, and a reliable man make all the difference to a cruise. They cost a little, but they are worth it.'

It was at this period that the first attempt was made to set up an agency through which boats might be booked. Ernest Suffling, the author of a number of books about yachting on the Broads, offered in 1895 to provide well-found yachts for parties wanting a holiday on the Broads, and by 1899 he claimed to be agent for 50 wherry yachts, sailing cutters and houseboats as well as a large steam launch: 'If you require a craft for Norfolk Waters I can accommodate you,' he promised.

The large steam launch mentioned by Ernest Suffling was by no means alone, for by the end of the century a number of private owners and boatyards were operating steamers on the North River as well as the Norwich River. One of the first to introduce day trips on the Broads in steam launches was C.C. Cooke, of Wroxham, who was running trips in the 1880s mainly for holiday-makers arriving by train at Wroxham station. Ambrose Thrower, also of

Wroxham, was by the end of the century operating the steam launch *Vivid*, which was built in 1875 and fitted with a neat vee twin engine made by the little-known Norwich engineering firm of Sturgess & Towlson; the engine is now preserved in the Bridewell Museum at Norwich. At Norwich two boat-owners at Pulls Ferry, A. Sabberton and C.F. Harrison, also had steam launches for hire; Sabberton charged 30s. per day for the launch *Cruiser*, which could also be had by the week.

The 1890s saw the setting up of the Norfolk Broads Yachting Company, a large organisation that had bases at Brundall (sold to C.J. Broom about 1905), Wroxham and Potter Heigham, and a head office in Norwich. The Wroxham premises were managed by Alfred Pegg, and operations at Potter Heigham were directed by Walter Woods, both of them men who became well known on the Broads. At the beginning of this century the syndicate had built up a fleet of three pleasure wherries, 22 yachts and a number of half-deckers, as well as many smaller boats.

The wherry *Dragon* was built for the company by Fred Press, the son of Coltishall wherry builder Herbert Press, at Wroxham in 1901. Two smaller pleasure wherries, the *Fairy Queen* and *Endeavour*, also belonged to the Norfolk Broads Yachting Company. When the company was sold up in a three-day auction at Wroxham at the end of the 1920 season, during which gross lettings had amounted to no less than £4,850, the *Dragon* fetched £725, the *Fairy Queen* £625 and the *Endeavour* only £550. The *Endeavour* was later converted into a motor wherry and renamed *Darkie*.

The earliest experiments with internal combustion engines for holiday craft on the Broads were made with large converted lifeboats such as the former Gorleston volunteer lifeboat *Friend of All Nations*, which became the motor cruiser *F.O.A.N.*, and the Yarmouth lifeboat *John Burch*, built by Yarmouth boatbuilder James Beeching in 1892, which after conversion to the motor cruiser *Crescent* about 1913 still showed clear signs of her origin in the cork padding round her hull. The *Crescent*'s engine was a twin-cylinder Brooke engine made by J.W. Brooke at Lowestoft, a four-cylinder engine of the same make being installed in the pleasure wherry *Black Prince*. One of the biggest and finest of these early conversions was the *Enchantress*, a former Thames steamer which was reputed to have been owned at one time by King Edward VII before he ascended the throne.

With the demise of the Norfolk Broads Yachting Company, Alfred Pegg set up at Wroxham in partnership with his son, while Walter Woods started working on his own account at Potter Heigham. Woods, the official builder of the Yarmouth One-design class, a half-decker rigged with a lugsail for the Great Yarmouth Yacht Club, was a member of a well-known boatbuilding family, for his brother Ernest was the designer in 1908 of the Yare and Bure One-design, a very attractive half-decker for the Yare and Bure Sailing Club. Ernest built the first of this class at Cantley on the Yare, but in the 1920s he moved to Horning, establishing a yard just below the ferry. There is a family tradition that he hired two wherries for the weekend to carry his equipment and stock

104 *Half-deckers racing at Horning Regatta in 1921. These are Yarmouth One-designs, built by Walter Woods at Potter Heigham for the Great Yarmouth Yacht Club and rigged with lugsails. The somewhat similar Yare and Bure One-designs for the Yare and Bure Sailing Club were designed by Walter's brother Ernest and were gunter-rigged.*

to the new location, and as there was no wind that weekend they had to be quanted down to Yarmouth and all the way up the North River in order to finish the job in the time available. He went on to build no fewer than 65 of the White Boats, as they were known, with his own hands and three more with assistance before his retirement in 1963, when the licence to build the boats went to Herbert Woods Ltd., of Potter Heigham.

One of the biggest boatbuilding firms on the Broads, Herbert Woods Ltd., was established in the 1920s by Ernest's nephew, who built his first cruiser in his spare time while working for his father Walter. Between 1926 and 1930 he launched nine boats of the 34ft. 'Speed of Light' class and five of the smaller 'Morning Light' class, stylish cruisers that owed nothing at all to the design of earlier craft. By 1939 the fleet totalled 45 motor cruisers and 20 yachts, and to accommodate the expanding business Herbert had built new boathouses below the bridge and excavated a network of dykes that was christened Broadshaven.

Alfred Ward, who started in business at Thorpe in 1913, was one of the first to hire motor cruisers in the early 1920s, followed quite soon by J.H. Jenner, who had come from his native Lowestoft to set up a boatyard not far from Ward's at Thorpe. In 1930 Jenner built the 36ft. cruiser *River Boy*, designed to provide the best accommodation in three cabins with 6ft. headroom throughout, and this set the standard for future cruisers; there was to be no stooping in the cabins of cruisers as there was in those of the sailing boats.

Another Broads institution had its beginning when Harry Blake and five friends from a tennis club in Dulwich, in south London, spent a holiday on the Broads in the wherry yacht *Olive*. At the end of their holiday Blake suggested to the owner, Ernest Collins, that he should act as agent, obtaining bookings for the yard and hopefully extending the six-week season. In 1907, his first year as agent, Blake wrote most of the bookings in a tiny pocket diary, but the following year he risked 4s. 6d. on a three-line advertisement in the *Daily Mail*; it brought in 400 replies, and Blake's agency was well and truly in business.

The first catalogue appeared in 1908, with a drawing on the cover of a boatbuilder with beard and peaked cap and a holidaymaker with slouch hat and drainpipe trousers. It was to all intents and purposes a list of Ernest Collins' fleet, and the preface makes it plain that at that time Harry Blake was acting primarily for this one Wroxham yard.

> We have great pleasure in presenting herewith our Illustrated Catalogue of Ernest Collins' Yachts, Wherries and Boats for Hire. We wish in the first place as Agents for <u>Ernest</u> Collins [the word Ernest was deeply underlined, in an attempt to avoid any confusion with the firm of Alfred Collins next door] to thank the numerous clients who have extended their hearty support to him for many years past, and also for their expressions of satisfaction with his Pleasure Craft, which we can safely say cannot be surpassed on the Norfolk Broads.

The 1909 list contained a total of 43 cabin sailing yachts available for hire from a baker's dozen of boatyards. These were Ernest and Alfred Collins, both at Wroxham; George Applegate at Potter Heigham; the Norfolk Broads Yachting Company Limited at Wroxham and Potter Heigham; A.R. Brown at St Olave's; Smith & Powley at Horning Ferry ('but parties can be met at Wroxham'); F. Miller & Company and W.S. Parker at Oulton Broad; Southgate Brothers at Stalham; E. Belmore at Great Yarmouth; Hart & Son, Wroxham or Thorpe; H. Howlett, Wroxham; and E. Cooper, Oulton Broad.

Among the vessels on offer were the wherry yacht *Goldfinch* from Alfred Collins, in charge of skipper William Rouse, late skipper of the 35-ft. cutter yacht *Vacuna*, and said to have been built only in 1909. George Applegate had the pleasure wherry *Dauntless* of 32 tons and the wherry yacht *White Rose*, and A.R. Brown had the pleasure wherries *Garnet*, *Leisure Hour* (25 tons) and *Industry* (23 tons), as well as the wherry houseboat *Herald* (22 tons). Smith and Powley had the pleasure wherry *Idler* and F. Miller had the pleasure wherry *British Queen* (28 tons), while W.S. Parker (who became chief draughts-man at John Chambers' yard at Oulton Broad) had the auxiliary wherry yacht *Rambler* of Oulton Broad, not to be confused with the pleasure wherry of the same name. She had been fitted with a 14 bhp Brooke three-cylinder motor in the cockpit only shortly before the list was prepared, and was one of the first boats on the Broads to be so equipped. Southgate Brothers had the wherry yacht *Wildflower*, of 45 feet by 12 feet with a white hull, clinker built, and a narrow washstrake. Then there was the 54-ft. pleasure

105 *The cover of the first list issued by H. Blake &*
Company in 1908, illustrated by a young artist named
W.D. Ford. That first edition was virtually a list of Ernest
Collins's yachts, wherries and boats, but in subsequent years
other boat hirers were included.

106 *Blake's 1913 Yachting List had a photographic*
design on its cover but continued with the landscape format
that was retained for many years.

wherry *Natal*, owned by E. Belmore, and the pleasure wherry *Elsie* of
Wroxham.

The list offers some good advice to clients about dealing with the
'attendants', and throws considerable light on the way in which a Broads
cruise was organised in the early years of the century:

> As regards boarding the attendants (if taken), the method generally adopted, and
> one which we recommend, is to cater for them yourselves. Another way is to allow
> them a certain sum a week for their board.
>
> The skippers and stewards will be found to be the most obliging of men; they
> are the best of good company, and willing to impart their knowledge of sailing to
> the novice; in fact, if you have not done this holiday before, their advice as to the
> cruise is invaluable, and can safely be followed. They will do their utmost to make
> your cruise enjoyable by taking you to the most interesting and picturesque parts
> of the Broads.
>
> Having settled your stores, we now come to the journey down. Before starting
> be sure you are well supplied with stock of tobacco, cigarettes and cigars, as you
> must remember one cannot step off the yacht into a shop to obtain fresh supplies,
> being surrounded by meadows and miles away from a village. Even when you moor
> at night near a village it's odds against you getting what you require in the way of
> tobacco and cigarettes.

There is also in the 1909 list an indication that the number of bungalows
along the rivers was increasing year by year:

> Should any of our clients after their cruise on the Broads think of renting a piece
> of land in East Anglia, and having erected thereon a bungalow similar to those

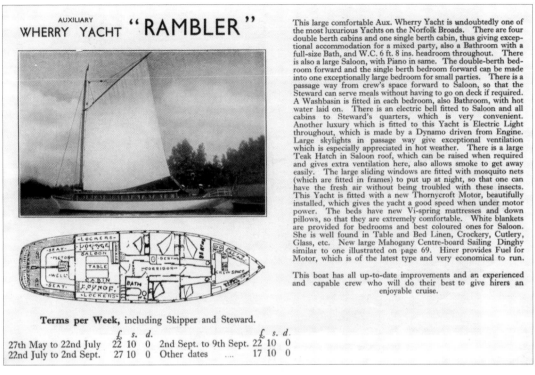

AUXILIARY
WHERRY YACHT "RAMBLER"

This large comfortable Aux. Wherry Yacht is undoubtedly one of the most luxurious Yachts on the Norfolk Broads. There are four double berth cabins and one single berth cabin, thus giving exceptional accommodation for a mixed party, also a Bathroom with a full-size Bath, and W.C. 6 ft. 8 ins. headroom throughout. There is also a large Saloon, with Piano in same. The double-berth bedroom forward and the single berth bedroom forward can be made into one exceptionally large bedroom for small parties. There is a passage way from crew's space forward to Saloon, so that the Steward can serve meals without having to go on deck if required. A Washbasin is fitted in each bedroom, also Bathroom, with hot water laid on. There is an electric bell fitted to Saloon and all cabins to Steward's quarters, which is very convenient. Another luxury which is fitted to this Yacht is Electric Light throughout, which is made by a Dynamo driven from Engine. Large skylights in passage way give exceptional ventilation which is especially appreciated in hot weather. There is a large Teak Hatch in Saloon roof, which can be raised when required and gives extra ventilation here, also allows smoke to get away easily. The large sliding windows are fitted with mosquito nets (which are fitted in frames) to put up at night, so that one can have the fresh air without being troubled with these insects. This Yacht is fitted with a new Thornycroft Motor, beautifully installed, which gives the yacht a good speed when under motor power. The beds have new Vi-spring mattresses and down pillows, so that they are extremely comfortable. White blankets are provided for bedrooms and best coloured ones for Saloon. She is well found in Table and Bed Linen, Crockery, Cutlery, Glass, etc. New large Mahogany Centre-board Sailing Dinghy similar to one illustrated on page 69. Hirer provides Fuel for Motor, which is of the latest type and very economical to run.

This boat has all up-to-date improvements and an experienced and capable crew who will do their best to give hirers an enjoyable cruise.

Terms per Week, including Skipper and Steward.

	£	s.	d.		£	s.	d.
27th May to 22nd July	22	10	0	2nd Sept. to 9th Sept.	22	10	0
22nd July to 2nd Sept.	27	10	0	Other dates	17	10	0

107 *'Undoubtedly one of the most luxurious Yachts on the Norfolk Broads', says the description of the wherry yacht* Rambler *on this page of* Norfolk Broads Holidays Afloat *from the 1930s.*

seen in the district, we recommend Messrs. Boulton & Paul Ltd., for this work. This firm having many years' experience in this particular work, and being right on the spot, can offer the best possible terms, and can be relied upon to carry out one's instructions.

By the time that third edition of the list was produced there were already power craft making their presence felt on the Broads. 'Clients hiring Motor Launches should be careful as to the spirit they use for them, and by obtaining Pratt's Perfection Spirit they may be sure they have obtained the best and most suitable for the engines used in these Broads Launches.' The yacht *Test* (21 tons), owned by G. Hazell, 50 feet long and 12ft. 6in. in beam, was among the craft advertised in the 1910 list. She later reappears as 'Motor cruiser *Test*' with a four-cylinder Darracq engine in the 1920 list, which contains a handful of motor boats and launches inserted at the end of the book.

In 1915 the agency moved to 22 Newgate Street, London, E.C., and the following year Harry Blake was instrumental in founding the Norfolk and Suffolk Broads Yacht Owners' Association to represent the many boatbuilders for whom the agency was by then acting. The First World War did nothing to blight the progress of the Broads holiday, but in the 1920 Blake's list was

Length 60 ft. A large handsome motor cruiser, fitted throughout in teak. A most luxurious craft. New 30/40 h.p. engine Silent running and economical. Fuel: paraffin, starting on petrol Has saloon, three double-berth bedrooms, and one single bedroom, bathroom (full size bath, hot and cold). Large kitchen well equipped with stoves, oven, pantry, etc. Exceptional upper deck room, which is ideal for sitting out. Wicker arm-chairs and tables are provided for having tea on upper deck. Beds fitted with Vi-spring mattresses and down pillows, and very comfortable. Wash basins in each cabin with hot water laid on. Self-emptying w.c. with flush pump. Piano in saloon, also folding wash basin with hot water. Drawers in saloon and bedrooms. Electric light throughout. Large sliding windows, mosquito nets for night. Electric bells from saloon and all cabins to steward's quarters. Completely fitted with everything of first-class quality for living and sleeping on board except towels. Crew—two in number—skilled engineer acting as skipper, and steward who attends to all cooking. Large new mahogany Centre-board Sailing Dinghy.

Terms per week, with two attendants—

7 June to 12 July, £23 15s.; 12 to 26 Ju.y, £28 5s.; 26 July to 30 August, £30; 30 August to 6 September, £23 15s. Other dates £19 10s.

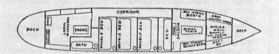

Please address all communications and applications to Blake's Ltd., 22, Newgate Street, London, E.C.

108 *A page from* Norfolk Broads Holidays Afloat *giving details of the* Enchantress, *which is reputed to have been at one time a Thames steam yacht owned by the Prince of Wales, later King Edward VII.*

a note: 'The Owners regret they have been compelled to revise the terms for the 1920 Season to help to meet the heavy increase in materials, etc., which has risen between 200 and 300 per cent since 1914.' On the credit side Harry Blake was able to claim a startling increase in his business over little more than a decade:

> 1908 We commenced business without a client
> 1920 Our connection is now over TEN THOUSAND, built up by recommendation of satisfied clients.

One of the largest motor cruisers ever to operate in the hire fleets appeared in the 1923 list. She was the *Panther*, an 80-ft. converted motor launch built for the Royal Navy in the First World War and used for patrol and anti-submarine work. The same list contained a motor cruiser also named *Panther*, built that year at Brundall and described as 'of a new type with a Kelvin Marine engine running on paraffin'.

By 1925 Blake's had three motor wherries in the list, the *Darkie* (Oulton Broad), *Black Prince* (Beccles) and *Leander* (Horning), all of them former sailing wherries with their masts and sails removed and an engine fitted. The first few transom-sterned motor cruisers were appearing in the mid-'20s, and the 1927 list had 36 pages of motor craft in contrast to the dozen motor cruisers in the 1922 list.

109   *The saloon of the motor cruiser* Enchantress *with a small piano for the entertainment of the passengers. With a length of 60 feet, this vessel was hired out with two attendants, a skipper-engineer and a steward.*

The number both of boatyards and of boats increased year by year, until in 1931 the 24th annual issue listed 495 boats, including well over a hundred motor cruisers, a type of craft that was to become even more important in later years. In the agency's 50th year it had grown to represent 40 Broads boatyards and *Norfolk Broads Holidays Afloat* offered no fewer than 462 motor cruisers, 213 sailing yachts, 85 sailing craft with auxiliary motors and 26 houseboats.

When the Norfolk and Suffolk Broads Yacht Owners' Association celebrated its 25th anniversary at the *King's Head Hotel*, Wroxham, on 7 December 1931, the chairman was Mr Leo Robinson. A photograph taken on that occasion, and now in the Blake's offices at Wroxham, shows the then members of the association.

With the Munich Crisis past, the 1939 edition of *Holidays Afloat* contained the self-congratulatory note that 'This 1939 Edition of 100,000 copies cancels all previous issues since 1908 and is copyright'. War broke out before the last holidaymakers had left the Broads, and production of the 1940 edition was in vain, because in June 1940 the Broads were declared a prohibited area into which outsiders were not allowed.

110 *Members of the Norfolk and Suffolk Broads Yacht Owners' Association met at the* King's Head *at Wroxham to celebrate the 25th anniversary of the Association in 1931.*

Blake's London offices at Broadland House, 22 Newgate Street, were badly damaged by bombing, so when the ban on visits to the Broads was eased in 1943 Harry Blake ran the business from his home at Croydon. The pre-war staff were all serving with the forces, but Harry and Mrs Blake carried on as best they could. With no petrol available for cruising, motor cruisers were let as houseboats.

With the return of peace in 1945 Harry Blake, at the age of 65, decided to retire and the agency was sold to the boat-hirers, who were anxious to gain more control over their lettings. New premises were found in London, and the first post-war *Norfolk Broads Holidays Afloat*, labelled an 'austerity edition', was produced in 1946.

It was still in the old horizontal format which had been introduced with the first issue in 1908, but it was only 64 pages. An introduction told of the changes that had taken place:

> Our many clients and friends will notice that our name has changed a little. Mr and Mrs Blake have now retired from the business and our address in Newgate Street, regretfully, no longer exists. All this has meant a certain re-arrangement of the Company with new and, we believe, better premises in Fleet Street. The senior staff are, however, largely unchanged ... This 1946 booklet is our first since the war. It is not as fully descriptive as we would like but, of course, paper rationing is still with us.

H.F. 'Jim' Brooker was invited by the boatowners to become General Manager, and the name changed from Blake's Ltd. to Blakes (Norfolk Broads Holidays) Ltd. Brooker, who took over in February 1946, had been responsible for the production and distribution of timber parts from the Fairmile Marine Co. to boatyards all round the coast, including Percival at Horning, Collins Pleasure Craft and Robinson at Oulton Broad and Herbert Woods at Potter Heigham, for the building of light coastal craft during the Second World War; before the war he had been contracts manager for Polytechnic Tours Ltd.

One of the changes introduced by the new management was a style change for the annual list. The 1947 edition was the first in a new upright format, and with colour photographs. It was a handy 'pocket' size, but seemed rather insignificant in an age of ever-increasing pressure, so in the 1970s we see it back to horizontal format but in a much larger size. Then in the mid-'70s it returned to the upright format, but still in the larger size, a little more than A4.

Harry Blake died in 1959, but his name lives on in the title of the agency he founded back in 1907. The Norfolk and Suffolk Broads Yacht Owners' Association had a membership of 33 boatyards in the late '40s, and by the time the agency celebrated its 70th birthday this had grown to forty. A dozen of the 40 members were new

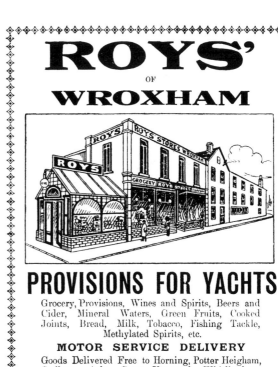

ROYS' OF WROXHAM

PROVISIONS FOR YACHTS

Grocery, Provisions, Wines and Spirits, Beers and Cider, Mineral Waters, Green Fruits, Cooked Joints, Bread, Milk, Tobacco, Fishing Tackle, Methylated Spirits, etc.

MOTOR SERVICE DELIVERY

Goods Delivered Free to Horning, Potter Heigham, Stalham, Acle, Great Yarmouth, Whitlingham, Brundall, Oulton Broad.

WIRELESS SETS, GRAMOPHONES AND RECORDS FOR HIRE

If you don't know what to take, write us; we will then send you a List of Goods suitable for the trip. We take back any Non-Perishable goods left over at end of cruise, and allow in full. To ensure early delivery please send your orders in advance. **Branches—Horning, Potter Heigham and Coltishall.**

TELEGRAMS: "ROYS."   TELEPHONE 99

111 *Beginning in 1895 with a shop in their native Coltishall, three members of the Roy family opened a second store in Hoveton St John in 1904 which was later advertised as 'The Largest Village Store in the World'. In a prime position just to the north of Wroxham bridge, the shop grew with the holiday trade, offering to take back any non-perishable goods left over at the end of the cruise. This advertisement from the 1930s shows that the firm had by then expanded by opening branches in Horning and Potter Heigham; it has since expanded beyond the Broads area.*

businesses, or old yards which had come under new management since the war. It was not only the membership that was growing but also the scale of operations; already the season was spread over six months rather than the six weeks that was the rule in the early years of the century, and some boatyards were prepared to hire craft outside the season. The numbers of craft owned by members of the Norfolk and Suffolk Broads Yacht Owners' Association and the rival Broadland Owners' Association had increased by 1978 to the point at which measures had to be taken to avoid congestion when hire craft returned to their home boatyards for the changeover; several yards advertised some of their boats 'Thursdays start only'.

The Broadland Owners' Association had its beginning in the early postwar years when W.B. Hoseason set up an agency at Oulton Broad that was to emulate Blakes and was to help promote the expansion of the holiday boating industry not only on the Broads but on other British waterways and in Europe. From the early 1970s both agencies expanded into other fields, advertising holidays on the English canals, the River Thames, Loch Ness and the Caledonian Canal, the River Shannon in Ireland, the Dutch waterways and the French canals.

A great increase in the number of pleasure craft using the Broadland waterways has brought problems of overcrowding, particularly in those parts most popular with holidaymakers. The increasing numbers of motor boats since the 1920s, often operated by inexperienced hirers who do not realise the effect their handling of the boats has on the river banks and on other users of the river, has brought serious results, particularly where wash from the boats has been one of the main causes of bank erosion.

In 1971 there were 10,177 boats registered on the Broads, and by 1995 this number had risen to over 13,000, though fortunately they were not all using the rivers at the same time. The 1995 total included 2,445 hire craft, more than half of them motor cruisers, and 10,640 private craft, of which some 3,500 were motor cruisers.[13] In fact the number of hire craft has declined from a peak of some 3,900 boats in 1979, but these craft are intensively used throughout a long summer season. In recent years there has been a tendency for some hire craft to remain in operation almost throughout the year, and whereas in the late 1940s the rivers were used hardly at all in midwinter, now a Christmas holiday on the Broads has become quite popular with the hardier strain of holidaymakers. In contrast, private craft tend to be used only for a comparatively few weeks when the owners are on holiday and at weekends throughout the summer.

Eleven

ECOLOGICAL DISASTER

Brought into being by man in the Middle Ages, the Broads suffered a serious decline in the 20th century from a variety of causes both natural and man-made. Towards the end of the century it had become obvious to all who used the Broadland rivers that serious damage was being done to the local environment, and by the 1980s it was clear that action had to be taken to remedy the increasingly dire situation if the Broads themselves were to survive.

Even in the previous century a few far-sighted people were sounding the alarm. The Revd Richard Lubbock noted in his book *Observations on the Fauna of Norfolk* (1845):

> Our marshes are more and more improved and drained, for the sake of pasturage … The fen is no longer enlivened by the note of the redshank, nor echoes to the scream of the quickly glancing tern; the boom of the bittern no longer is heard at nightfall; the ruff, formerly so common amongst us, singular in habits and beautiful in plumage, always eagerly sought by the epicure and bird preserver, has in most places nearly vanished.[1]

It has to be admitted that Lubbock seems himself to have had a hand in reducing the bittern to near extinction, for during a snipe and duck shooting expedition in 1819 he killed 11 bittern 'without searching particularly for them'. He also asked a marshman to shoot some bearded tits for him 'for preservation' but regretted that when he received them they were spoilt by having been killed with large shot. He supplied the marshman with dust shot, and as a result received six birds killed at one shot.

By the end of Queen Victoria's reign more than one bird had been lost as a breeding species. 'Probably the Black Tern and Bittern will never again rear their young in Broadland,' said the Revd M.C.H. Bird in his chapter on bird life in Dutt's book, published in 1903, but in 1911 Emma Turner, a pioneer bird photographer, and Jim Vincent, the legendary Hickling keeper, found that the bittern had returned to breed in Norfolk. The bittern continued to nest in the Broads, and in 1923 B.B. Riviere estimated that 16 or 17 pairs were breeding in Norfolk.[2] I remember seeing a bittern in reedbeds at Barton Turf somewhere about 1950, and a few years later I saw one fly across the Acle New Road as I cycled towards Yarmouth; I have seen others since,

112 *'He looked like a tall, gaunt old woman masquerading in bird's attire', was Emma Turner's description of the young bittern she and Jim Vincent discovered at Hickling on 8 July 1911. This historic photograph was taken by Miss Turner early the following morning; it was found pasted into a copy of her book* Broadland Birds, *published by Country Life in 1924.*

but they have to be sought. Sadly, the bittern declined in the 1960s, and by 1970 the number in the county had been reduced to 28 booming males. Today the Royal Society for the Protection of Birds and the county wildlife trusts are endeavouring to manipulate their reserves to provide the right kind of reed bed and waterway so as to attract the bittern and to encourage it to breed.

It is a process that had its beginning in the early years of the 20th century when three bird lovers, Edwin Montagu, Lord Lucas and Sir Edward Grey (later Lord Grey of Falloden) purchased part of the Hickling estate, which they established as a private nature reserve, only the second such reserve in the country. Within a year or so Lady Lucas purchased the Horsey estate, just to the east of Hickling, which was also declared a nature reserve. Aided by Jim Vincent, these early conservationists and their successors at Hickling turned the estate into a haven for breeding birds and visiting migrants, at the same time developing it as a shooting estate.

Jim Vincent, who was the son of an earlier keeper of the Hickling estate, was engaged at the age of 16 by Edwin Montagu, then an undergraduate at Cambridge, to help him build up his collection of birds and eggs. When in 1912 Montagu, Lord Lucas and Sir Edward Grey made their purchase Montagu engaged Jim as head keeper of the Whiteslea estate, instructing him to improve the existing habitats for breeding and migrating birds and to increase the number of wildfowl on the estate. It was an inspired choice, for Jim made it his life's work.

Nobody knew more about the birds of Hickling than Jim Vincent, and successive employers gave him almost a free hand in developing the estate. His knowledge of birds and his accumulated experience of flooding, cutting, draining and grazing the marshes to attract waterfowl and other birds was used over the years to turn the estate into one of the finest of its kind anywhere in the country. Nobility and royalty were attracted to the shoots at Hickling, King George V twice shooting on the Broad as a guest of Lord Desborough, who had taken over the estate in 1926. King George VI came not twice but many times, and more recently the Duke of Edinburgh and Prince Charles have been among the visitors. In January 1961 the Duke was among the last to enjoy a weekend's duck and coot shooting at Whiteslea; all shooting ceased on Hickling Broad and Heigham Sounds at the beginning of February that year.

As a result of his work Jim Vincent became known far beyond his own county, and the stories told about him are legion. In 1930 he was invited by George V to spend three days at Sandringham as the guest of the royal family, an accolade that has been accorded to few head gamekeepers. Perhaps it was as well that Jim was undaunted by the high-ranking people who came to Hickling; his sister Ida told an amusing tale of how he got his own back on those who did not do as he told them:

> My brother Jim used to get up to a lot of mischief, particularly with some of the important visitors who came to Whiteslea for the shooting. Some of these Lords and Sirs he couldn't get on with, as they didn't do what he told them when they went shooting. Jim had a favourite trick how to get his own back on them. Sometimes they would stay for the evening flight until it was too dark to see anything, and this would mean crossing a ligger over a dyke to reach their punt. Perhaps one of these Lordships, whom Jim didn't like, would reach a ligger and say he couldn't see it. He had a job to know where to put his feet. So Jim, who had already crossed, would stand in the middle of it facing his Lordship. He then struck several matches to show the way over. His Lordship slowly walked the ligger when Jim would light no more matches, saying he was sorry but he hadn't got any more. Of course, the light from the matches had blinded his Lordship, who now didn't know where to put his feet. The next thing that happened was his Lordship fell off the ligger into the dyke, and crawled out smelling something terrible![3]

Jim Vincent died in 1944, the same year that Lord Desborough decided to sell the estate. It was purchased by Christopher Cadbury, who had been a frequent visitor to Hickling, and some friends and given by them the following year to the Norfolk Naturalists' Trust, an organisation established in 1926 by the far-sighted Dr Sydney Long. This pioneer organisation, which remained for 20 years the only such naturalists' trust in the country, acquired its first Broadland reserve in 1928 when it bought the 26-acre Starch Grass at Martham, a nesting ground of both bitterns and harriers, following that two years later with the purchase of Alderfen, a landlocked broad between Neatishead and Irstead surrounded by 50 acres of reedbeds, marsh and farmland.

Many other county trusts were formed on the lines of the Norfolk Naturalists' Trust in the years after the Second World War, and the Norfolk Wildlife Trust – the name was changed in line with the policy of the Society for the Promotion of Nature Conservation – is now one of 47 local wildlife

113 *A holidaymaker gathers marsh flowers while the steward of the wherry yacht does the washing up, but G.C. Davies warned that 'the possessors of the Broads set as much store by their bulrushes and water lilies as the admiring visitor, therefore, do not gather any off the Broads.'*

charities in Britain. It has 18,000 members, eight thriving local groups and more than 1,000 active volunteers employed in maintaining and looking after 40 nature reserves in the county. The trust owns nine broads and five areas of ancient woodland as well as ten kilometres of coastline, and has five visitor centres that attract an estimated 250,000 visitors each year, one of them being a floating thatched wildlife centre on Ranworth Broad opened by the Queen in 1976. Its counterpart organisation in Suffolk has reserves at Carlton Marshes and Oulton Marshes on the River Waveney, and is currently engaged in a two-year task of restoring dykes and clearing scrub at Oulton Marshes so that it will be possible to manage the reserve in a sustainable way through grazing and mowing.

While on the one hand the concept of nature reserves was being developed by naturalists, on the other the increasing popularity of the Broads as a holiday destination led to a marked degree of disturbance in those areas that proved most attractive to visitors. The kind of yachtsmen that George Christopher Davies sought to interest in the region were those who valued the seclusion and wildness of these little-frequented waterways, but a result of the publicity he provided through the publication of *The Handbook to the Rivers and Broads of Norfolk and Suffolk* was that the Broads became popular also with a more extrovert and often less well-behaved class of holidaymaker.

Early editions of *The Handbook* had only a short preface, the one in the first edition of 1882 looking forward to the publication of his larger book which came out the following year, but when in 1888 Davies was asked by his publishers, Jarrold and Sons, to revise his *Handbook*, he found it necessary to write a much longer introduction. 'Each year the tourist stream increases … and the Rivers and Broads of Norfolk and Suffolk are fast becoming one of the most popular of English playgrounds,' he wrote.

> I should like to put the brake on a little in one respect. One guide-book writer appears to treat the riverside meadows as commons, and suggests that yachtsmen should bring lawn-tennis sets and cricket materials with them. Pray don't take such absurd advice … The riparian owners are generally willing to afford the well-

THE BROAD DEMONS.
enjoying(?) themselves.

114 *Davies also warned against running steam launches at full speed past moored yachts and anglers. This sketch appeared in* The Graphic *of 8 September 1888.*

> behaved public all reasonable facilities for enjoyment. Let this be repaid by the public refraining from potting away at waterhens and pigeons, or other birds on the banks ... A great point to remember is, that the possessors of the Broads set as much store by their bulrushes and water lilies as the admiring visitor; therefore, do not gather any off the Broads.[4]

Having berated 'the bottle shooters, coot potters, and noisy revellers, the swan's egg robbers and grebe destroyers, the persons who use one's boat-houses as luncheon rooms or dust bins', he went on to set out what he called 'the hitherto unwritten rules' of behaviour on the rivers and broads. They included an injunction to men to bathe only before eight in the morning as 'ladies are not expected to turn out before eight, but after that time they are entitled to be free from any annoyance' and a statement that 'steam launches must not run at full speed past yachts moored to the bank, particularly when the occupants of the latter have things spread out for a meal'. Most of these rules continued to be included in future editions, right up to the 50th and last, but that about bathing before 8 a.m. lapsed when bathing suits became more generally worn.

Quite clearly the growth of the leisure industry was having an impact on the region that was not always to its benefit, but few could foresee the problems that lay ahead. While Jim Vincent enthusiastically worked on the creation of his employers' nature reserve at Hickling and studied the birds, others worked on various different aspects of the Broads. At Sutton Broad Eustace and Robert Gurney established a freshwater biological station where a scientific study was made of the aquatic fauna, work that was brought to a premature end by the outbreak of war in 1914.

The war threatened to have an impact in other ways. A proposal in 1913 that the Admiralty should take over Hickling Broad for use by flying boats when weather conditions prevented flying from the Yarmouth air station might have proved devastating, but it was not proceeded with at the time.[5] Even when the Broad was taken over in August 1918 under the Defence of the Realm Act it was used only very occasionally as an emergency landing place for marine aircraft, and it soon settled back into its natural state when the Armistice came.

The suggestion of a flying boat base on the Broads does not appear to have been raised during the Second World War, but a number of airfields were built in the area, the most important of them being RAF Coltishall, which remains in use today. Built in 1939-40 as a bomber station, this airfield, largely in the parish of Scottow but immediately north of the village from which it takes its name, opened as a fighter airfield in 1940. Its squadrons played a role in the Battle of Britain, assembling each day at Duxford to work as part of the Duxford Wing.

During the wartime years Coltishall had two satellite stations, one to the west at Matlaske and the other at Ludham, in the heart of the Broads. Ludham airfield, lying between that village and Catfield, received a visit from King George VI and Queen Elizabeth on the afternoon of 28 January 1943. The royal party arrived just as two pilots of No. 167 Squadron landed their Spitfires after shooting down a marauding Junkers Ju88, and it is said that the King showed great delight at their success.

One of the great fears as Britain prepared to repel invasion in 1940 was that the Luftwaffe would attempt to land troop-carrying aircraft on the Broads. A joint Army-Navy unit based at Wroxham took over a number of day launches that had been available for hire to peacetime holidaymakers and fitted each of them with Lewis machine guns, carrying out regular patrols of the waterways. By 1941 the Army had taken full charge of the river patrols. Harry Blake, who operated the biggest boat-hiring agency from offices in London, packed a weekend case and went down to Wroxham as civilian adviser to the Resident Naval Officer there. He was quickly ordered to arrange for holiday craft to be moored out in the middle of broads to serve as obstacles to the landing of enemy seaplanes; some broads were obstructed by piles driven into the bottom and linked together by wires for the same purpose. The contents of his weekend case proved inadequate, for though Blake had expected to be away from home just a few days his work developed so much that he did not complete it until April 1942.

The *Ferry Inn* at Horning was a favourite watering hole of pilots from the Coltishall-based squadrons, and some of them lost their lives when the place was destroyed by bombs on the night of 26 April 1941; altogether it is thought

115 *The* Horning Ferry Inn *that was destroyed in an air raid on the night of 26 April 1941. The replacement inn was itself destroyed by fire in 1965 when smuts from a chimney fell on to the thatched roof.*

that 22 people died in the raid, five of them people who had left Yarmouth in an attempt to escape the bombing of that town. In an English-language broadcast later William Joyce, better known to British listeners as 'Lord Haw-Haw', claimed that the raid had destroyed a 'warship factory'. In fact only four of the 15 bombs dropped caused damage, the others falling in the riverside marshes.

It does seem likely that the bombs were aimed at H.T. Percival's boatyard, which was at that time building vessels for the Royal Navy, but aeronautical historian Huby Fairhead has pointed out that Horning was the site of one of three 'Starfish' decoy sites designed to draw enemy raiders away from Norwich. When activated, the decoy lights and fires resembled the Midland & Great Northern Joint Railway's City Station yard at Norwich – and the Horning site was in use on the night of the raid.

Percival's boatyard, which built ten 112ft. Fairmile B-type motor launches for patrol and rescue work and two 105ft. support landing craft, designed to give artillery support to invasion forces landing on a defended beach, was only one of a number of Broadland yards engaged in the building of small vessels for the services. Leo Robinson at Oulton Broad built five Fairmile MLs, plus one at their Tewkesbury yard on the River Severn, and one motor torpedo boat, while the nearby yard of Collins built eight Fairmile motor launches and two Fairmile D-class motor torpedo boats. The smaller harbour defence motor launches (HDMLs) were built in some numbers by Leo Robinson at Oulton Broad and on the Severn, Graham Bunn at Wroxham and Herbert Woods at Potter Heigham and at a number of other yards operated by the company in other parts of the country. In addition Herbert Woods built target-towing launches for the RAF and also airborne lifeboats designed to be dropped from aircraft to ditched aircrews.

Broadland yards including those of H.C. Banham at Horning, J.E. Fletcher and Leo Robinson at Oulton Broad, E.C. Landamore and Jack Powles at Wroxham, and Pleasure Craft Limited at Lowestoft built landing craft of various kinds for use in combined operations and in the invasion of Europe.

The larger craft built in the upriver yards such as Percival's MLs had to be taken to Yarmouth for fitting out. Negotiating the Bure bridges at Yarmouth was a difficult matter since there was limited clearance and the tidal conditions had to be observed carefully; too low a tide and the craft would ground, too high and it would not pass safely under the bridges. The wheelhouse and deck fittings would be installed only after the bridges had been successfully passed.

Shipyards such as Brooke Marine, Richards Iron Works and East Anglian Constructors at Lowestoft, George Overy at Oulton Broad and Fellows at Yarmouth were involved in the construction not only of motor torpedo boats and motor launches but also of motor fishing vessels and motor minesweepers. Indeed, Richards were parent yard for the building of the 90-ft. motor fishing vessels, which meant that they controlled the construction of this type of craft throughout the country.

It was in the post-war years that concern was increasingly expressed at the many problems that were seen to beset the Broads. Indeed, as early as 1945 a Broads Conference was called to consider the problems and requirements of the area, and that body recommended that a central planning committee be set up. A Broads Joint Advisory Planning Committee was established in 1947 with members representing local authorities, navigation and drainage interests, fisheries and water supply authorities, commercial boating interests, the agricultural executive committee, naturalists and landowners, but proposals that the Broads should be one of the National Parks, the first of which were established in 1949, were not followed up. The opportunity was lost, and conflicting local interests were left to fight over the carcase as the situation became rapidly worse.

What had gone wrong? The extraordinarily rich growth of aquatic plants in the alkaline waters of the Broads proved to be the underlying cause of one of the basic problems, for as the vegetation died down each winter it rotted and dropped to the bottom. The gradual deposition of silt led to broads becoming shallower over the centuries, and in some of the less deep cuttings reedswamp plants such as reed and lesser reedmace was able to colonise the Broads, leading to the formation of a mat of vegetation which would eventually be invaded by tussock sedge, lesser pond-sedge and saw-sedge. Once a depth of just three feet was reached the build-up of reedswamp and loss of open water could be surprisingly rapid; at the beginning of the 20th century there was still a relatively large expanse of open water at Sutton Broad, but by the 1950s there was nothing more than a narrow channel kept open artificially for navigation.

Some of the smaller, shallower broads such as Carleton Broad, south of the Yare in the parish of Carleton St Peter, and Thurne Broad have disappeared, and others have largely grown up in the past 200 years, leaving only a small area of open water in the midst of overgrown peat cuttings. In a number of areas it is only dredging carried out in the interests of navigation that has prevented the growing up of once-extensive broads.

In the course of the 20th century, and particularly since the Second World War, there were considerable changes in land management which resulted in areas of marsh and fen going out of use and changing drastically in appearance. The demand for reed, sedge and marsh hay declined sharply, and the abandonment of traditional practices allowed scrub to gain a foothold on reedbeds and marshes that had hitherto been kept clear by cutting. In time alder and birch colonised once-productive wetland, which soon became carr or wet woodland. Riverside trees that had been either cut down or pollarded in the days of wherry trading were left to grow tall, to the dismay of sailing men; sometimes they became top-heavy and were blown over by gales, their roots being torn out of the insecure ground to leave holes in the river bank.

In one small part of the Bure valley the area of open water diminished from 114 acres in 1845 to 15 acres in 1958, the area of grazing and mowing marshes, reed and sedge beds from 345 acres to 190 acres. In the same period the acreage of woodland and carr increased from 51 to 305 acres.

That was bad enough, but in the second half of the 20th century it became apparent that water quality was declining and that the Broads were dying. Nitrogenous run-off from heavily fertilised agricultural land and phosphates discharged from sewerage plants into the rivers were enriching the water so that the growth of algae was stimulated to the extent that the water turned green and sunlight was unable to penetrate below the surface. In the absence of that sunlight aquatic plants were unable to grow. The once-rich flora of the Broads was virtually wiped out; outbreaks of botulism played havoc with wild-fowl on the northern broads, and fish were poisoned by toxins released by an algae, *Prymnesium parvum*.

Early holidaymakers had been attracted to the Broads by the wildlife; now there were fears that future generations of visitors would find little or no wild-life at all. 'I look upon it as a desert,' said a distraught Ted Ellis in 1975. 'It was a marvellous area, a living paradise of wildlife, but now masses of things are dead. It's a tragedy.' Scientists at the University of East Anglia gave the startling news that 11 of the 28 broads they had studied appeared to be completely devoid of aquatic vegetation, and in a further 11 the plants were showing poor growth. If nothing were done it was feared, with good reason, that by the end of the century the Broads would be just a series of sterile, muddy lakes.

Where once one could look down past the water lilies and through the crystal-clear water to see water soldier growing up from the bottom of Barton Broad, now one saw only a green liquid that had the appearance of pea soup. On the edge of the broad, and along the banks of the rivers, the reed fringe that had protected the shore from the wash of passing motor cruisers was mysteriously dying back. Only in a few marsh dykes unconnected with the rivers was there anything like the old richness of aquatic plants, the same wealth of invertebrate life that used to be general in the Broads.

The Norfolk Naturalists' Trust took the initiative in calling for a co-ordinated programme of study to resolve the underlying causes of the disaster that was afflicting Broadland. Believing that no single organisation had the manpower, the financial support, the scientific and technical knowledge and the authority to perform such an investigation, the trust called for the inauguration of a long-term project with a full-time project director working from the University of East Anglia.

In 1961 the National Parks Commission had come to the conclusion that it would be inappropriate to designate the Broads a National Park, but in 1976 the Countryside Commission decided to consult with interested parties on the possibility of the area, or part of it, becoming one. Opposition came from, among others, the boat hirers, and the idea was again shelved. And then a new threat became apparent, this time a threat to the landscape itself. Farmers were being encouraged by the government to deep drain the former grazing marshes and to plough them up for the production of cereals, generous grants being made available to facilitate work that would completely change the appearance of the district. Instead of the green marshes inhabited by grazing cattle one looked out across flat fields of golden wheat, much of it destined to go into store rather than to the mills.

As the dykes were deepened and the water table lowered the water in the dykes turned bright orange, a contrast with the green soup of the Broads. This effect was particularly serious in the area of the upper Thurne and Horsey Mere, where the land had been flooded by seawater on many occasions over the centuries. The formation of iron pyrite (ferric sulphide) by bacterial reduction of sulphates derived from the seawater causes no problems while the water table remains high, but when the soil is drained the pyrite is oxidized to form soluble iron and sulphuric acid, the soluble iron being precipitated as ferric hydroxide, commonly known as ochre. When the drainage water from the acid-sulphate soil is discharged into a dyke the acidity is neutralised and large quantities of ochre produced, colouring the water and causing serious silting up of the drainage channels. Aerial photographs show the ochreous water from the Brograve Level, converted to arable during the 1960s, flowing down the Waxham Cut from the Brograve pump into Horsey Mere, part of which is turned orange. Horsey Mere is a nature reserve of international importance.

In 1981 there came a proposal from the internal drainage board to install new pumps at Berney Arms and Seven Mile House, on the Yare, to improve the drainage of the Halvergate marshes so as enable farmers to use the land for arable farming. The scheme would have cost some £2,000,000, with a grant of more than 40 per cent coming from the Ministry of Agriculture, and would have irrevocably changed the landscape of the lower Yare valley. 'We are using an increasing amount of public funds to drain the marshes for cereal production which will swell the EEC grain mountain, and are destroying unique wildlife habitats that can never be recreated,' said Norwich North MP David Ennals in the House of Commons. 'Much more priority must be given to conservation.'

The tide was about to turn.

Twelve

NEARLY A NATIONAL PARK

Changing farm economics persuaded many of the farmers with land in the drained marshland areas to contemplate turning their marshes into arable land in the 1970s and 1980s. It was not as radical a change in principle as it might have seemed, for crops such as mangolds and corn had been grown on the marshes in the 19th century, but in practice the developments were to have a devastating effect both on the landscape and on wildlife because of the way farmers approached the task of conversion.

To enable them to use machinery economically it was necessary for the farmers to increase the size of the fields used for growing cereal crops, and drastic alterations were made to the drainage systems. The old dykes were filled in, with a corresponding loss of wildlife habitat, and the marshes were levelled, filling in any old salt marsh creeks that survived, removing the higher margins that had resulted from the dumping of dredging spoil and material cleared from the dykes, and levelling other bumps and hollows that had given the grazing marshes their character.[1]

In some cases the improvement of the marshes resulted in the entire drainage system being filled in and replaced by a much more restricted layout of steep-sided drains. The water in the new drains was far shallower than in the original dykes, and very few aquatic plants grew in them. The result was often a loss of wildlife habitat which was the more serious since the marsh dykes had become the last stronghold of plants and animals ousted from the broads and rivers by the disastrous changes taking place there.

Environmentalists were dismayed by such operations and the effect they had on the area's wildlife. One who was prepared to give a lead was a young Norfolk-born botanist, Andrew Lees, who in the late 1970s set up Broadland Friends of the Earth to campaign against what he saw as the desecration of the Broadland landscape typified by the deep drainage and dyke infilling that took place in the area administered by the Muckfleet and South Flegg Internal Drainage Board at that time. When in 1984 farmer David Wright gave notice of his intention to drain and plough up part of the Halvergate Marshes for corn production, Andrew led protesters in a sit-down on the threatened land.

Though the National Farmers' Union contended that the ploughing up of the marsh would not have a serious impact on marshland wildlife, the local

116 *Disc-ploughing arable land on Halvergate Marshes on a misty day in July 1987, with Berney Arms Mill to the south. Two years earlier this land had been grazing marsh.*

Friends of the Earth were successful in harnessing public opinion by making known the enormous damage that would be caused both to the landscape and to the wildlife if the whole of the Halvergate area were brought under the plough. Intense pressure from the group eventually led to the setting up of the Broads Grazing Marshes Conservation Scheme, under which payments were made to farmers who agreed to manage their land in the old way.

It was a time of confrontation between farmers forced by economic factors to abandon livestock in favour of arable farming and conservationists aghast at environmentally damaging schemes encouraged by the agriculture ministry's substantial grant aid. Happily the gap between the two was bridged by a widely respected civil servant, Quentin Hill, who became the ministry's project officer when in 1987 the experimental conservation scheme was superseded by the Broads Environmentally Sensitive Area scheme, which extended to the whole Broadland area. While neither the original scheme nor its successor was entirely satisfactory to all those involved, Quentin Hill made it work, and the ploughing up of the marshes was halted. It was a tribute to his qualities that farmers were quick to enrol in the Broads ESA scheme, and that during its first year no fewer than 374 agreements were negotiated. At the time of his tragic death in 2002 Quentin Hill was described by Chris Durdin, the local chief of the Royal Society for the Protection of Birds, as 'one of the unsung heroes'.[2]

Changing agricultural practices were among the factors listed as posing a threat to the area in the first report, *What Future for Broadland?*, issued by the Broads Authority in 1982. The Authority had been set up in 1978 and had begun work on its strategy and management plan the following year, and *What Future for Broadland?* was the result of three years of intensive research involving the University of East Anglia. In 1977 the Countryside Commission had seen 'a national park plan as the management tool which would enable a Broads authority to pursue agreed objectives, placing at the fore-front measures to conserve the Broads as a natural resource of national significance for its environmental qualities', but strong local opposition to the principle of a National Park had ensured that the Broads Authority did not have all the powers it needed to deal with the problems.

117 *This memorial stone outside Wickhampton church commemorates Andrew Lees, who was instrumental in saving the Halvergate Marshes from the plough. Working with Friends of the Earth, he succeeded in persuading the Ministry of Agriculture, Fisheries and Food to create the Broads Grazing Marshes Conservation Scheme.*

For one thing the Broads Authority did not have control of navigation, the Great Yarmouth Port and Haven Commissioners opposing the transfer of part of their powers to give the new authority direct management of the waterways. It seemed that the lack of co-ordinated action that had bedevilled the Broads for so many years was likely to continue, and the new body, little more than a joint committee of local authorities, would prove unequal to the daunting task of putting right all the things that had gone so badly wrong with the Broads. Nevertheless, the authority set to work with a will to find solutions to some of the problems that beset the area. Would it be possible to revive the dying Broads and to bring back the wildlife that had been lost?

Cockshoot Broad, a small broad on the Woodbastwick side of the Bure a short distance downstream of Horning Ferry, was chosen for one of the early experiments. Part of the Bure Marshes National Nature Reserve, Cockshoot was owned by the Norfolk Naturalists' Trust, which expressed a willingness to take part in an attempt to reverse the processes that had already led to the virtual death of the broad. In summer there was barely six inches of water, green with algae and incapable of supporting either water plants or other wildlife, above several feet of mud containing large concentrations of phosphorus. The loss of aquatic plants was reflected in a drastic reduction in the number of birds visiting the broad.

The first essential was to isolate the broad by damming both Cockshoot Dyke, which connected it to the River Bure, and Old Hall Dyke, which led into Ranworth Broad. The dam in Old Hall Dyke was completed early in 1982, but

Cockshoot Dyke was left open so that two floating pumps could be brought in to suction-dredge the dyke and the broad, the mud being pumped to a settlement lagoon in an alder carr north-east of the broad. In three months 40,000 cubic yards of mud were removed, and after the departure of the floating pumps Cockshoot Dyke was dammed to separate the broad from the river.

Levels of nitrate and phosphate dropped dramatically as soon as the broad was cut off from the river, and within a month the water was clear enough for the bottom to be seen. Recovery was so rapid that seeds which had been buried in the mud for perhaps 30 or 40 years were germinating just two or three months afterwards, and water lilies and water weeds were growing in the dyke. Recovery in the broad itself was retarded by the action of large numbers of birds that descended on the broad and ate the plants faster than they could grow.

Not all broads could be isolated from the rivers, and action was needed to improve the quality of the water in the rivers themselves. Anglian Water installed phosphate-stripping equipment at the sewage treatment works which discharged into the River Ant, and in the 1980s they implemented a five-year phosphate removal programme at sewage works on the Bure. Was there a possibility of restoring a broad without cutting it off from the river?

118 *A young volunteer planting waterlily rhizomes in Cockshoot Broad in 1985.*

In 1987 a small broad in a loop of the Bure a little over a mile above Wroxham Bridge, Belaugh Broad, was cleared of contaminated mud by mud-pumping. Although the link with the river was left open the water in the broad cleared, though the water plants were very slow in re-establishing themselves. Large-scale restoration work was also carried out on Hoveton Great and Little Broads and the landlocked Alderfen Broad.

In its first ten years the Broads Authority carried out vital investigations into the causes of the disastrous decline in the Broadland environment and made a start on tackling the daunting task of bringing the region back to life. It

lacked statutory powers, its only powers being those delegated by the local
authorities, it had no control of navigation on the local waterways, and it
was always short of funds. Clearly
something altogether stronger and
more effective was going to be needed
if the problems besetting the area
were to be dealt with in a way that
would ensure the survival of this
unique wetland region.

Backed by the local councils, the
Council for National Parks and the
Broads Authority itself, the Countryside Commission recommended to
the government that the Broads
should be cared for by a single body
with adequate powers and sufficient
funding to manage the whole area,
both land and water. Despite the
intransigence of the Great Yarmouth
Port and Haven Commissioners, the
Norfolk and Suffolk Broads Bill became law in 1988, setting up a new
Broads Authority with statutory powers, including those of navigation,
and the new body began its work on
1 April 1989.

There was still local opposition to
the principle of the Broads becoming a National Park, and the Broads
Act of 1988 stopped short of giving

119 *A mudpump operated by English Nature at work on the Woodbastwick nature reserve in 1997. Mud dredged from the dyke is being thrown into the alder carr.*

the area that title. Yet, as the new Authority declared in a pamphlet entitled
The Broads; Britain's newest and very special National Park, the area had become
a National Park in all but name, sharing the same protection as the Lake
District, the Yorkshire Dales and the eight other parks.

Much was being achieved, but the story was not one of continuous success. The research done at the University of East Anglia by Brian Moss and
others was beginning to pay off, but there was to be no easy way of unrav-
elling the complicated web of cause and effect that had led to the catastrophic
decline of the local environment. Volunteers who spent time and effort in
transplanting water soldier (*Stratiotes aloides*) from unpolluted marsh dykes
to Barton Broad found that the plant could not survive in the enriched and
algae-ridden water of the broad. The answer had to be sought in a much
more ambitious and costly scheme that would restore the water quality and

120 *The Norfolk Wildlife Trust's floating conservation centre at Ranworth, opened by the Queen in 1976.*

at the same time remedy the many other ills that were afflicting the second largest of the Broads.

A great deal of careful planning went into the formulation of a restoration project for Barton Broad that began in 1995 and was expected to cost over £2,000,000; in the end it cost some £3,000,000. This was to be a massive mud-pumping operation, much bigger than anything so far attempted, to remove some 300,000 cubic metres of phosphate-rich mud from the bed of the broad, which had silted up to the extent that much of the water area was inaccessible to anything more than small rowing boats. The mud was piped from the floating dredgers to three settlement lagoons on fields to the west of the broad, where bunds or embankments were constructed to contain the mud.

At the same time that the dredgers were removing silt from the broad, biomanipulation techniques, developed by the Broads Authority and the Environment Agency in liaison with European partners, were employed to help return the water to its former healthy state. Specially designed fish barriers were used to seal off sections of the broad from which fish were removed by electro-fishing; the fish are temporarily stunned by an electric current passed through the water, making it possible to put them into tanks for transport to other waters where they can safely be released. It is all a matter of giving nature a helping hand.

121　*Wigeon on Buckenham Marshes in winter, with the old Buckenham steam drainage pump in the background.*

122 *A conservation team of Broads Authority 'Beavers' digging a turf pond at Broad Fen on the River Ant to provide a new habitat for aquatic plants and invertebrates.*

When the water is clean and healthy plants grow beneath the surface, pike will lurk among the plants, emerging to predate on the shoals of smaller fish and ensuring that only the fittest survive to adulthood. Also hiding among the water plants are microscopic animals such as water fleas (daphnia) which feed on the algae, those tiny plants which in large numbers make the water cloudy and prevent larger plants from growing. In the right conditions the pike keep down the numbers of fish that prey on the water fleas, the water fleas prevent the algae from multiplying, and the plants grow in the clear water and provide a hiding place for water fleas and pike alike.

When everything gets out of balance, as has happened in the Broads, the plants die, the pike cannot hunt among them for small fish, the fish multiply and eat up all the daphnia, and so the algae multiply to the point where they turn the water cloudy and the plants die ... as the circle continues conditions become worse and worse until an ecological disaster ensues. Only by removing the fish, albeit temporarily, allowing the daphnia to thrive and eat up the algae can the scientists break the circle and bring about a restoration of clear water, as is being done in Barton Broad. It is actually possible to discern the relative clarity of the water inside the fish barriers as the water fleas, freed from predation by small fish, devour the algae.

Biomanipulation of this kind has also been used in the Rollesby, Ormesby, Filby group of broads to improve the quality of the water, which is extracted by Essex and Suffolk Water for Yarmouth's public supply.

As part of the Barton Broad Clear Water 2000 Project, which received a grant of £1.15 million from the Millennium Commission in addition to financial help from other sponsors, efforts are being made to restore the reed fringes around the broad which have died back partly as a result of grazing by geese which feed on the green shoots of the reed. Loss of the reedbeds that border both rivers and broads has been a long-standing problem throughout the Broads; another factor in this phenomenon is undoubtedly erosion caused by wash from motor vessels using the waterways and damage by boats ramming the banks, the first being countered by the imposition of speed limits and by experiments in designing boats that will produce less wash.

Education plays a large part in the Broads Authority's work; as navigation ranger Martin Joslin remarked after an altercation with the driver of a speeding motor cruiser on the Ant, it is the younger members of the family that are most likely to see the point of speed limits when it has been explained to them. A spin-off from the Barton Broad project was the construction of the Barton Freshwater Ecology Centre at How Hill, just downstream from the broad. School parties as well as adults attend courses run by the How Hill Trust, an independent educational trust set up in 1984 to operate what was styled the Environmental Centre for the Broads in a large Edwardian house built for himself by a Norwich architect, Edward Boardman.

How Hill, standing atop a gravel hill that dominates the valley of the Ant, remained the Boardman family home until 1968, when the estate was sold up and the house and 360 acres of marshes, woodland and gardens were acquired by Norfolk County Council for £37,000 to become a residential education centre. When he opened the centre in 1968 naturalist Ted Ellis remarked that the County Council had given the public a share in the How Hill paradise, but the running costs of such a paradise were high, and in 1983 Norfolk Education Committee decided to sell it.

The Broads Authority acquired the marshes and the little marshman's cottage known as Toad Hole Cottage, which is now a combined museum and information centre, and insurance giant Norwich Union bought the house, leasing it to the How Hill Trust for continued use as a residential education centre. Former schoolteacher David Holmes took up the post of director of the Trust the following year, and soon groups of youngsters, some of them from urban schools, were arriving to enjoy the experience of dyke-dipping and to learn about the lives of dragonflies, daphnia, fish and frogs in ideal surroundings; happily the dykes at How Hill have not suffered to a serious degree the decline that has afflicted so many parts of Broadland. The building of the new ecology centre with its laboratory and teaching room has greatly enhanced the facilities for school parties.

When the children are not in residence courses are held for adults. These include a 'winter birds' course each January that has proved surprisingly popular,

some people coming back year after year to search for marsh harriers, hen harriers, bitterns and bearded tits. Sometimes the river and the dykes are frozen over, but this does not deter the regulars; one year the weather was so hard that it was even feared that those taking part would be unable to leave for home at the end of the course, the disappointment being that the weather cleared in time.

David Holmes and his wife Sue are still running How Hill with undiminished enthusiasm nearly 20 years on, and in 2002 they faced a further challenge when Norwich Union in an almost unparallelled act of corporate generosity decided to hand over the house as a gift to the How Hill Trust.

The marshes at How Hill are cared for by the Broads Authority's marshman, Eric Edwards, who is as much an enthusiast for the Broads as Sue and David and is well known to all who visit the centre. He is also known in a much wider field through his appearances in television programmes and his frequent exposure in newspapers and less ephemeral publications, for he is one of those people who is never too busy to make himself available to help others.

123   *Broads Authority marshman Eric Edwards preparing a bundle of reeds on Reedham Marshes beside the River Ant. In spite of the name these marshes are nowhere near the village of Reedham, which lies on the Yare.*

Although Eric likes to cut his reed with a scythe in the old-fashioned way he also uses a motor-scythe developed from a Japanese rice-harvester. Mechanisation speeds up the work considerably, but it can result in the quality of the cut reed being lower than when cut by hand. When mowing with a scythe a man will stop every now and then to whet his scythe and keep a keen edge on the blade; be cannot halt the mower and remove the blades for sharpening every so often in the course of a day's work, and the result can be that the reed is less cleanly cut; a ragged end to the cut read will give an inferior finish and will wear less well, giving a shorter life to a thatched roof. That, Eric says, could explain why in recent years so much of the reed used in this country has been imported from Hungary, where the economics of labour have not up to now encouraged mechanisation.

Eric is a hardy fellow and thinks little of the discomforts of standing up to his knees in water on a bitter January day as he cuts the reed, but few young men would care to join him in his work. For Eric the pleasure of seeing bearded tits around him picking up the seeds of the reed he has just gathered helps make up for the misery of freezing hands and feet, but few there are prepared to take over when he and others like him reach retirement age. One of the aims of the Broads Authority is to recruit younger people who will learn the skills that Eric and others have honed during their lives on the marshes.

Without men to harvest the products of the fens, the reed, sedge and marsh hay, the fens themselves will disappear under encroaching scrub and woodland. In the second half of the 20th century the area of open fen in the Broads declined by about a third, and if the process is allowed to continue the result will be a drastic change in the Broadland landscape, and a further decline in the local wildlife.

Volunteer working parties spend a good deal of time clearing scrub from the marshes, but with so large an area to be managed willing

124   *The Broads Authority's Fen Harvester discharging chopped marsh vegetation into a second tracked vehicle which blows the material along a pipe to a tractor-hauled trailer standing on firm ground at the edge of the marsh.*

volunteers cannot entirely cope with the task that has to be done. Faced with this fact, the Broads Authority, English Nature and their partner organisations have been investigating the possibility of developing sophisticated machines to harvest fen vegetation and so regenerate the wetland areas while providing renewable energy supplies. With the help of European Union funding a highly specialised mechanical harvester capable of coping with wet, soft and uneven terrain has been developed; this machine has a very low ground pressure so that it does not compact the ground in the way that most machines do. The harvester cuts the vegetation into small pieces that can be blown along a flexible pipeline up to 1,000 metres long to a lorry standing on firm ground.

125 *Volunteers from the Norfolk Naturalists' Trust clearing sycamores alongside the River Yare at Brundall in 1983. Since the sailing wherries ceased to trade on the rivers, trees have been allowed to grow unhindered along the banks.*

Designed for the Broads Authority by consultant engineer Nick Ash, the new harvester produces a material that can be dried and used for a variety of purposes. Marsh litter can provide animal feed in pellet form, animal litter, or biofuel, either loose or as briquettes suitable for use on a domestic fire, a wood burner or a boiler. Related experiments have also been carried out with a self-contained boiler and generator that can be stationed in the vicinity of the marshes and can supply electricity to the national grid. The results of the Norfolk project will be relevant far beyond the Broads, and progress is being keenly followed by colleagues in many other countries, particularly France,

126 *The pleasure wherry* Hathor, *operated by Peter Bower, passing the old steam pumping station at Buckingham on the Yare in August 2001. In the distance is the sail of the wherry yacht* Olive.

the Netherlands, Rumania, Poland and the Ukraine. The fen harvester has even greater potential as a means of producing local renewable energy in the vast wetlands of eastern Europe than in the Broads.

Two of the most characteristic features of the old Broads landscape were the sailing wherries and the drainage windmills employed to raise water from the marsh dykes into main drains or rivers. It seemed likely not so long ago that both would disappear from the local scene, yet thanks to the efforts of a few enthusiasts they have survived into the 21st century to be enjoyed by local people and holidaymakers alike.

It was in 1949 that Roy Clark, then a bookseller in Norwich, took a leading part in forming the Norfolk Wherry Trust to restore the wherry *Albion* and return her to trading under sail on the Broadland rivers. Several sympathetic

127 *The wherry* Albion, *owned by the Norfolk Wherry Trust, passing Burgh Castle on her way up th
Waveney on her centenary trip in May 1998.*

companies promised to support the project by providing cargoes, but attempts
to turn the clock back in that way rarely succeed, and eventually the idea of
keeping a wherry in trade had to be given up. Instead the *Albion* took to
charter work, carrying parties of Scouts, Sea Cadets and other young people
who slept in hammocks in the hold on cruises along the Broadland rivers.[3]
    With the support of its now widespread membership the Wherry Trust has
kept the *Albion* sailing, in spite of her increasing age which has necessitated

constant attention and repeated expensive refits, some carried out by volunteers led by boatbuilder Mike Fuller. The Duke of Edinburgh sailed aboard *Albion* when she celebrated her centenary in 1998; he had supported the Trust years earlier when it made an appeal for funds to keep the wherry sailing.

Two other enthusiasts in the cause of restoration are Barney Matthews and Peter Bower, of Wherry Yacht Charter, who have restored the wherry yachts *Olive* and *Norada* and the pleasure wherry *Hathor* and operate them from a base at Wroxham, providing what their brochure describes as 'Edwardian-style holidays'. The *Olive* was built by Ernest Collins at Wroxham in 1909 and the *Norada*, known for some years as the *Lady Edith*, by the same company in 1912, so both were showing signs of age when the two partners embarked on their restoration. The *Hathor* was built by Daniel Hall at Reedham in 1905 for members of the Colman family and had been cut down to a houseboat when they acquired her in 1985 and set about rebuilding her and restoring her to sail.

An even more ambitious restoration scheme was that carried out by Vincent Pargeter and his wife Linda when in 1981 they raised the derelict trading wherry *Maud* from her resting place at Ranworth and set to work rebuilding her. It was a task that occupied them for some 18 years before the *Maud* took her place alongside the Norfolk Wherry Trust's *Albion* and other craft on Wroxham Broad one very wet day in the autumn of 1999.

Since then they have acquired Clippesby mill, one of the Bure drainage mills, with the idea of restoring that to working order. Meanwhile Vincent, one of the few working millwrights, is fully occupied on repairs to other mills, including other Broadland drainage windmills. In 2002 he completed work on Thurne Dyke Mill so that the sails could turn again, watched by a large gathering of interested local people, on a memorable Sunday afternoon. The owner of the mill, Bob Morse, had acquired the mill from the Repps, Martham and Thurne Internal Drainage Board in 1949 to preserve it from decay, and Ludham millwright Albert England had helped save it from dereliction at that time.

Ambitious plans for the restoration of other drainage mills have been made by the Norfolk Mills and Pumps Trust, an organisation that began life as the Norfolk Windmills Trust in 1963. To preserve the surviving machinery

128 *David Holmes setting the sails of Clayrack Mill shortly after its rebuilding by Richard Seago.*

the Trust fitted temporary aluminium caps to some of the more complete marsh mills pending money becoming available for full repair, a most commendable initiative. Less creditably, the little hollow post mill re-erected on Clayrack Marsh north of Ludham by Richard Seago has deteriorated for lack of routine maintenance, an illustration of the need for periodical attention if decay is not to set in.

Closely paralleling the story of the How Hill Environmental Centre is that of the Percy Hunter & Sons boatyard, also at Ludham. The business was set up by Percy Hunter and his sons in 1932, and the fleet of sailing yachts that they built and operated was distinctive in that it contained no motor craft, only sailing yachts that doggedly retained not only a traditional appearance but also many features that have disappeared from other fleets over the years. The wooden boats still have varnished hulls, auxiliary motors have never been fitted, and there is no electrical installation, lighting still being by oil lamps set in gimbals; almost the sole concession to progress has been the replacement of twin Primus stoves by gas cooking equipment. It is this dogged adherence to tradition, and to traditional standards of maintenance, that attracts connoisseur hirers to the Womack Water yard.

At a time when education had a meaning that was not dominated by classrooms and the National Curriculum, the yard and its fleet of 13 cabin yachts was acquired by Norfolk Education Committee as a schools sailing centre, but in 1995 the cash-strapped Committee decided to sell the yard and the yachts to help plug the hole in its budget. The outcry caused by this decision was very similar to that aroused by the sell-off of How Hill a decade earlier, and the outcome was somewhat similar: a charitable trust was set up to buy the yard and its yachts and to maintain them for the future. In an age of fibreglass bathtubs propelled by diesel engines, with television sets in the saloon and fitted showers if not bathrooms, the Hunter fleet is available to

129 *Graham Cooper, one of the workers at the Hunter Fleet boatyard at Ludham, engaged in the building of a traditional 28-ft. sailing yacht in September 2001.*

those diehard yachtsmen who believe that the only proper way to see the Broads is from a sailing yacht with minimal modern trimmings.

As the Hunter fleet was being taken over by a specially formed trust, the Museum of the Broads was being laid out in a boatshed at Potter Heigham that had been part of the Herbert Woods yard. The museum opened there in 1996, and after some four years was transferred to premises at Stalham Poor's Staithe. Sadly there is no room in this museum for the keel that was raised from its resting place at Postwick in 1985 and has been deteriorating almost ever since; it is a great pity that it was not left where it was until a place could be found where it could be conserved and put on proper display.

Such developments as these have gained the support of the Broads Society, which was formed in 1956 to provide a platform for all who care for the Broads and, as one of the Society's brochures put it, to fight for the future of Broadland. At a time when different bodies wrestled with each other to promote their own interests, the Broads Society spearheaded a campaign to establish one single authority to manage the Broads, and they hailed the creation of the Broads Authority as a success for their efforts.

At the helm of the Broads Authority for the first 22 years of its existence was Professor Aitken Clark, who had the task not only of setting up the new organisation but of inaugurating the programme of research that established

130   *The stock of a new sail being hoisted into the poll end of Turf Fen mill on the How Hill estate durin*
restoration of the mill in 1987. It was impossible to get a crane to the site, so the job was done in the traditiona
way using block and tackle.

the causes of decline and the possible cures for the many ills that beset the
region. He remained in post when in 1988 the Norfolk and Suffolk Broads
Act brought into being a new and stronger Broads Authority with powers
enabling it to tackle problems that had hitherto been beyond its control.
When the time came for his retirement he was succeeded by a geographer

131 *Geese fly by as though in salute as the rebuilt wherry* Maud *spreads her sail for the first time on Wroxham Broad on 20 September 1999.*

and town planner, Dr John Packman, who celebrated his appointment by taking part in the Three Rivers Race in June 2001; perhaps he wondered if it was an augury of metaphorical stormy waters ahead when the race was abandoned because of strong winds that capsized some of the participating boats and damaged others.

Changes in organisation were not long in appearing, designed by the new chief executive to produce greater efficiency and closer working between navigators and conservationists. The shake-up paved the way for a new emphasis that is to be reflected in a new name for the Broads Authority, eventually to be known as the Broads National Park, though at the time of writing the legislation bringing the change of name into effect is not yet in place.

Much has already been done to bring the Broads back to life, and much more is planned. Faced with changing holiday trends, with more holidaymakers travelling abroad and fewer coming to the Broads, the Broads Authority also has proposals to rejuvenate the Broads holiday trade by encouraging the modernisation of the hire fleets, improving riverside public houses and providing new and better leisure facilities. The holiday trade, which is worth an estimated £146 million and employs some 2,000 people, is after all vital to the region, and the number of people taking boating holidays has halved in the past twenty years. A bold strategy is required if the region's economic base is to be safeguarded at the same time that the environment is also not merely safeguarded but restored.

There are still many other problems to be addressed, and the work required will not prove either cheap or easy. The Broads Authority has not only called for a stronger relationship between the national parks and the Department for Environment, Food and Rural Affairs but has made it plain that, if it is to achieve what it is setting out to do, it will need to double its current funding of £4.2 million and have a capital programme of £40 million; currently there is no capital programme at all.

Is this asking too much? With officials advocating planned retreat in the face of rising sea levels, there are those who will say that it is asking far too much. If forecasts of global warming resulting in coastal breaches that could lead to widespread flooding of low-lying areas are correct, however, the Broads could disappear, as some recent writers have predicted. If such a disaster is to be avoided something more than an increase in government funding might be required.

It is not merely a matter of the local economy at stake, or regional prestige. It has been seriously suggested that the Broads should be designated a World Heritage site.

GLOSSARY

...lect words in use in or pertaining to the Broads district

...ah Ague, a form of malaria, was once common in the ...ter parts of East Anglia, including the Broads. This ...nunciation is given by Major Edward Moor, whose ...*folk Words and Phrases* was published in 1823. The ...ease, *Plasmodum vivax*, was spread by the mosquito ...*opheles maculpennis,* which is still to be found on the ...adland marshes. Besides causing the deaths of many ...ellers in the Broads area, this disease was almost ...tainly responsible for the deaths of King James I and ...ver Cromwell. Improved drainage of the marshes ...ring the 19th and 20th centuries reduced the mosquito ...pulation, and this together with modern preventative ...dicine led to a sharp decline of ague in this country, ...ugh it still occurs in northern Holland.

...os Tufted ducks.

...bbing A method of fishing for eels in which a bunch ...worms threaded on worsted is fastened to the end of ...ine attached to a pole or stick. The line is gently ...bbed' up and down until an eel bites into the bundle ...worms, its teeth becoming entangled in the worsted. ...s then possible to haul the eel out of the water and ...ke it off the 'bab' into the bottom of the boat or into ...ne suitable receptacle. William Dutt recalled in *The ...rfolk Broads* how a marshman on the Waveney told him, ...When you feel a little pull at th' line jist hyst it up ...efully an' drop the' worams inter th' keeler. Ony you ...ustn't be too hasty about it, or you may shake him orf ...d luse him. Thas how I mean," he went on as he ...ught up an eel wriggling on the end of his line, and ...ocked it off the bab by swinging it against the inside ...the tub.'

...r-cutter A short-handled implement with a blade set ...the same plane as the handle, used by marshmen to ...t back the shore of a dyke.

Bargoose and bargander The shelduck, female and male. Also known as a Bay-duck.

Binns A term for the deck edge of a wherry. The overhanging binns were protected by the binn iron, an iron strip with a rounded outside face that was nailed all round the binns. The bends were the wales or rubbing strakes employed in shipbuilding in the 17th and 18th centuries, and the wherrymen's term might well have been derived from this.

Black curlew The glossy ibis, a bird from eastern Europe which has occasionally been seen in the Broads. In his *Observations on the Fauna of Norfolk* (1845) the Revd Richard Lubbock says that 'fifty years back it was seen often enough to be known to gunners and fishermen as the Black Curlew'.

Black poker The tufted duck.

Black star Bog rush (*Schoenus nigricans*).

Black-weed Bur reed (*Spargranium ramosum*).

Blue darr The black tern, a passage migrant that was at one time commoner in East Anglia than it is now. The second element of the name could be derived from the word dart.

Blue hawk The male hen harrier, which is of a distinctive blue-grey colour.

Boke load A wherryman's term for a cargo that is loaded up above the level of the right-ups or coamings, sometimes with the hatches laid on top.

Bolder The true bulrush (*Scirpus lacustris*), which was formerly cut on the Broads for rush weaving and similar purposes. In 1879 this name was quoted as 'bowder rushes', an example of the local habit of failing to pronounce the letter L.

Bor A common term of address among men, very likely derived from the Dutch *buur* or *buurman*, neighbour. It is not the same as the word boy, which is usually pronounced '*booey*'.

Bottle-bump A name for the bittern, which is known in Dutch as a *Roerdomp*. The first element of the name is the local term **buttle**, also used for this bird; the second is descriptive of the male bird's boom.

Bottle tom The long-tailed tit, which is also known as the **featherpoke** from its meticulously constructed nest.

Bottom-fying A term used for cleaning out mud and rotting vegetation from a marsh dyke.

Broad arrow Arrowhead (*Sagittaria sagittifolia*).

Brawtches, brotches Otherwise broaches, those split rods of willow or hazel, sharpened at each end, twisted and bent in the middle and used by thatchers to secure the rods or rizzers that hold down the thatch. In some parts of England known as spars. 'A fell of such wood is divided into hurdle-wood and broach-wood', Forby tells us; the former is the stouter rods, the latter the more slender. In a 15th-century source we find 'Broche for a thacstere'.

Brush, to To cut or trim a hedge. **Brushings** are the twigs that result from the operation, as in 'brushwood'. A French origin is usually ascribed to the word 'brush', but in this case one might do better to look to the northern European languages.

Bulrush Local name for the greater reedmace (*Typha latifolia*).

Bunk Marsh angelica (*Angelica sylvestris*).

Bush-weed Water crowfoot (*Ranunculus* spp).

Carnser, carnsey A causeway across low-lying or marshy land, or a raised pathway. The Revd Robert Forby spells it Caunsey, which brings the word a step nearer to its apparent Latin derivation.

Carr Wet, marshy woodland containing mainly alder. Natural succession is for open water to silt up until a depth is reached at which reed and rush can grow; reedbeds form and then unless the reeds are managed alders and birches will seed, in time forming carr.

Cat's-tail, Fox-tail The Mare's-tail (*Hippuris vulgaris* primitive plant found growing in wetland and in wa said to be a descendant of a plant family that was pro in prehistoric times, perhaps when the dinosaurs roan the earth. Linnaeus gave it the name *Hippuris*, fr hippo, the Latin for horse, but Forby remarks, 'Here must correct the great naturalist; this plant is surely m like the tail of a cat than that of a horse'.

Cauliflower weed Water crowfoot (*Ranunculus* spp)

Chatter-pie A magpie, a clear allusion to its harsh cl tering call.

Cheat The sedges (*Carex riparia* and *C. acutiformis*), r canary-grass (*Phalaris arundinacea*) and other grasses a sedges regarded as 'small stuff' present on a marsh primarily for reed.

Church-hole One's last resting place, the grave.

Clung Limp, like a cabbage that has been picked a left lying all day in the sun.

Cobble The stone of fruit such as plums and peach

Cobs Gulls. The black-headed gull was sometimes kno as a Scoulton cob, from the large colony at Scoulton t was first recorded in the 17th century.

Coburg A wooden wedge-shaped fairing which preven the mainsheet from fouling the protruding part of cabin stovepipe on a wherry. The wooden chimney, wh might be either a short one or a long one, was made fit on top of the coburg. It seems likely that the te came into use shortly after the marriage in 1840 Queen Victoria and Prince Albert of Saxe-Coburg, w also gave his name to a type of bread loaf, a dress fab and a hat.

Cockey A drain or sewer. In Norwich the Cockey wa stream running down to the Wensum from the vicir of the castle; it gave its name to Cockey Lane, now L don Street.

Cornelian Mezereon (*Daphne mezereum*), a rare nat plant of wet woodland.

Cowbird The yellow wagtail, which was often fou among cattle on the marshes feeding on the inse disturbed by the grazing animals.

Crome A long-handled implement with tines set at rig angles to the shaft, used for hauling weed from a dy river. The word has a Celtic root; *crom* is the Welsh for ooked, and the right-angled tines might be likened to crooked fork. A **muck crome** is a similar tool used for king muck from carts when spreading manure on the elds.

owd A verb meaning to push a barrow, from the Dutch *uien* with the same meaning. Hence a **crudburra** (rowdbarrow) is a wheelbarrow.

ag Dew. One of those words that has come to us from andinavia; in Swedish it is *Dagg*, in Norwegian *Dogg* d in Danish *Dug*.

icky Usually pronounced dicka, this is a dialect word r a donkey. The well-known Barking Dicky in estlegate, Norwich was once a public house known as e *Light Dragoon*; the ill-painted sign showed a soldier ounted on a horse which appeared to have its mouth de open, hence the allusion to a barking donkey. A orfolk man meeting another in a foreign place might k, 'Ha' yar fa'er got a dicka, bor?', to which the cor ct answer is, 'Yis, an' he want a fule ter roide him. ill ya come?'

ckey-bird The oystercatcher or sea-pie. A dickey was a irt front, and the white chest of the oyster catcher can rtainly be likened to a gentleman in a dress shirt.

idapper The little grebe, or to give it its alternative mmon name, the dabchick. No doubt both didapper d dabchick originated in the bird's diving habit.

o A whole book might be written on the uses of the rd **do**, sometimes written **du**. Perhaps the best example the use of the word is a Norfolk labourer's explana on of how his 'guv'nor' rebuked him for some isdemeanour or other: 'My master he say, he do, that I did do as I oughter do I shon't do as I do do, he do.' nother good example is: 'She dun't do as she oughter , do she wun't do as she do do.' It can be compared the modern German *doch*, meaning 'yet', 'well', or ut', and the Danish *dog*, meaning 'though', 'yet' or en 'if'.

odder-grass Quaking grass (*Briza media*).

ow The wood pigeon. The word is pronounced to yme with cow. It appears to be of Norse origin; the orwegian for a pigeon is *due*, pronounced 'doer'. It uld also be a variant pronunciation of dove.

raw-latch A most expressive compound word for a sneak g fellow who might also be termed an eaves dropper.

Draw-water The goldfinch. This little bird with its startling colouring was often kept as a cage bird, and in captivity it could be taught to draw water for itself with a thimble and chain, hence the name draw-water. *See also* **King Harry**.

Drift, driftway A road leading from the higher ground on to the marshes along which cattle were driven to the grazing marshes.

Dwile A floorcloth, a word which has entered the dialect direct from the Dutch, in which it is spelt *dweyl*. The 'traditional' sport of dwile flonking, in which a floorcloth is soaked in beer held in a chamber pot and then hurled at the opposing team, is a spoof game introduced in the 1960s and first played in the Bungay area.

Dydle A long-handled tool with a metal ring at one end on which is fastened a piece of net, used to dredge out mud from a broad or a dyke. The same word is also used as a verb to describe the operation of removing mud using such an implement. It was known to Thomas Tusser in the 16th century:
A sickle to cut with, a didall and crome
For draining of ditches that noyes thee at home.

Dyke, dike A word of Old English origin, also found in Dutch and some other languages, which has come to have two quite dissimilar meanings. In the Broads area it is normally used of a drainage ditch, but in the Fens and elsewhere it means an earthen bank, as it does in the Netherlands. The Devil's Dyke is an impressive earthwork of indeterminate date stretching from near Newmarket to the fen edge at Reach in Cambridgeshire, and there are other linear earthworks similarly called dykes. The word is by no means peculiar to East Anglia.

Eel pick A spear which would be driven into the mud; eels would become jammed between the springy tines. In Norfolk and Suffolk the pick was made of sheet iron. Also known in some areas as an eel pritch, and in the Fens as a gleave.

Eel sett A large net spanning a river for the catching of migrating eels. The net extends from bank to bank and thus traps all the eels as they swim downriver on their way to the sea. The upper part of the net is fastened to a rope bearing a number of wooden floats and made fast to a stout pole on each side of the river, while the foot of the net is fastened to a second rope, the warp, which is weighted to hold it firmly to the river bottom. From the mouth the net tapers into two, three or four bosoms, to each of which is attached a pod, a long cyl inder of net stretched tightly over hoops. A line from the end of each pod enables the fisherman to lift the pod to remove the catch. It is possible to lower the net to the river bed to allow vessels to pass over it. Years ago there were numerous setts on the Broadland rivers, but only one now survives.

Fare A much-used dialect word which derives from the same root as the German *fahren*, to go. Forby records it as merely to seem, but it is used in a number of other senses which are best detailed by example. A countryman might say of a sickly neighbour, 'She fare wholly bad', while a comment on the weather might be 'thet fare t' be rainin' like thass never goin' t' stop'. And as two men part after a night in the local one will say to the other, 'Fareyewell, moind how ye goo'.

Fen nightingale A frog.

Ferret's-tail Hornwort (*Ceratophyllum* spp).

Fiddlesticks Marsh figwort (*Scrophularia aquatica*).

Firetail The redstart.

Fishleaf Water plantain (*Alisma plantago-aquatica*).

Foxtail *See* Cat's-tail.

French spink The brambling. The word spink is derived from the bird's call note.

Fresher A young frog.

Fulfer Probably a variant pronunciation of fieldfare, a winter visitor, but also used for the resident mistle thrush. Indeed, the fieldfare was sometimes known as a French fulfer, in contradistinction to the English fulfer or mistle thrush.

Furrow-chuck The whinchat.

Fuzhacker The stonechat and whinchat. A combination of furze and hacker or stutterer, a word of Saxon origin.

Game hawk The peregrine, which the Revd Richard Lubbock records as having bred on the spire of Norwich Cathedral, 'to the great annoyance of the pigeon fanciers of this city'.

Gargut root Bear's-foot (*Helleborus viridus*).

Gladdon The Norfolk name for lesser reedmace (*Typha augustifolia*) and yellow flag (*Iris pseudacorus*), cut on the Broads for the making of horse collars and frail baskets.

Both, as Ted Ellis explains, are plants with sword-shap leaves, from *gladius*, a sword.

Goose tansey Silverweed (*Potentilla anserina*), a comm native plant of waste ground, roadsides and dam meadows.

Gotch-belly A good round belly much resembling t shape of a gotch, an earthenware jug of a very round form.

Go-to-bed-at-noon, John-go-to-bed-at-noon The Goat beard (*Tragopogon pratensis*), whose flowers open in t morning but close again before dinnertime.

Grass-weed, Fennel-weed Fennel-leaved pondwee (*Potomogeton pectinatus*).

Grup In modern usage the drain leading from the ed of the road into the roadside ditch to clear water fro the road. However, Forby defines it as 'a trench, n amounting in breadth to a ditch. If narrower still, it is grip; if extremely narrow, a gripple'. There appears be a Scandinavian origin; in Faeroese *gropa* is to dig hole. An associated word is **grooping**, the cutting of groove, as in coopering; the cooper used his **groopir iron** to make the groove around the inside of the barr to receive the head.

Guleham The yellowhammer, possibly from the Nor *gul* for yellow.

Gull A miniature ravine cut by a fast-flowing strear There is a public house at Framingham Earl, betwee Norwich and Loddon, whose sign shows a seagull; it w actually named after the nearby drainage channel. Forb defines gull as a verb meaning to sweep away by force running water and also as 'a breach or hole made by th force of a torrent'. It is presumably related to gully ar gully-hole, the mouth of a street drain or of any oth kind of drain for that matter.

Hain Dialect word for raise. When patent sails replace the old canvas sails on the marsh mills of the Broa region some of the brick towers were hained by buildir a vertical section on top of the tower. In other circur stances it might be said that a worker had 'hed his wag hained'. The word is derived from the Anglo-Saxon *heig* to heighten.

Hair-weed *See* **Grass-weed**.

Ham A small bay or inlet. Leathes Ham at Oulton is good example, though it was separated from Lak thing when the railway embankment was built across in 1846. The word is much used of inlets on the Broads, but it is also used on the coast.

Hansel The first money taken by a tradesman in the day. The tradesman was apt to spit on it 'for luck' before pocketing it.

Happennies-and-pennies Frogbit (*Hydrocharis morsus-ranae*).

Harnser A heron, an old name that was well known to Shakespeare: in *Hamlet* a character says, 'I know a hawk from a handsaw', a sentence that has puzzled many a schoolboy down the years. In 1766 Pennant wrote that not to know the Hawk from the Heronshaw, was an old proverb taken from this diversion [heron-hawking]; but in course of time, served to express great ignorance in any science'. Forby spells the word harnsey, but remembering the Norfolk habit of changing a 'y' sound into 'a', as in dicka, it is perhaps better spelt as we have done. It is in origin not a dialect word at all but a contraction of the old word heronsew or heronshaw, a diminutive of heron. In the *Squire's Tale* Geoffrey Chaucer wrote, 'I wal not tellen … of hir swannes nor of hir heronsewes'. Whether you call him a heron or a harnser, the grey heron, a bird which is increasing in number on the Broads, knows his own name, which he announces as he flaps away, 'Fraank!'

Harnser-gutted Lanky and lean, like the heron.

Hassocks Tussock sedge (*Carex paniculata* and *C. propinquata*), a typical plant of Broadland. Such hassocks were sometimes cut and used as kneelers, or hassocks, in parish churches.

Herb tuppence Creeping Jenny (*Lysimachia nummularia*), a native plant of wet meadows and ditches.

Highlows A covering for the foot and ankle, too high to be called a shoe and too low for a boot, says Forby. Major Moor adds that they are tightly laced in front, midleg high, with a thong or lace known in Suffolk as a whang. A correspondent in the *Eastern Daily Press* some years ago stated that the original highlows were 18th-century military boots, mentioned as such in Thackeray's novel *The Virginians*. The word is often quoted as a dialect word, but it has a much wider usage.

Hornpie The lapwing or green plover.

Hover A floating island of reed broken away from a reedbed by storm-force winds. Many of the reedbeds surrounding broads are little more than floating mattresses, and it is not difficult for a storm to wrench a section free; on one occasion a huge hover from the south side of Heigham Sounds drifted downriver and blocked Potter Heigham bridge. Spurden notes the word hovvers or huvvers, meaning dried flags used as fuel. Whereas turves were blocks of peat taken from beneath the surface, hovvers were pared from the surface and one face was made up of grass and sedge.

Keeler A tub, usually made by a cooper, for a variety of purposes. A wherry carried a **hand-killer**, a small wooden handbasin, square in form, which was normally kept under the sternsheets and filled from the river.

Kentishman A hooded crow (*Corvus corone cornix*), once a more common winter visitor to East Anglia than it is now. Arthur Patterson remarks in *Nature in Eastern Norfolk* (1905) that 'it performs a useful office in devouring carrion, a continual and abundant supply of which is always to be discovered in the vicinity of tidal waters', but goes on to add that 'in severe winters the Hooded Crow certainly shows its predatory instincts, and will not only seize upon wounded fowl, but even snap up small birds in the very presence of the gunner'.

King-cup The marsh marigold (*Caltha palustris*).

King George The peacock butterfly.

King Harry A goldfinch. Perhaps a folk memory of the splendid attire of King Henry VIII led to this name being given to what is, after all, one of our most resplendent little birds. More likely, however, is the explanation that the name comes from the Norse *hæren*, meaning an army, a reference to the goldfinch's habit of going about in small flocks in search of seeds. Also known as a **draw-water**.

Lace-weed *See* **Grass-weed**.

Lamb's skin Floating sheets of algae whose filaments form a skin on the surface of the water.

Lantern men Will-o'-the-wisps, caused by spontaneous combustion of marsh gas (methane). Nevertheless, no such down-to-earth explanation would satisfy old-time marshmen, who believed them to be supernatural and far more dangerous, and had many a story to bear out their belief. Also known as a **Hobby lantern**. Forby spells it the old way, hobby lanthorn, and seeks to explain the term by pointing to the motion of a will-o'-the-wisp, 'as if it were a lanthorn ambling and curvetting on the back of a hobby' (a pony or small horse).

Laughing goose The white-fronted goose.

Ligger A plank laid across a dyke as a footbridge. The same word was also used for a device used for catching pike, generally known as a trimmer. This is a short piece of round wood with a length of fishing line attached, weighted and hooked. The line is wrapped around the stick, leaving some three feet loose. The hook is baited and the device put into the river or broad; if a pike or eel takes the bait the line runs off the stick. On the Broads a ligger was often made from a bundle of reeds or rushes.

Lijahs Small straps worn just below the knees to hold up the trouser legs. These were an essential part of the worker's clothing when trousers were made of heavy, stiff material in order to give his legs freedom of movement.

Loon The great crested grebe, a common bird of inland waters that breeds on nearly every broad.

Lucam, lucomb A dormer window, or the projecting hoist of a water mill, steam mill or malting by which the sacks of grain were hoisted to the garner floor or bin floor. The *Oxford English Dictionary* has *lucarne*, and suggests an origin from the French, but the East Anglian lucam seems more likely to have been derived from Dutch, in which the word *loker* is used for a hole or aperture.

Maidenhair grass Quaking grass (*Briza media*).

Mardle Can be used either as a verb, to gossip or chat, or as a noun, 'we had a rare good ol' mardle, he and I'. It has been suggested that it derives from the talking that went on around the retting pit, but in fact the word in this sense is derived from the Old English *moedlan*. Rather oddly, neither Forby nor Moor gives mardle in this sense; it appears in Spurden's supplement to Forby as 'a jolly meeting' or 'to indulge in such jollity'; Spurden gives maudle as the verb to gossip, but then adds an example, 'Tom and I stood mardling (or maudling) by the stile'.

Mare's fat Marsh fleabane (*Pulicaria disenterica*).

Martin snipe The green sandpiper.

Maund A basket, especially the open basket used for sowing seed broadcast and also a basket used for herrings or sprats. The word is Anglo-Saxon, but there is a possibility that it was introduced into the East Anglian dialect from the Dutch; *mand* is still found in Dutch and Flemish. In Coverdale's Bible of 1535 we read, 'Like as a partrich in a maunde, so is the hert of the proude'. Major Moor says, 'A large sort of basket out of which

seed corn is sown by broadcast', while John Greaves M tells how a 'boat maund' was used to land herrings the beach at Yarmouth; each maund held about 2 fish. Fitzgerald in his *Sea Words and Phrases Along the Suf Coast* comments that he always heard it pronounc 'maand', which is close to the modern Dutch.

Mawther A dialect word for a girl or young woman. I possibly a variant of the word mother, and might derived from Scandinavian; it is perhaps significant t in some Norwegian dialects *mor* (mother) is used of gi and of course it was common in East Anglia to addr women as 'mor'.

Meag, meak A cutting tool allied to a scythe with straight handle and a blade set at right angles to handle, used for reed-cutting and for harvesti gladdon, etc.

Meece The plural of mouse.

Nat-hills Tussock sedge (*Carex paniculata*).

Needle rush Hard rush (*Juncus inflexus*).

Penny-weed *see* **Ha'pennies-and-pennies.**

Pickcheese The blue tit. It is said that cheese was co monly used by boys for baiting the traps they used catching tits.

Pickerel-weed Water soldier (*Stratiotes aloides*), a on prolific aquatic plant with stars of leaves resembli thistles. Changes in the Broads over the past fifty ye have almost extinguished this plant, and efforts ha been made by the Broads Authority to re-establish it Barton Broad and other waters. Early attempts fail because the water quality was not sufficiently improve Also used of the water plant *Pondeteria cordata*.

Pin-rush Local name for the hard rush (*Juncus inflex* and sea rush (*Juncus maritimus*).

Pipe A charge of powder or shot. Writing in the 182 Major Moor says, 'Some 30 or 40 years ago, t conveniences of patent powder-flasks and shot-belts, w suitable charges, were not much used among us; a we carried our powder in one bag, and our shot another, with the bowl of a tobacco pipe in one both.' Although the pipe-bowl was no longer used as measure at the time he compiled his *Suffolk Words a Phrases*, the term pipe was still sometimes used as measure, and he wrote of having heard it said of a lo duck-gun that 'she'll carry tew pipes of each'.

...ncher Forby, Major Moor and the Revd Walter Skeat list plancher as a dialect word, but a glance at the ...ford English Dictionary shows that its use is, or at any ...e was at one time, by no means confined to East ...glia. The dictionary does, however, quote Forby in ...e of its examples. The word is clearly from the Old ...ench plancher. There is a lovely reference in the Paston ...ters in 1449: 'They ben scarse kne hey fro the ...wncher'. In some instances the word seems to have ...en used for an upper floor, but this might be merely ...indication that in earlier times the ground floors were ...t boarded but of rammed earth. Major Moor is some-...at more specific: he defines plancher as the floor of ...bedroom, especially the part near the bed's foot. The ...rd is also used as a verb, meaning to cover a floor ...th boards.

A specific East Anglian use of the word is for the ...vering board of a wherry, but it has been pointed out ...at this is no more than a mispronunciation of ...nksheer, the outermost deck plank covering the timber ...ads of the frames, otherwise known as the covering ...ard.

...ker The reedmace, either lesser or great; a typically ...scriptive dialect word for a plant whose head reminds ...e of the poker used to stir up a fire.

...kers or **Redheads** Norfolk name for pochard, a duck ...ich has been extending its range in recent years. A ...nter visitor to the Broads.

...llard A tree which has had its head, or poll, cut off so ...at new branches grow from the top of the stem or tod. ...ajor Moor attributed the popularity of pollarding in ...ffolk – 'this barbarous custom', he called it – to the ...ct that the loppings or stowins were the tenant's per-...uisites, whereas a timber tree belonged to the landlord. ...ere is, however, another reason: the roots of trees ...anted alongside marsh or fenland roads helped to ...otect the road edge, but if the tree were allowed to ...ow to its full height it would easily be blown down in ...storm; pollarding not only produced a good crop of ...eful poles every few years but reduced windage and ...couraged the tree to produce a good root system.

...llywiggle A term used for the tadpole. Sir Thomas ...owne, the Norwich doctor-naturalist, noted in 1646 ...at 'the spawne is white, contracting by degrees a ...acknesse, answerable ... unto the porwigle, that is, that ...imal which first proceedeth from it'. Forby refers to ...lliwigs or purwiggy, and traces its origin to periwig, ...ough he observes that 'one of the little animals bears ...much resemblance to that antiquated article of finery, ...e wig with a long queue, as to a pot-ladle, by which

name we also call it'. Well, in 1529 a 'perwyke' was made for the king's fool; but the word 'polwygle' in the sense of a 'wyrme' had appeared about 1440, some years be-fore the peruke seems to have made its mark on the English fashion scene.

Pot-ladles A Norfolk name for tadpoles, derived from their shape. According to the supplement to Forby's vocabulary compiled by the Revd W.T. Spurdens, another name used for the little tadpole was dish-ladle.

Pudden, pudding A toad. Pudding Moor, the roadway in Beccles running at the foot of the cliff along the edge of the marsh, is said to have gained its name from the toads found there.

Puddenpoke, oven tit or **ovenbuilder** The willow tit, from its beautifully constructed nest. These names are also used for the chiffchaff, which builds a very similar nest.

Puit A black-headed gull or Scoulton cob.

Pulk or **pulkhole** In Norfolk, a small pool or marsh pond, or an inlet among the reedbeds on the margin of a river or broad. In Suffolk, a small pond used for domestic water supply to a nearby dwelling.

Pyewipe The lapwing or peewit.

Quant A long pole bearing a turned wooden 'bott' at one end and an iron-shod toe, together with a wooden foot to prevent it sinking into the mud, at the other. It is employed to propel a wherry, a reed lighter or other boat in shallow waters, in a calm or against the wind when tacking is impossible because of the narrowness of the waterway. It was also used to give a wherry a set off from the bank, either to assist her in going about or to enable her to creep along the lee shore. A full-size wher-ry's quant used to be 22 feet long, but this was increased to 24 feet when the Norwich River was dredged to a greater depth; handling so large a quant requires con-siderable skill as well as stamina. Yacht quants are much smaller.

Queech, squeech An untilled, rough bushy corner of a field, according to Major Moor. There is also a sugges-tion of a wet place. This is a once-common word that has survived only in the dialect; it is recorded as far back as the 15th century. *See also* **Spong**.

Rafflejack The corncrake, a bird which began to decline towards the end of the 19th century and now appears in East Anglia only as a migrant on passage. The dialect name is descriptive of its grating call.

Rafty Cold and damp, as in 'rafty old weather' or 'a rafty morning'. It has been suggested that the word originated in the late 18th or early 19th century when Napoleon was threatening to invade England with an army carried on rafts, but this ingenious explanation of the word fails when one finds it in use in the mid-17th century. Its real origin is obscure.

Ransack To search for something that is missing; originally in a legal sense to search a house or person for stolen goods. From the Old Norse *rannsaka*, to seek.

Rattle-basket Yellow rattle (*Rhinanthus minor*), a marsh plant whose seeds rattle in the pods as the wind blows.

Ratweed The name used in the Broads for lesser duckweed (*Lemna minor*).

Reed pheasant Broadland name for the bearded reedling (*Panurus biarmicus*) or bearded tit. This distinctive bird of the reedbeds belongs to the babblers (*Timaliidae*) and not to the tit family. In the 19th century the activities of gunners and collectors brought this little bird to the brink of extinction, and in 1898 it was estimated that no more than 33 pairs had nested successfully in the whole of Norfolk. The bearded tit became a protected species in 1895 and has at times greatly increased its numbers, but it is extremely vulnerable in prolonged periods of bad winter weather.

Roger, Sir or **Rodges blast** A sudden, violent whirlwind. Forby in his *Vocabulary of East Anglia* (1830) gives: '**Roger's-Blast**, s. a sudden and local motion of the air, not otherwise perceptible but by its whirling up the dust on a dry road in perfectly calm weather, somewhat in the manner of a water-spout. It is reckoned a sign of approaching rain.' There is here a suggestion that the word was then of general East Anglian usage, but today it is most often heard in the Broads region.

Christopher Davies has something to say of the **rodges-blast** in *Norfolk Broads and Rivers* (1883): 'It is really a rotary wind-squall or whirlwind, and is most likely to occur with a south-west wind. Sometimes the blasts are very violent, and come without warning. Even if you see one coming over the marsh, convulsing the grasses or lifting the reed-stacks high in the air, you cannot tell whether it will strike you or not, its course is so erratic. It may wreck a windmill fifty yards away, and leave the water around you unruffled. It may blow the sail of one wherry to pieces, and another wherry close by will be becalmed. Occasionally you may see a dozen wherries in the same reach, all bound the same way, with their sails now jibing, now close-hauled, now full and now shaking, with the fitfulness of the wind.

Sometimes, in a large reed-bed, you may see the ree[d] all laid flat in a circle, or in a carr the trees uproot[ed] for a space, where a rodges-blast has descended. N[ow] and then, although rarely, a veritable watersp[out] crosses the country, and does great damage when [it] breaks.'

The spelling varies considerably, with several of t[he] correspondents whose letters were reprinted in *Bro[ad] Norfolk* in 1893 referring to the phenomenon as a S[ir] **Roger**. One of them refers to a tradition that the nam[e] was derived from 'the unquiet spirit of Sir Rog[er] Ascham', but it was of much earlier origin. About 14[..] John Lydgate wrote that

I haue herd seid of ful yore agon
A whirl wynd blowing nothing soft
Was in old Englissh callid a Rodion,
That reiseth duste & strauh ful hih alofte.

The pronunciation of the word is made plain by t[he] alternative spelling 'Rodjon'. Rodges-blast or Sir Rog[er] the name is derived from a word of unknown origin th[at] in the 15th century was spelt rodion or rodjon.

Rond The swampy margin of a river or broad betwee[n] the water's edge and the river wall. A word deriv[ed] possibly from Old Norse but found also in Dutch a[nd] German, meaning a bank or border. In some parts [of] the country the same word was used for the skirts of [a] field. The Dutch word *rand*, meaning a rim or ridge [of] hills, has found its way into Witwatersrand, the elevate[d] ridge in the south Transvaal which forms the barri[er] between the Vaal river and the Olifants river; the Ra[nd] became famous for its gold mines.

Rond-stuff Rond-grass (*Glyceria maxima*).

Saddlebacks A descriptive term for the black-backed gu[lls,] both the Great (*Larus marinus*) and the Lesser (*Lar[us] fuscus*). The Great black-backed came to East Anglia [in] their tens of thousands for the Autumn or Home Fis[h]ing.

Scuppet A shovel with parallel sides which are turne[d] upward and even a little inward, and a T-handle. Maj[or] Moor also mentions a **skaffel**, which he describes as [a] small scuppet used in draining 'and in out-hawling [or] feying narrow bottomed ditches'. Both words are use[d] by Thomas Tusser, who farmed in Suffolk.

Sea-pie The oystercatcher.

Serpent's tongue Arrowhead (*Sagittaria sagittifolia*), [a] water weed which grows in some of the marsh drai[ns] and in the upper reaches of some of the Broadland rive[rs.]

e-gladdon The greater reedmace (*Typha latifolia*).

e-reed, soft reed The reed canary-grass (*Phalaris ndinacea*) and also second-growth reed (*Phragmites munis*), which lacks the flowering plumes and is of erior quality for thatching.

oe-awl The avocet. The dialect name is presumably a erence to the bird's upturned beak.

b Alluvial ooze, particularly the soft mud that gathers the bottom of a dyke as a result of silting and the cay of aquatic vegetation. Possibly adopted from the tch (in modern Dutch *slobber* is sludge or slush), it is word of some antiquity; John Norden (1548-1625), o was in 1593 'authorised and appointed by her jesty to travil [sic] through England and Wales to make ore perfect descriptions, charts and maps', referred in *Speculum Britanniae* to land which 'fortefies it selfe h heaped mountes of sande, slub and pibble-stones'. jor Moor remarks that 'wet, poachy ground, recently dden by cattle, is said to be slubby, or all of a slub', d adds that 'walls raised from the ooze of rivers require be slubb'd over, that is, the interstitial chinks or fissures sed by evaporation, require to be filled up with more the slub, or alluvial deposit'.

bbing out The operation of removing slub from a ke or drainage ditch. It might be done with a mud-ppet, a shovel or scoop sometimes made of wood.

ft rush, soft water-rush The blunt-flowered or fen rush *ncus submodulosus*), a common plant of the mowing marshes.

ile A stout wedge of wood tipped with iron and used clay or gravel pits to let down large quantities of terial at once. This operation was known as 'caving'. word that has come to us from Dutch, it is also used a pile for such work as supporting an embankment. is likewise our pronunciation of *spoil*', adds Major oor to his definition of the word.

ong The Revd Sir John Cullum says simply a narrow p of land, and the Revd Robert Forby adds 'such as a ong active fellow might clear in a *spang* or leap'. Major oor is more explicit, describing it as 'an iregular, nar-w, projecting part of a field, whether planted or in ass. If planted, or running to underwood, it would be lled a squeech or queech [q.v.]. Spinny is another definite word applied like dangle, reed, shaw &c. to egular bushy plots or pieces of land'.

oonbeak A descriptive name for the shoveller, a duck at feeds by filtering its food off the surface of the water.

aithe A quay, wharf or landing stage. The word, which is by no means confined to East Anglian dialect, appears to be derived from an Old Norse term for a landing stage; it is found wherever Viking influence was strong. On the Broads almost every riverside town and village had its staithe, sometimes owned by the parish but some-times by private landowners, a difference that has in several cases led to conflict and law suits.

Stank A wooden dam put across a stream or dyke to stop the flow of water.

Star-grass, starch-grass The bog-rush (*Schoenus nigricans*), a common plant of mowing marshes.

Swipe, swape, swike or **swake** The handle of a pump. In the case of the wherry's wooden-cased pump the word was used for the pump itself, which is not surpris-ing when one finds that around 1700 a swipe was 'an Engine to draw up Water'. It is a word of Anglo-Saxon origin.

Tenchweed The broad-leaved pondweed (*Potamogeton natans*), a plant with bronze-tinted floating leaves found in quiet bays around the Broads and in the deeper Broadland dykes.

Thack, twig-rush The great saw-sedge (*Cladium mariscus*), which can dominate the fen and have a strong influence on the natural development of a Broadland landscape.

Tod The stump of a tree. The word is also used of the trunk of a pollarded tree, one which has had its head (poll) cut off so that new branches shoot from the top.

Trunk-way A culvert carrying the water of a ditch under the approach to a gateway. In general usage it is a box-like passage, usually made of wooden boards, for passing air, light or water, but in Norfolk and Suffolk the word was used to refer to an arch of brick or masonry as above. Forby remarks that the name doubtless arose from the use of hollowed tree trunks for the same purpose 'in ancient and simpler times, and even now [1830] in the few woody parts of both counties'.

Tussock A clump of matted grasses or other vegetation, particularly of the tussock sedge (*Carex paniculata*), which has played a significant part in the growing up of the Broads. It eventually forms huge, close-set stools as much as three or four feet high and begins to crowd out reeds and other aquatic vegetation. Such tussocks were some-times cut and trimmed to provide rough seating in cottages or hassocks for churches, as Forby describes: 'These hassocks in bogs were formerly taken up with a part of the soil, matted together with roots, shaped, trimmed, and dressed, a sufficient part of their shaggy and tufted surface being left, to make kneeling much easier than on the pavement of the church, or the bare boarded floor of a pew.'

Upland 'Higher and drier ground, as contradistinguished from fen-land,' says the Revd Robert Forby. An **Uplander** or **Uplandman** is an inhabitant of the uplands.

Wakes Patches of clear water on an otherwise frozen broad.

Whelm Half a hollow tree laid under a gateway to carry the water of a ditch. 'A bad substitute for a brick arch',

says the Revd Sir John Cullum in his list of words in u at Hawsted in the 18th century. See also **trunk-way**.

Willow-weed The great hairy willowherb (*Epilopia hirsutum*) and amphibious bistort (*Polygonum amphibiur*

Wrong A term used for a crooked timber, usually a tr bough, much sought after by shipbuilders to form t curved timbers and knees. It is a word which has con to us from the Old Norse *wrange*, bent or curved. A ve similar word is still used in Norwegian and Swedish f a ship's ribs.

EARLY BOOKS ON THE BROADS

Surprising numbers of books have been written and published about the Broads over the past 120 years, and most of those that pre-date the Second World War are now eagerly sought by collectors. There have even been books in French (*En Wherry: Trois semaines dans les Broads du Norfolk*, published in Paris in 1892) and German (*Die Norfolk Broads: Auf Flussen und Seen im Sudosten Englands*, Hamburg, 1994).

Possibly the commonest of the early books is George Christopher Davies's *The Handbook to the Rivers and Broads of Norfolk and Suffolk*, published by Jarrold & Sons in fifty editions over a period of some forty years, the first appearing in 1882 and the 50th, with illustrations by W.L. Rackham, some time in the 1920s. Like other titles in Jarrolds' 'Holiday' series, the *Handbook* can be found in various bindings, for early issues were available at a half-crown in 'cloth elegant' or for a shilling in illustrated boards; the cloth version had a pocket inside the back cover that originally contained a copy of *Jarrolds' Map of the Rivers and Broads of Norfolk and Suffolk*, though today the pocket is often empty. Editions dating from the early years of the 20th century have card covers printed with a picture in colour with the title rendered as *Jarrolds' Illustrated Guide to the Rivers and Broads of Norfolk and Suffolk*; sometimes the title page declares it to be the *Handbook*, sometimes it bears the same title as the cover. There is also *The Tourist's Guide to the Rivers and Broads of Norfolk and Suffolk* which appears to be the *Handbook* in a smaller format and at a cheaper price, and a slim 24-page version from the 1920s called on the title page *Rivers and Broads of Norfolk and Suffolk* but having on the cover exactly the same design as the 206-page *Handbook*.

A year after the first appearance of the *Handbook* Davies produced *Norfolk Broads and Rivers; or, the water-ways, lagoons, and decoys of East Anglia*, illustrated by a dozen photographs, all but one of them taken by Davies himself. The copper plates from which these illustrations were printed had only a limited life, and for that reason the second edition of 1884 had only seven of the illustrations, converted into steel engravings. It has been said that the books of Davies were largely responsible for popularising the Broads as a holiday playground, but another book of his, *The Swan and her Crew; or the adventures of three young naturalists and sportsmen on the Broads and rivers of Norfolk*, which had appeared in 1876 and continued to appear in various editions right up to the 1930s, had an even greater impact on the younger generation. Arthur Patterson was one who in his youth was enthralled by the adventures of Frank Merrivale and his friends in their home-made catamaran. 'I well remember how we youths who followed on the heels of the Breydon men like spaniels went excited over one copy of *The Swan and her Crew* which the Yarmouth bird stuffer lent us to read in rotation ... That little book took hold of me more than ever did Robinson Crusoe, my patron saint,' Patterson wrote.

Another local author who produced a guide to the Broads was Harry Brittain, a Norwich bank manager who for more than 17 years sailed the rivers in the *Buttercup* and later became the owner of the wherry *Zoe* and brought out *Notes on the Broads and Rivers of Norfolk and Suffolk* in 1887, with second and third editions in the following two years. The pleasure wherry *Zoe* featured in a little book by Norfolk antiquary-solicitor Walter Rye, whose *A Month on the Norfolk Broads* came out in 1887. The lawyer-author fell into the trap of including a story told him by his skipper, Tungate, about how a Norwich banker who had committed suicide was said not to have done so at all but to have absconded to Spain; he found himself in difficulties over that story, and a second edition appeared with the offending paragraph altered to refer only to 'the various myths as to his sad end prevalent in the district, which were of the curious character usually connected with sudden and tragical deaths'.

It was a somewhat different indiscretion that led to Peter Henry Emerson's *Birds, Beasts, and Fishes of the Norfolk Broadland* appearing in two slightly differing editions. His description of the sexual prowess of a male swan had been too explicit for Victorian times, and in a prefatory note to the second issue he said that certain passages 'which were held, whether rightly or wrongly need not here be discussed, to make the book less suitable to general reading, have been left out or changed ...'. Emerson was a pioneer of what he termed 'naturalistic photography' and with his artist friend Thomas Goodall compiled *Life and Landscape on the Norfolk Broads*, which was published in 1886 or 1887 and is illustrated with 40 plates in platinotype, a photographic process. The interest in early photographs espoused by academics and collectors in America has led to this volume fetching quite extraordinary prices at auction; a faulty copy with one of the more sought-after plates missing made £14,000 in a New York saleroom in October 2002.

At the time of its publication *Life and Landscape on the Norfolk Broads* did not enjoy great success, perhaps because its selling price put it out of reach of all but the richest of readers. Early advertisements state that 750 copies of the ordinary edition in green cloth and 100 copies of the de luxe edition in vellum were being produced, but later advertisements make it plain that only 175 copies of the ordinary edition and a mere 25 copies in vellum had been put on sale. Later titles such as *Pictures of East Anglian Life* and *Pictures from Life in Field and Fen* were illustrated with photo-etchings and are not so wildly sought by millionaire collectors and American universities; they too seem to have been printed in much lower quantities than the original advertisements announced.

At the other end of the scale are those ephemeral publications produced by the Great Eastern Railway at their printing works at Stratford in the 1890s, to encourage travellers to visit the Broads by train, and the lists of boats published by such as the Norfolk Broads Yachting Company. Most ephemeral of all must be the little gift book printed in Saxony in the late 19th century containing paintings done by an artist who had almost certainly never seen the Broads; happy the collector who finds a copy in its original envelope.

Too many authors rushed into print after spending a short time on the Broads, and their efforts aroused the scorn of an anonymous reviewer writing in the magazine *Nature* in 1897 of 'A Batch of Guide-Books to the Norfolk Broads' which included the ninth edition of Davies's *Handbook*:

> Surely no spot in the British Isles has been so 'be-guided' as the Norfolk Broads. For the last twenty years the literature of the subject has been on the increase, till hardly a magazine or newspaper exists from Blackwood to Exchange and Mart which has not opened its pages to the flood of contributors on this apparently fascinating subject; and the whole has culminated in a shower of guide-books which enliven the railway bookstalls with their gay exteriors, rendering it difficult to say which of the twain is the more largely advertised – Colman's mustard or the Norfolk Broads. The bulk of the articles are of the feeblest sort by people who, having spent a few days on the Broads, returned to their distant homes imbued with the erroneous impression that they were qualified to enlighten the world with regard to the features and peculiarities of a tract of country difficult of access and still more difficult to appreciate, and the very names of whose towns and villages they had not learned to spell correctly.

The criticism was fully justified in some cases, but the collector is unlikely to be put off by the errors of these carpet-bagging scribblers. Rather will he smile at their foibles as he adds another little volume to his shelf; the search might be long, but the satisfaction in finding a rare publication is not to be denied.

NOTES

1 WATERY LANDSCAPE, pp.1-8

1. J.M. Lambert and J.N. Jennings, C.T. Smith, Charles Green and J.N. Hutchinson, *The Making of the Broads: A Reconsideration of their Origin in the Light of New Evidence*, Royal Geographical Society Research Series No.3 (1960).
2. Report on Broadland (1965), p.20.
3. E.A. Ellis, *The Broads* (1965), pp.225-8.
4. Stewart Linsell, *Hickling Broad and its Wildlife* (1990), pp.15-16.
5. *Broads Plan 1997. The Strategy and Management Plan for the Norfolk and Suffolk Broads* (Broads Authority, Norwich, 1997).

2 THE GREAT ESTUARY, pp.9-19

1. R. Rainbird Clarke, *East Anglia* (1960), p.48; John Wymer, 'The Neolithic Period' and Peter Murphy, 'Early Farming in Norfolk', *An Historical Atlas of Norfolk* (1993), pp.26-8.
2. Clarke 1960, p.52.
3. Paul Johnston, *The Seacraft of Prehistory* (1980), pp.121ff.
4. Clarke 1960, p.51.
5. Wymer 1993, p.26.
6. Clarke 1960, pp.66-7; *Proceedings of the Prehistoric Society* 2 (1936), pp.1-51.
7. Clarke 1960, p.91.
8. A. Davidson in *East Anglian Archaeology* 49.
9. *Geography* 4.5.2.
10. P. Bidwell (ed.), *Hadrian's Wall 1989-1999* (1999), p.76.
11. Cf. A.J. Morris, in *Proceedings of the Suffolk Institute of Archaeology*, 24 (1949), pp.100-20.
12. *Norfolk Archaeology* 5 (1859), pp.146-60; *East Anglian Archaeology* 20 (1983).
13. *East Anglian Archaeology* 20, p.11.
14. M. Gelling, *Signposts to the Past* (2000 edn.), p.67.
15. Greville J. Chester, 'A Brief Sketch of the Antiquities of the Valleys of the Waveney and Yare', *Norfolk Archaeology* 4 (1855), pp.314-15.
16. *Norfolk Archaeological Journal* 46, pp.331-49.
17. G.J. Levine, *A Concise History of Brundall and Braydeston* (1979).

3 SETTLERS AND INVADERS, pp.20-45

1. Kenneth Penn in *Saxon* 30 (1999).
2. Kenneth Penn in *A Festival of Norfolk Archaeology* (1996), p.42.
3. Norman Scarfe, *Suffok in the Middle Ages* (1986), p.25.
4. H.O. Coxe (ed.), 'Rogeri de Wendover Chronica', summarised by Dorothy Whitelock, *Proceedings of the Suffolk Institute of Archaeology* 31 (1968), p.229.
5. Charles Green, 'East Anglian Coast-line Levels since Roman Times', *Antiquity* 35 (1961), pp.21-8.

6. Barbara Cornford, *Eastern Daily Press*, 6 July 1990.
7. Sue Margeson in *A Festival of Norfolk Archaeology* (1996), pp.47ff.
8. Francis Blomefield, *History of Norfolk* (1806), 4, p.260.
9. Antonia Gransden, *Legends, Traditions and History in Medieval England* (1992), pp.98, 104.
10. C.R. Hart, *The Early Charters of Eastern England* (1966).
11. See Hornington in Eilert Ekwall, *The Concise Oxford Dictionary of English Place-names*, 4th edn. (1960), p.251.
12. J.R. West, *St Benet of Holme 1020-1210* (1932).
13. Joan Snelling, *St Benet's Abbey, Norfolk*, revised W.F. Edwards (1983), p.3.
14. A.L. Poole, *From Domesday Book to Magna Carta 1087-1216* (1951), p.338.
15. E.P.L. Brock, *Journal of the British Archaeological Association* 36 (1880), pp.15-21.
16. Blomefield 1806, 4, p.527.
17. Barbara Dodwell, 'The Monastic Community', *Norwich Cathedral, Church, City and Diocese, 1096-1996* (1996), p.253.
18. *Ibid.*, p.232.
19. W.A.S. Wynne, *St Olave's Priory and Bridge* (1914); K.R. Davies, *Ministry of Works Guide to St Olave's Priory* (1949).
20. *Index Monasticus* (1821), p.24.
21. S.J. Noel Henderson, *The Story of Hickling Priory 1185-1536* [1976].
22. William White, *History, Gazetteer and Directory of Norfolk* (1864), p.433.
23. Quoted in William A. Dutt, *The Norfolk Broads* (1903), p.304.
24. M.R. James, *Suffolk and Norfolk* (1930), p.148.
25. Joan M. Snelling, *St Benet's Abbey, Norfolk*, revised by W.F. Edwards (1983), p.13.
26. S. Heywood, 'Round-Towered Churches', *An Historical Atlas of Norfolk* (1993), p.56.
27. H. Munro Cautley, *Suffolk Churches and their Treasures*, 5th edn. (1908).
28. *Ranworth: A Village and Church on the Broads* (1908).

4 THE RIVER CROSSINGS, pp.45-56
1. Cal. Pat. Rolls 1 Henry IV, p.232.
2. Cal. Pat. Rolls Henry V, 7 June 1421.
3. Cal. Pat. Rolls Henry V, 5 June 1421.
4. Cal. Pat. Rolls Henry V, 6 July 1420.
5. Cal. Pat. Rolls Henry V, 3 October 1419.
6. Cal. Pat. Rolls Henry V, 24 June 1420.
7. *St Olave's Priory and Bridge* (1914), pp.61-2.
8. E.A. Labrum (ed.), *Civil Engineering Heritage, Eastern and Central England* (1994), pp.129-30.
9. Charles Green, 'Broadland Fords and Causeways', *Norfolk Archaeology* 32, p.320.
10. William White, *History, Gazetteer and Directory of Norfolk* (1864), p.437.
11. NRO, WKC 7/109 404x5; Percy Millican, 'The Rebuilding of Wroxham Bridge in 1576: A transcript of the account book', *Norfolk Archaeology* 26 (1938), pp.281-95.

5 THE MAKING OF THE BROADS, pp.57-64
1. C.T. Smith, 'Historical Evidence', *The Making of the Broads*, RGS Research Series No. 3 (1960), p.63.
2. H.C. Darby, *The Domesday Geography of Eastern England* (1971), p.117.
3. *Ibid.*, p.127.
4. Smith, 1960, p.82.
5. *Ibid.*, p.73.
6. *Ibid.*, p.88.
7. *Ibid.*, p.96.
8. *Ibid.*, p.95.
9. Neville Williams, *The Maritime Trade of the East Anglian Ports 1550-1590*, Oxford University Press (1988).
10. C.J. Palmer, *The Perlustration of Great Yarmouth* (1874), vol.3, pp.285-6.

11. W.A. Dutt, *The Norfolk Broads* (1903), p.136.
12. C.F. Carrodous, *Life in a Norfolk Village. The story of old Horning* (1949), pp.19-23.
13. NRO, PD251/41, quoted in Colin Wells, 'Post-medieval turf-digging in Norfolk', *Norfolk Archaeology* 43 (2000), p.473.
14. Dutt 1903, p.308.
15. W.A. Dutt, *Wild Life in East Anglia* (1906), p.200.
16. Barbara Cornford, 'The Commons of Flegg in the Middle Ages and Early Modern Period', in *Commons in Norfolk* (Norfolk Research Committee, 1988), p.20.
17. M.C.H. Bird, 'The rural economy, sport and natural history of East Ruston Common', in *Transactions of the Norfolk and Norwich Naturalists' Society*, vol.8 (1909).
18. Wells, p.479.

6 FARMING AND DRAINING, pp.65-84

1. Barbara Cornford, 'Water Levels in the Flegg Area', *Norfolk Research Committee Bulletin* 28 (1982), p.18.
2. BL Cotton Nero Dii; the Latin text is published with introduction by H. Ellis in the Rolls Series (1859).
3. Barbara Cornford, 'The Sea Breach Commission in East Norfolk 1609-1743', *Norfolk Archaeology* 37 (1980), p.137; Cal. Pat. Rolls, 11 July 1564.
4. 7 Jacob. 1 cap xx.
5. R.R. Teasdel, 'The Dutch inscription in Haddiscoe Church, Norfolk', *Norfolk Archaeology* 25 (1935), pp.449-50.
6. N.J.M. Kerland, 'Aliens in the County of Norfolk, 1436-1485', *Norfolk Archaeology* 33 (1965), pp.200-12.
7. Cornford 1980, p.140.
8. *Ibid.*, p.142.
9. *Faden's Map of Norfolk*, Larks Press edition, 1989.
10. W. Marshall, *The Rural Economy of Norfolk* (1795), 2, p.270.
11. R.E. Pestell, 'Brograve – immortal name of marshland', *East Anglia Life*, November 1966.
12. NRO, WD8 384 x 5.
13. *White's Directory of Norfolk* (1845), p.491.
14. *Eastern Daily Press*, 26 January 1929.
15. Rex Wailes, 'Norfolk Windmills: Part II, Drainage and Pumping Mills including those of Suffolk', *Transactions of the Newcomen Society* 30 (1955-57), p.163.
16. Pers. comm., Vincent Pargeter.
17. *Norwich Mercury*, 25 February 1832.
18. *Norwich Mercury*, 15 June 1833.
19. *Kelly's Directory of Norfolk*, 1879.
20. R.H. Clark, *Steam Engine Builders of Norfolk* (1988), pp.10-11.
21. *Norwich Mercury*, 13 March 1582.
22. Joan Snelling, *St Benet's Abbey, Norfolk* (1971).
23. *Eastern Daily Press*, 6 June 1945.
24. Anthony J. Ward, 'Smoke drifting over the reeds', *Journal of the Norfolk Industrial Archaeology Society*, 6, no.2, p.46.
25. *White's Directory of Norfolk* (1845), p.294.
26. Ward, pp.48-54.
27. *Norwich Mercury*, 16 September 1882.
28. *White's Directory of Norfolk* (1890).
29. W.A. Dutt, *The Norfolk Broads* (1903), pp.182-3.
30. Anthony Buxton, *Fisherman Naturalist* (1946), pp.106-8.

7 RIVERS AND WATERWAYS, pp.85-110

1. Daniel Defoe, *Tour through the Whole Island of Great Britain* (1724).
2. W. Hudson and J.C. Tingey, *The Records of the City of Norwich* (1906), vol.1, pp.277-8.

3. *Ibid.*, vol.2, p.171.
4. *Ibid.*, vol.1, p.142.
5. *Ibid.*, vol.2, p.391.
6. Peter Brown, 'Winterton-on-Sea: village survey', *Journal of the Norfolk Industrial Archaeology Society* 6 (2000), p.79.
7. Tom Williamson, *The Norfolk Broads: A Landscape History* (1997), p.76.
8. 22 Charles II cap.16.
9. H.R. de Salis, *Norfolk Waterways* (1900).
10. 13 Geo. III cap.37.
11. Percy Millican, *History of Horstead and Stanninghall* (1937).
12. de Salis 1900.
13. *White's Directory of Norfolk* (1855), p.408.
14. 52 Geo. III cap. 69.
15. *Norwich Mercury*, 16 April 1825.
16. *Ibid.*, 9 April 1825.
17. *Ibid.*, 18 June 1826.
18. de Salis 1900.
19. *Norwich Mercury*, 23 January 1830.
20. *Norfolk Chronicle*, 20 May 1820.
21. J.W. Robberds, illus. James Stark, *Scenery of the Rivers of Norfolk* (1834), plate 16.
22. *Norwich Mercury*, 2 July 1832.
23. *Ibid.*, 16 July 1831.
24. NRO, Y/PH109.
25. Peter Brown, 'Norwich Lock', *Journal of the Norfolk Industrial Archaeology Society* 6 (2000), pp.47-53.

8 KEEL AND WHERRY, pp.111-29

1. W. Hudson and J.C. Tingey, *The Records of the City of Norwich* (1906-10), 1, pp.223-4.
2. *Ibid.*, pp.140-1.
3. Francis Blomefield, *History of Norfolk* (1806), 4, p.70.
4. R. Malster, *Wherries and Waterways* (1971), p.57.
5. C.J. Palmer, *The Perlustration of Great Yarmouth* (1874), vol.1, p.395.
6. *Norwich Mercury*, 2 November 1782.
7. *Norwich Mercury*, 13 April 1785.
8. NRO, Y/C38/3.
9. J.G. Nall, *Great Yarmouth and Lowestoft, A Handbook for Visitors and Residents* (1866), p.415.
10. *Norfolk Chronicle* and *Norwich Mercury*, 23 October 1779.
11. E.W. White, *British Fishing-Boats and Coastal Craft, Part II: Descriptive Catalogue and List of Plans* (Science Museum, 1952), p.14.
12. Malster 1971, pp.59-66.

9 EXPLOITING A WETLAND, pp.130-42

1. Richard Lubbock, *Observations on the Fauna of Norfolk, and more particularly on the District of the Broads* (1845), p.53.
2. Lubbock, 3rd edn (1879), p.96.
3. G.C. Davies, *Norfolk Broads and Rivers* (1882), p.145.
4. H. Stevenson, *Birds of Norfolk*, continued by Thomas Southwell (1890), pp.170-7.
5. W. Hudson and J.C. Tingey, *The Records of the City of Norwich* (1910), 2, p.125.
6. Francis Blomefield, *History of Norfolk*, vol.4 (1806), p.530.
7. Lubbock 1845, p.137.
8. *Norfolk Broads and Rivers; or, the water-ways, lagoons, and decoys of East Anglia* (1883), p.119.
9. There is an excellent description of smelt fishing in W.A. Dutt, *Wild Life in East Anglia* (1906), pp.151-64.
10. Nathaniel Kent, *General View of the Agriculture of the County of Norfolk* (1796), p.53.

11. For a detailed account of the drainage of the Halvergate marshes *see* Tom Williamson, *The Norfolk Broads: A Landscape History* (1997), chapter 3.
12. *White's Directory of Norfolk* (1855), p.533.
13. Nathaniel Kent 1796, p.167.
14. R.W. Farman, 'Reeds and Thatch', *Eastern Daily Press*, 14 January 1948.
15. Robert Forby, *The Vocabulary of East Anglia* (1830), pp.285-6.
16. 'East Anglian Words' by the Revd W.T. Spurdens, *Reprinted Glossaries XX*, English Dialect Society (1879), pp.76-7.
17. Richard Lubbock 1845, p.89.

10 WATERY PLAYGROUND, pp.143-72
1. W. Hudson and J.C. Tingey, *Records of the City of Norwich* (1910), 2, p.67.
2. J.W. Robberds, illus. James Stark, *Scenery of the Rivers of Norfolk* (1834), text to plate 10.
3. *Suffolk Chronicle*, 29 August 1840.
4. W.M. Blake, 'The old Maria', *Yachting Monthly*, November 1933.
5. Nicholas Everitt, *Broadland Sport* (1902), pp.240-1.
6. *Ibid.*, p.243.
7. L.E. Bolingbroke, quoted in G.C. Davies, *Practical Boat Sailing for Amateurs* (1986), pp.48-9.
8. Everitt 1902, p.249.
9. *Ibid.*, p.251; Charles Goodey, *120 Years of Sailing* (1980), p.10.
10. *Eastern Daily Press*, 26 March 1926.
11. H.M. Doughty, *Our Wherry in Wendish Lands* (1901).
12. Keble Chatterton, *The Water-ways of Norfolk and Suffolk* (1899).
13. Broads Authority, *Broads Plan 1997*, pp.99-100.

11 ECOLOGICAL DISASTER, pp.173-80
1. Richard Lubbock, *Observations on the Fauna of Norfolk, and more particularly on the District of the Broads* (1845), p.53.
2. B.B. Riviere, *A History of the Birds of Norfolk* (1930), p.134.
3. Stewart Linsell, *Hickling Broad and its Wildlife* (1990), p.47.
4. G.C. Davies, *The Handbook to the Rivers and Broads of Norfolk and Suffolk*, 11th edn (1888), pp.xiv-xvi.
5. C.F. Snowden Gamble, *The Story of a North Sea Air Station* (1928), pp.60-1, 420.

12 NEARLY A NATIONAL PARK, pp.181-200
1. Martin George, *The Land Use, Ecology and Conservation of Broadland* (1992), p.262.
2. *Eastern Daily Press*, 17 May 2002.
3. Martin Kirby, *Albion: The Story of the Norfolk Trading Wherry* (1998).

SELECT BIBLIOGRAPHY

Brittain, Harry, *Notes on the Broads and Rivers of Norfolk and Suffolk*, Argus Office, Norwich, 1887; 2nd edn, 1888; 3rd edn, 1889

Campbell, J. and Middleton, C., *The Man Who Found the Broads, A Biography of George Christopher Davies*, Hamilton Publications, Gorleston, 1999

Davies, George Christopher, *The Handbook to the Rivers and Broads of Norfolk and Suffolk*, Jarrold & Sons, London, 1882; 3rd edn, 1883; 11th edn, 1888; 18th edn, 1891; 23rd edn, 1894; 41st edn, *c*.1901; 50th edn, illustrated by W.L. Rackham, *c*.1920

Norfolk Broads and Rivers; or, the water-ways, lagoons, and decoys of East Anglia, William Blackwood & Sons, Edinburgh, 1883; 2nd edn, 1884

The Swan and Her Crew; or the adventures of three young naturalists and sportsmen on the Broads and Rivers of Norfolk, Frederick Warne, London, 1876; 7th edn, 1892. Jarrolds, London, n.d. [*c*.1920s]. New edn revised by Hugh C. Davies, Methuen, 1932

Dutt, W.A., *The Norfolk Broads*, Methuen, London, 1903; 2nd edn, 1905; 3rd edn, 1923; 4th revised edn, 1930

Wild Life in East Anglia, Methuen, London, 1906

Ellis, E.A., *The Norfolk Broads*, Collins, London, 1965

Emerson, Peter Henry and Goodall, Thomas, *Life and Landscape on the Norfolk Broads*, London [1887]

Emerson, Peter Henry, *Wild Life on a Tidal Water*, London, 1890

A Son of the Fens, London, 1892

On English Lagoons: being an account of the voyage of two amateur wherrymen on the Norfolk and Suffolk rivers and Broads, David Nutt, London, 1893

Birds, Beasts, and Fishes of the Norfolk Broadland, David Nutt, London, 1895; 2nd edn, 1895

Marsh Leaves, Stratford, Essex, 1898

Everitt, Nicholas, *Broadland Sport*, R.A. Everitt & Co., London, 1902

Ewans, Martin, *The Battle for the Broads*, Terence Dalton, Lavenham, 1992

George, Martin, *The Land Use, Ecology and Conservation of Broadland*, Packard Publishing, Chichester, 1992

Holmes, David, *The Norfolk Broads*, Sutton Publishing, Stroud, 1996

Back to the Broads, Sutton Publishing, Stroud, 1998; Lucas Books, 2001

Hutchinson, Sheila, *Berney Arms: Past & Present*, Sheila and Paul Hutchinson, 2000

The Halvergate Fleet: Past & Present, Sheila and Paul Hutchinson, 2001

Kiessler, Bernd-Wilfried, *Die Norfolk Broads: Auf Flussen und Seen im Sudosten Englands*, Edition Maritim, Hamburg, 1994

Lambert, J.M. and Jennings, J.N. *et al.*, *The Making of the Broads: A Reconsideration of Their Origin in the Light of New Evidence*, Royal Geographical Society, London, 1960

Linsell, Stewart, *Hickling Broad and its Wildlife*, Terence Dalton, Lavenham, 1990

Lubbock, Richard, *Observations on the Fauna of Norfolk, and more particularly on the District of the Broads*, Norwich, 1845; 2nd edn, 1848; new edn with additions by Thomas Southwell and a memoir by Henry Stevenson, etc., Jarrold & Sons, Norwich, 1879

Malster, Robert, *Wherries and Waterways*, Terence Dalton, Lavenham, 1971; revised edn, 1986

    The Broads, Phillimore, Chichester, 1993

Moss, Brian, *The Broads*, Harper Collins, London, 2001

Moss, Brian, Madgwick, Jane, and Phillips, Geoffrey, *A Guide to the Restoration of Nutrient-enriched Shallow Lakes*, Broads Authority, Norwich, 1996

Patterson, Arthur, *Broadland Scribblings*, Norwich, 1892

    Man and Nature on the Broads, Thomas Mitchell, London, 1895

    Notes of an East Coast Naturalist, Methuen, London, 1904

    Nature in Eastern Norfolk, Methuen, London, 1905; 2nd edn, 1906

    Wild Life on a Norfolk Estuary, Methuen, London, 1907

    Man and Nature on Tidal Waters, Methuen, London, 1909

    Through Broadland in a Breydon Punt, H.J. Vince, Norwich, 1920

    The Cruise of the Walrus on the Broads, Jarrolds, London, 1923

    Wildfowlers and Poachers: fifty years on the East Coast, Methuen, London, 1929

    A Norfolk Naturalist: observations on birds, mammals and fishes, Methuen, London, 1930

    Through Broadland by Sail and Motor, Blakes Ltd, London, 1930

Suffling, Ernest, *The Land of the Broads. A Practical Guide for Yachtsmen, Anglers, Tourists, and other Pleasure-Seekers on the Broads and Rivers of Norfolk and Suffolk*, L. Upcott Gill, London, 1885; 2nd edn, 1887. Benjamin Perry, Stratford, Essex [1892]; 7th edn, Benjamin Perry, [1895]

    The History and Legends of the Broad District, Jarrold & Sons, London [1891]

    The Innocents on the Broads, Jarrold & Sons, London, 1901

    How to Organise a Cruise on the Broads, Jarrold & Sons, London [1897]

Tully, Clive, *The Broads: The Official National Park Guide*, Pevensey Guides, 2002

Williamson, Tom, *The Norfolk Broads: A Landscape History*, Manchester University Press, 1997

INDEX

NORWICH

Timber Yards
Flour Mills
Breweries
Maltings

RIVER WENSUM

Hobrough's Dockyard

Trowse Eye

Chalk Pits &
Limekilns

Trowse Mills

RIVER YARE

POSTWICK

BRUNDALL

Surlingham
Brick Works

Surlingham Ferry

Bramerton
Woods End

Rockland Staithe

ICE HOUSE SURLINGHAM

BUCKENH

LANGLE

Bishop's Bridge, River Wensum, Norwich

The Mill, Loddon, River Chet

Lo

1 0   1   2   3   4   MILES
FURLONGS